This book studies the way that the central act of Christian worship (variously known as the Eucharist, the Lord's Supper, the Holy Communion and the Mass) has been treated in the thought and practice of the Evangelical tradition in the Church of England. Evangelicals are not noted for their emphasis on the Eucharist, and Christopher Cocksworth's study is innovative in its demonstration that – at its times of strength – the Evangelical tradition has held the Eucharist in the highest regard. As well as providing a thorough historical survey from the sixteenth century to the present day, the book develops a theology of the Eucharist which, whilst consistently evangelical, is also thoroughly ecumenical.

EVANGELICAL EUCHARISTIC THOUGHT IN THE CHURCH OF ENGLAND

EVANGELICAL EUCHARISTIC THOUGHT IN THE CHURCH OF ENGLAND

CHRISTOPHER J. COCKSWORTH

*Anglican Chaplain, Royal Holloway and Bedford New College,
University of London*

CAMBRIDGE
UNIVERSITY PRESS

Published by the Press Syndicate of the University of Cambridge
The Pitt Building, Trumpington Street, Cambridge CB2 1RP
40 West 20th Street, New York, NY 10011-4211, USA
10 Stamford Road, Oakleigh, Victoria 3166, Australia

First published 1993

Printed in Great Britain at the University Press, Cambridge

A catalogue record for this book is available from the British Library

Library of Congress cataloguing in publication data

Cocksworth, Christopher J.
Evangelical eucharistic thought in the Church of England /
Christopher J. Cocksworth.
p.   cm.
Includes bibliographical references.
ISBN 0 521 40441 X
1.   Lord's Supper–History. 2.   Evangelicalism – Church of England.
I. Title.
BV823.C59 1992
234'.163–dc20   92-5041   CIP

ISBN 0 521 40441 X hardback

To Charlotte, my wife

Contents

PART 3   THEOLOGICAL ANALYSIS

Preface

In one way, writing a book is an individualistic affair. But in another way, it is a corporate exercise. Although the responsibility for what lies in these pages is entirely mine, there are many people who have helped me along the way. The Bishop of Guildford, the Rt Revd Michael Adie, has given unswerving support from the very beginning. Dr Richard Bauckham and the Revd Dr Kenneth Stevenson have given their invaluable advice, direction and guidance through their supervision of an earlier form of this work, which was successfully submitted for a Ph.D degree to the University of Manchester. The Revd Mark Wilson and the people of Christ Church, Epsom allowed me time and space to adapt and revise the work for publication. Also to this end, Mr Alex Wright of Cambridge University Press has given wise advice throughout and Mrs Freda McCormick of Epsom has worked hard to prepare the final details of the typescript. And my father-in-law, the Rt Revd David Pytches, has never ceased to encourage and enthuse me. Without the very special help and counsel of all these people, this book could not have been written.

There are many others who have given freely of their expert knowledge in specialist areas, including Dr George Bebawi, the Revd Dr Francis Bridger, the late Revd Dr Geoffrey Cuming, the Revd Peter Lewis, the Ven. Trevor Lloyd, the Revd Noel Pollard, the Rt Revd Brian Skinner, the Revd Canon Tom Smail, the Revd Dr Bryan Spinks and the Revd Dr Gordon Wakefield. To all of them I am very grateful. My debt extends to the Rt Revd Colin Buchanan for his guidance in the initial stages of the project and for the generous loan of his private correspondence dating from the debate over the Second Series communion service. I am also grateful to the Rt Revd Eric Kemp for permission to quote from his correspondence to Colin Buchanan during this period.

Although so many have contributed to the beginning, continuing and completing of this book, they can take no share of the blame for any faults it may have. I am fully aware that to write on, as well as to participate in, the Lord's Supper is a serious matter, about which we must examine ourselves. If any feel that I have written in an unworthy manner, they must advise and correct me. I should like the book to be seen as the work of an Evangelical Christian who has known the presence of the redeeming Lord in the most holy Supper, and who has found others – both past and present – within the evangelical tradition who have known the same. With their help I have sought to grasp something of the mystery of the Eucharist in a way that is authentically evangelical and truly catholic. If in some way this book helps others to a deeper knowledge of the One who makes himself known in the breaking of the bread, I shall be glad.

This book is dedicated to my wife Charlotte, who has made her own sacrifice for its completion and for whom also I give my thanks and praise.

Abbreviations

CBRP	Church Book Room Press
CEEC	Church of England Evangelical Council
CELC	Church of England Liturgical Commission
CEN	*Church of England Newspaper*
CIO	Church Information Office
CMS	Church Missionary Society
CPAS	Church Pastoral Aid Society
CUP	Cambridge University Press
DLT	Darton Longman & Todd
EH	J. E. Rattenbury, *The Eucharistic Hymns of John and Charles Wesley*
Ev.H.	J. E. Rattenbury, *The Evangelical Doctrine of Charles Wesley's Hymns*
FAL	*Further Anglican Liturgies*, edited by C. O. Buchanan
GB	Grove Books
GLS	Grove Liturgical Study
GMWS	Grove Ministry and Worship Series
GROW	Group for the Renewal of Worship
GWS	Grove Worship Series
HAL	G. J. Cuming, *A History of Anglican Liturgy*
H & S	Hodder & Stoughton
HLS	*Hymns of the Lord's Supper*
IVF	Inter-Varsity Fellowship
IVP	Inter-Varsity Press
LACT	Library of Anglo-Catholic Theology
LH	Latimer House
LS	Latimer Study
MAL	*Modern Anglican Liturgies 1958–1968*, edited by C. O. Buchanan
MHB	*Methodist Hymn Book*

MMP	Marcham Manor Press
NOL	*News of Liturgy*
NTS	*New Testament Studies*
OUP	Oxford University Press
PEER	*Prayers of the Eucharist Early and Reformed*, edited by R. C. D. Jasper and G. J. Cuming
SCM	Student Christian Movement
SJT	*Scottish Journal of Theology*
SPCK	Society for the Propagation of Christian Knowledge
WCC	World Council of Churches

Introduction

CHAPTER I

The movement, the thesis, the method

THE EVANGELICAL MOVEMENT

To define and analyse the Evangelical grouping within the Church of England is a difficult task.[1] The breadth of contemporary Evangelicalism, which spans Reformed rigorists on the one side and Charismatic innovators on the other – with a good deal in between – makes a straightforward identification, quite apart from a simple definition, almost impossible. At this stage I shall attempt a more general definition, which covers the general sweep of Evangelical identity, and leave a more detailed analysis to the end of the chapter and to a note at the beginning of part 2.

Even in their most embattled and therefore unified times, Evangelicals have been notoriously difficult to organize into a distinct party, and have preferred to see their mutual alignment in terms more of adherence to common principles than of institutionalized structure. Although they recognize their immediate origins in the Revival of the eighteenth century, they have always seen themselves in continuity with an evangelical tradition stretching back from the eighteenth-century Evangelicals to the Puritans, to Luther and the other Reformers, to Augustine, to Paul and indeed to Christ himself. Hence Evangelicalism in its classic form has seen itself not as one tradition amongst many, each with an equal claim on the truth, but as the custodian of pure New Testament faith: 'It is, we maintain, the oldest version of Christianity, theologically regarded, it is just apostolic Christianity itself.'[2] *Packer.*

This is a big claim to make. It has its source in the two underlying elements of the Evangelical consciousness: the existential and the theological. Within Evangelicalism there exist side by side a strongly pietistic strain and a unified theological structure. It is tempting for its prosecutors and defenders to start and finish with its recognizable

3

theological tenets. However, despite Evangelicalism's conviction that it possesses a revealed deposit of truth which must not be compromised, it has not seen this in terms of an abstract theological system but as a theological edifice built on the foundation of God's redemptive involvement with the soul. In other words, piety and theology form one interdependent structure, which provides the Evangelical with a coherent way of understanding.

Gospel and Bible: the relationship between piety and theology

The categories of Narrative Theology and the Sociology of Knowledge can be of some help in delineating more clearly the relationship between piety and theology. Narrative Theology seeks to unite experience and reflection in an epistemological whole, by defining the redemptive process in terms of an interaction between the personal identity of the individual and the corporate identity of the community. The former is the personal search for meaning and the latter is the community's interpretation of Scripture. The 'collision' between the two is a revelatory self-disclosure in which the individual finds his meaning in the truth about God as held and communicated by the community.[3]

The language of the Sociology of Knowledge is similar: 'Society, identity and reality are subjectively crystallized in the same process of internalization'.[4] An individual perceives a sense of identity through an apprehension of reality as it is communicated by the society. Individuals are able to make sense of themselves and their world because they have been provided with a convincing plausibility structure by the mediating structures of a given community. 'Meaning' (that is, objective reality) confronts, invades and then pervades 'Identity' (that is, subjective reality) by the mediation of a set of attractive principles.

When John Stott described Evangelicals as 'Gospel people' and 'Bible people',[5] he was referring to the sort of dialectic identified by the categories of Narrative Theology and the Sociology of Knowledge. The Gospel is the essence of Christianity. The appointed means for its preservation and communication is the Bible. Similarly, when defining 'Evangelical Religion', J. C. Ryle made use of the same relationship:

[for] a religion to be really 'Evangelical' and really good, [there] must be the Gospel, the whole Gospel, and nothing but the Gospel, as Christ

prescribed it and expounded it to the Apostles; – the truth, the whole truth, and nothing but the truth; – the terms, the whole terms, and nothing but the terms, – and in all their fulness, all their freeness, all their simplicity, all their presentness.[6]

Here, for both Ryle and Stott, 'Gospel' is not just a message, still less personal belief, but rather the joining of the two. In other words, it is engaged message. Thus we may simplify the relationship between piety and theology into apprehension of the Gospel and communication of the Gospel.

I have said that Evangelicals see themselves in a tradition of spirituality which holds certain theological priorities in common. And I have implied that they do so not (primarily) in order to maintain a coherent and unified scheme, but because these theological priorities articulate the reality at the heart of the faith – the encounter between Christ and the individual. The appeal to Scripture finds its final justification not as a gift of propositions from God but as a text that has its root, its confirmation and its authentication in a continuity of experience:

Night and day I pondered until I saw the connection between the justice of God and the statement 'the just shall live by his faith'. Then I grasped that the justice of God is that righteousness by which through grace and sheer mercy God justifies us through faith. Thereupon I felt myself to be reborn and to have gone through open doors into paradise (Luther).[7]

The existential grasp of God's absolute salvific grace is rooted in a confrontation with Scripture and leads to a series of rudimentary theological insights: we are incapable of saving ourselves (utter helplessness of man), but Christ has achieved our salvation for us (sole sufficiency of Christ's work), leaving our part as only the recognition of his part (justification by faith) and full participation in the life of the Church (priesthood of all believers).

Writing from the storm centre of the Evangelical reaction to Ritualism at the turn of the century, Henry Wace described the essence of Protestantism as its rediscovery of the doctrine of original sin: 'That is the real point, from which the whole movement of thought and spiritual experience starts.'[8] Whatever theological qualifications modern Evangelicals might want to give to the concept of original sin, they would agree with Wace's identification of the utter helplessness of man before God and the complete helpfulness of God towards man in Christ, as the basis of Luther's Gospel and the

central concern of the Evangelical movement as it looks back to him
and beyond him to the Pauline Gospel.

Conversion: assurance, holiness, evangelism and fellowship

The fundamentals of Evangelicalism as listed by most Evangelical
apologists are not exhausted by the Reformation priorities so far
discussed.[9] They extend to several characteristics of spirituality: an
emphasis on the Spirit's role in assuring the believer of the salvation
received and in effecting the signs of that salvation in the person's life,
a concern for evangelism, a conviction of the necessity of conversion
and a desire to meet with like-minded Christians.

The hallmark of Evangelical spirituality is often seen to lie in its
emphasis on conversion. Whilst this is often misunderstood, the
significance Evangelicals attach to conversion does provide a helpful
insight into the character of the movement:

> Begin by considering what the Evangelical means by conversion and before
> you know where you are you are face to face with the majesty and holiness
> of God, the sinfulness of man, the divine compassion and the divine
> Redeemer, the new birth, the new life.[10]

Conversion is thus the category Evangelicals use to describe the
experiential apprehension of the reality of the Gospel as it is mediated
by the principal theological tenets.

Similar revelatory moments to Luther's could be echoed from
countless heroes of Evangelical history as well as from the grass roots
of Evangelical Church life. However, Evangelicals do make a
distinction between the state of conversion and the experience of
conversion. The means of the appropriation may be through a
definite experience, a movement of faith or participation in the
corporate memory. The way is secondary. What is primary is its
realization in the life of the individual. In short, if it is an authentic
encounter with the truth of God it will have ramifications for the
emotional, ethical and spiritual life of the believer. There will be a
consciousness of salvation (assurance), a working out of salvation
(holiness), a desire to communicate that salvation (evangelism), and
an eagerness to join with those who are also conscious of their share
in the same salvation (fellowship).

In summary, there is an experiential core at the heart of Evangelicalism – a meeting between the individual and God in the person of

Jesus Christ. This is not necessarily the experience of the blinding light on the road to Damascus. It may be rather more akin to a non-sacramental Emmaus-road experience: the encounter with Christ in the present arises from the encounter with Christ in the Scriptures. As this encounter often breaks through inherited assumptions, the Bible is placed above its interpretation in the community. Just as the Jewish hermeneutic failed to provide Cleopas with the suffering Messiah from Nazareth so did the medieval Church's understanding obscure from Luther the freeness of the Gospel's message. At its best, Evangelicalism has been prepared to follow this through consistently and apply the same principles to its own stake in the Protestant heritage.[11] However, this is a difficult challenge to meet, for as has been shown, there is a close, almost indivisible link between piety and theology in the Evangelical framework: a grasp of the Gospel, enabled by the presentation of a theology, results in a given spirituality.

The distinguishing mark of Evangelicalism may be seen to lie in the particular mix and interaction between experience and theology which it contains and displays. When trying to define the distinction between Evangelicalism and other forms of Churchmanship, J. C. Ryle described it in terms of a theology held in a distinctive set of proportions.[12] Thus other traditions may hold to the same theological beliefs, but with proportionally different emphases. He used a baking illustration to show that use of the same ingredients does not guarantee the same outcome. What counts is the measures and methods used. In terms of the foregoing analysis, it could be said that emphases in Evangelical theology and their interrelationships are in direct relation to the recipe set by the experience of the Gospel.

THE THESIS

Disagreement and division between Evangelicals and other (particularly more catholic-minded) Christians have often centred on the Eucharist. Luther's charge in his 'Babylonian captivity' shows that the Sacrament became a focus in the Reformation protest:

By far the most impious of the bondages in which the sacrament is held is that at this day there is no belief in the Church more generally received or more firmly held than that the Mass is a good work and a sacrifice. This alone has brought in an infinite flood of other abuses.[13]

The Reformation understanding of the Gospel stood so at odds with the inherited sacramental doctrine that the two appeared to be irreconcilable. *Justification by faith* involved a direct relation between the individual and God mediated only by Christ, not by the Church. The *total sufficiency of Christ's work* involved a completed, past act requiring only acknowledgement and apprehension, not contribution or extension. The *utter helplessness of man* made any attempt at active, participatory involvement in the maintenance of Christ's work invalid, futile and even blasphemous. The *priesthood of all believers* involved open access for all, not a closed shop for some.

Nevertheless, though the mainstream Reformers rejected the sacramental principle of the medieval system, that is, the causal relationship by which the Church in its divinely appointed presence (institution) and action (sacraments) participates in the salvific work of Christ, they did not want to displace the (dominical) sacraments from a central place in the theology and spirituality of their own system. They might have abandoned medieval sacramentalism, but they did so only in order to recover an authentically evangelical form of sacramental experience.[14] The polemic of much sixteenth-century Protestant comment on the Eucharist should not detract from the robust and dynamic sacramental spirituality which was waiting to find expression. Cranmer tried to hold the two together in his Declaration of 1553 (though in so doing he also highlighted the tension): 'Therefore, when ye see the Sacraments at My Table, look not so much at them as at that which I promise you through them, Myself, the food of eternal life.'[15]

The three points just touched upon (the relationship between the Eucharist and the Gospel, the apparent theological problems of combining an Evangelical theology with a sacramental spirituality, and the presence of a positive regard for the Eucharist within the Protestant consciousness) set the scene for an outline of the contentions of this study. They will be related first to the general history of Evangelicalism and then to the more recent period.

The contentions

Evangelical history

The first contention of this study is that within Evangelicalism there is a theological and empirical basis for the centrality of the Eucharist. On theological grounds, if the concept of the Gospel and the interpretation of the Bible preserved in the Evangelical tradition (as judged by the standards of its own criteria) is to have any Christian authenticity and credibility, it must have a significant place for the Eucharist, for the Sacrament has an intimate connection with the biblical Gospel:

This is my body which is for you...For as often as you eat this bread and drink the cup, you proclaim the Lord's death until he comes (1 Cor. 11; 24, 26).

On empirical grounds, the very annals of Evangelical tradition which have been called upon to validate the more familiar Evangelical tenets of faith also reveal a spirituality of sacramental reality. From Paul to Augustine, from the pre-Reformation movements of reform to the Reformers themselves, from the Puritans to the Wesleys and their Evangelical peers of the eighteenth and early nineteenth centuries, the Eucharist has been found to be a dynamic context for an encounter with Christ. The first contention, therefore, is quite simply that if Evangelicals are Gospel people and Bible people, they must be also, in some sense, Eucharist people.

The second contention is that there are significant theological forces which militate against the expression of an Evangelical form of sacramental faith. These stem from the Reformation break with a theology which incarnated Christ in the life and liturgy of the Church, in favour of a theology of direct spiritual interaction between the individual and God in Christ. They can be seen in Luther's paradoxical commitment to the real presence, alongside his radical emphasis on justification by faith. The two appear to be juxtaposed rather than theologically related, thus giving the impression of an isolated anachronism due more to the psychology of the man than to the truth about God. At first sight, Zwingli appears the more consistent. By working through the logic of the Reformation he arrived at a more or less symbolic concept of the Sacrament in which it was reduced to a witness of something that happens by means other than itself. Bucer, Calvin and Cranmer may have tried to steer a middle way but, as the rubric for the Communion of the Sick in the Prayer Book shows, the crucial challenge to the Evangelical Protestant is to identify the *real value* of the Eucharist over and against that of hearing and believing the Word:

But if a man...do not receive the Sacrament of Christ's Body and Blood: the Curate shall instruct him that if he do truly repent him of his sins, and stedfastly believe that Jesus Christ hath suffered death upon the Cross for him, and shed his Blood for his redemption, earnestly remembering the benefits he hath thereby, and giving him hearty thanks therefore; he doth eat and drink the Body and Blood of our Saviour Christ profitably to his soul's health, although he do not receive the Sacrament with his mouth.[16]

The third contention is that, as well as theological forces, there are also historical forces working against the expression of an evangelical form of eucharistic spirituality. Such historical factors need to be defined in fairly broad terms as those which have influenced or determined the contemporary culture and consciousness of Evangelicalism. The following criticism of Zwingli's and Oecolampadius's eucharistic theology by Calvin points to a very real dynamic in the quest for a Protestant sacramental theology:

they laboured more to pull down what was evil than to build up what was good. For though they did not deny the truth they did not teach it so clearly as they ought to have done.[17]

We shall see that the extent to which the dynamic is active will be in close relation to the perceived threat from other, alternative systems.

This points to the fourth contention, which is that, when the historical context is sympathetic, the sacramental instinct inherent within Evangelicalism will begin to emerge and flourish. Such a climate may be produced either through the weakness of the negative historical forces at that particular moment (in relation to the survival of the particular Evangelical grouping), or through the health and creativity of the internal life of the grouping itself.

The fifth and final contention is that a sympathetic historical climate is not in itself sufficient to sustain the development of a healthy Evangelical expression of sacramental spirituality. Some attempt to grapple with the theological forces is needed in order to ensure that the sacramentalism remains Evangelical and that the Evangelicalism remains sacramental.

The recent period

Evangelicalism has experienced enormous changes in recent decades. For reasons which will become clear, our attention will be focused on the period just before 1960 to soon after 1980. During these years Evangelicals showed a growing concern to place the sacraments and especially the Eucharist in a more central position in their practice and theology. We may account for this in terms of the changing environment in which Evangelicalism found itself. Broadly speaking, there were three factors which changed the way in which Evangelicals viewed themselves and others within the Church. The first was the gradual strengthening of their political position within the Church of England. The second was the ecumenical climate of the wider Church. The third was the influence of the Charismatic Movement on Christians of all types, including Evangelicals.

The winds of change forced Evangelicals to review critically their own state of theology and spirituality. Many found it necessary to distinguish the essentials from the extras, the core from the culture, and in so doing identified missing motifs and retarded understandings in both. Although this was a general feature of Evangelicalism's life (even to the extent of creating the acknowledged identity problem at the end of the 1970s), the process was particularly noticeable in an increasing appreciation of the Eucharist amongst Evangelicals. Evangelicals began to engage with the theological forces within the Protestant system which inhibit sacramental expression, and which are most consistently and radically emphasized in their own tradition. However, the process remained at an early stage: it was rudimentary and instinctive rather than developed and systematic. If the rising sacramentalism observable in this period is to be sustained in later decades, the process of theological reflection and integration must also continue. If it does not, then the sacramental quest will be quashed when the historical context becomes less hospitable, and it will die the death of a burst of enthusiasm inadequately rooted in a consistent conceptual framework.

There are signs that this change of context is already happening at the beginning of the 1990s. Pragmatic concerns for evangelism and Church growth have become priorities for the end of the century and beyond. These emphases are, of course, nothing new for Evangelicals, but they have recently taken on a new precedence. Along with other branches of the Church, Evangelicals are concentrating attention on the creation and initiation of new converts rather than on the renewing and upbuilding of present Christians but, unlike at least the Catholic end of the Church (in all its manifestations), they are not doing so from a position of a thoroughgoing practical commitment to the centrality of the Eucharist supported by a developed and coherent theological structure. The particular challenges for the

Church at this stage of its history underline the need for the process of systematic reflection on the place of the Eucharist in Evangelical theology and spirituality.

THE METHOD

The first task, in part 1, is to survey the broad sweep of Evangelical eucharistic thought from the Reformation to the beginning of the 1960s. The aim is to meet the challenge set by Max Warren in 1946 that Evangelicals should:

> study afresh our whole doctrine and practice with regard to the Lord's Supper in the light of the practice and teaching of men to whom all Evangelicals look back with veneration. I suggest that this will involve us in a rediscovery of certain emphases which have too commonly been lacking, and for lack of which we are in want of an Evangelical expression of Eucharistic worship which gives worthy form to the central insights of our tradition.[18]

Such an attempt need not, however, be restricted to those occupying places of honour upon the Evangelical mantelpiece, but may be extended to significant individuals and movements that sought to maintain and defend the basic Reformation insights which Evangelicals hold dear.[19] The brief, therefore, is not to offer an extensive history but rather to chronicle an Evangelical strand mainly, but not exclusively, within the Church of England, in order to identify the factors which have helped or hindered the expression of an Evangelical form of sacramentalism. No study of Evangelical doctrine can be credible without a grounding in the theology of the mainstream *Reformers*, and so it is with the thought of Luther, Zwingli, Calvin and Cranmer that I begin. The rest of the study will focus on England (with occasional reference to Scotland) and move from the seventeenth-century *reinterpreters* of the Reformed tradition to the *revivalists* of the eighteenth. I shall conclude with the *reactors* to Tractarianism and Anglo-Catholicism in the nineteenth and twentieth centuries.

The task of part 2 is to chart the characteristics of eucharistic thought amongst Anglican Evangelicals in recent decades. The period from just before 1960 to soon after 1980 was one of dramatic change in the life of Evangelicalism as it responded to the considerable developments in the life of the Church. As these decades span the period of liturgical revision, the publication of the ecumenical statements which touch on the Eucharist, and the consolidation of the movements and influences affecting the spirituality of the Church, I shall concentrate on them in depth – though with reference to developments up to the end of the 1980s and the beginning of the 1990s. Evangelical involvement in and reaction to the liturgical revision of the Eucharist will be analysed. The impact of the Ecumenical Movement upon Evangelicals' understanding of the Eucharist will be assessed. The place of the Eucharist in Evangelical piety – particularly in terms of the influence of the Charismatic Movement – will be considered. The aim will not be to provide an exhaustive phenomenological analysis but rather to assess how the tradition of a positive Evangelical regard for the Eucharist, as identified in the general survey, was received and used amidst the specific features which marked the years from just before 1960 to soon after 1980. Thus, I shall attempt to show how the various theological methods and historical influences which have plagued or profited an Evangelical expression of a eucharistic spirituality were operative during this period.

The task of part 3 is to use resources which the tradition has at its disposal, both from within its own history and from the contemporary debate in the wider Church, to continue the process of theological reflection and integration, which has been identified as already happening and which is in need of further development. The classic themes of the sacramental function of the Eucharist, the experience of the eucharistic presence and, finally, the sacrificial dimension of the Eucharist will be then explored. The challenge will be to express the intrinsic relationship between Gospel, Bible and Sacrament, which is implied by the Pauline statement that 'as often as you eat this bread and drink the cup [Sacrament], you proclaim the Lord's death until he comes [Gospel]'; (1 Cor. 11 : 26) ; and by the dominical saying, 'This is my Body [Sacrament] which is given for you [Gospel]' (Luke 22 : 19) ; and by the Emmaus experience : 'he interpreted to them in all the scriptures [Bible] the things concerning himself [Gospel] ... When he was at table with them, he took the bread and blessed, and broke it, and gave it to them [Sacrament]. And their eyes were opened and they recognised him [Gospel], (Luke 24 : 27, 30).

Again, limits must be set. I am not attempting to answer the detailed liturgical questions which are inevitably raised in any theological discussion of the sacramental, Christological and sacrificial dimensions of the Eucharist. Neither am I attempting a definitive systematic treatment. Rather I am pointing to the directions that Evangelical theology must travel if it is to defend and extend its rediscovery of the central significance of the Eucharist in the life of the Church. In the language of the Sociology of Knowledge, I am examining the coherence of the plausibility structure which has a tendency towards minimizing the significance and necessity of the Eucharist. To do so, I shall have to consider whether the elements which mediate the meaningful world-view to the Evangelical consciousness have been sufficiently related to the anatomy of both Gospel and Bible. I shall have to look at what happens as those mediating structures begin to be altered by, for example, spiritual experience (Charismatic Renewal), or the widening of one's circle of 'significant others' (Ecumenical Movement), or a creative herme-neutic within one's own tradition (made possible by increased political confidence). And I shall have to consider ways in which the 'partial transformation' (that is, integration) of centrality for the Eucharist into the contemporary Evangelical system may be main-tained and developed without creating the need for an 'alternation' (that is, an abandonment of Evangelicalism in favour of an alternative system more readily compatible with a sacramental theology and spirituality). The means and methods of partial transformation are key issues for contemporary Anglican Evangeli-calism. They represented the challenge behind both the identity problem, which Evangelicals talked much about in the late 1970s and early 1980s, and the claim that Evangelicalism is losing direction and distinctiveness, which has been voiced at the end of the 1980s and the beginning of the 1990s.[20]

In conclusion, it is worth considering whether the work of religio-educational psychologists may help to identify the dynamics of the contemporary life of Anglican Evangelicalism. These psychologists trace a series of stages in an individual's journey to faith: an intuitive grasp is consolidated by affinitive group solidarity and moves, eventually, to an independently reasoned position.[21] An application of J. W. Fowler's delineation may provide a useful perspective on the history of Evangelicalism: the movement was forged out of an experiential, intuitive discovery of religious meaning and develop-ment into a cohesive, self-affirming grouping which defined that meaning in relative isolation from competing and undermining explanations. However, it has now emerged into a period of self-confidence which has, in turn, bred a healthy self-criticism in which it is aware of its possible deficiencies and sensitive to the alternatives. Fowler describes this phase – conjunctive faith – in the following way:

Stage 5 involves the integration into self and outlook of much that was suppressed or unrecognized in the interest of Stage 4's self-certainty and conscious cognitive and affective adaptation to reality. This stage develops a 'second naiveté' (Ricoeur) in which symbolic power is reunited with conceptual meanings. Here there must also be a new reclaiming and reworking of one's past. There must be an opening to the voices of one's 'deeper self'. Importantly, this involves a critical recognition of one's social unconscious – the myths, the ideal images and prejudices built into the self-system by virtue of one's nurture within a particular social class, religious tradition, ethnic group or the like.[22]

Fowler's description of conjunctive faith resonates in a remarkable way with the profound changes which have been happening in the life of Evangelicalism over the last thirty years. The 'symbolic power' of fundamental features of the movement have sought expression in 'conceptual meanings' which are not merely a repetition but 'a reclaiming and reworking of one's [corporate] past'. This has involved both a 'critical recognition of... the myths, the ideal images and prejudices built into the system' and 'an opening up to the voices of one's "deeper self"'. Signs of this liberation into the deeper self include a deeper contact with the sacramental, pentecostal and ecumenical dimensions of Christian experience and the missiological and hermeneutical complexity of Christian service.

Clearly, some Evangelicals are either regretful over the movement's entry into this phase of development or impatient with its length and complexity. Regret is expressed by those who bewail contemporary Evangelicalism's departure from the traditional characteristics of classic Evangelicalism. For them the majority of Evangelicals have lost their commitment to the central doctrines of the movement and betrayed its cause by compromise in the campaign to restore the Church of England to its authentic evangelical–Protestant identity.[23] Impatience is expressed by those who feel that the process of integration has created such diversity within Evangelicalism that it has lost its cohesion and its distinctiveness. For them Evangelicalism is in danger of becoming so broad in its make-up that it fails to speak with a clear voice and take a firm lead and so forfeits the opportunity decisively to influence – even determine – the future of the Church.[24] However, on purely pragmatic grounds, those who feel that by either attempting the process of integration or by taking too long over it, Evangelicals have lost their chance to affect the future course of the Church of England, cannot fail to be challenged and encouraged by the presence of an Archbishop of Canterbury who represents precisely the liberation which so much of Evangelicalism has been experiencing and the integration for which it has been striving.[25] And on more theoretical grounds, the basic characteristics of Christian existence require both individuals and movements to be open to a deeper apprehension of the fullness of God's revealed truth. In terms of Fowler's analysis of faith development, there is a remaining stage to be reached after conjunctive faith, and that is the realization of faith's full potential. The extent to which this is reached depends on the success of the liberating and integrating process of the earlier stage.

We must not be further side-tracked into attempting a phenomenology of Evangelicalism's past and present or into making a prediction about its future. Our task is more precise. It is to survey the broad history of one aspect of Evangelicalism's theological life, analyse its passage through one period of rapid change, and then present ways of developing its consistency with the fundamentals of Evangelical theology and experience as they are reflected upon in the light of the contemporary theological world in all its ecumenical breadth.

PART I

Historical survey

CHAPTER 2

The Reformers' bequest

MARTIN LUTHER

It is right to begin our historical survey with Luther, not only because, propelled by his radical commitment to the Gospel and the Bible, he was the pioneer of the Reformation, but also, because he believed that the Sacrament itself expressed the reality of the Gospel.

The Eucharist, for Luther, was the 'testament', or sign, of the promise of our justification by God's forgiveness through Christ's death. It cannot at the same time be a sacrifice, except of prayer, praise and thanksgiving. It speaks of what has been achieved for us *to receive*, not what remains for us *to do*. In his earlier work (for example, 'Treatise on the New Testament') Luther explored the concept of Christ's heavenly offering of *us in himself* to the Father in the eucharistic celebration: 'Not that we offer the sacrament, but that by our praise, prayer, and sacrifice we move him and give him occasion to offer himself for us in heaven and ourselves with him.'[1] But these thoughts became eclipsed in his later writings, on the one hand, by the debate on the doctrine of the presence of Christ within the Reformation and, on the other, by the intensification of the polemic with Rome. Throughout his work he wanted to ensure that the Eucharist could not be described in any sort of sacrificial way which would imply our co-operation with the salvific process beyond that of believing and receiving the promise. Here, of course, he was followed by the other Reformers:

I am here combatting that opinion with which the Roman Antichrist and his prophets have imbued the whole world – viz. that the mass is a work by which the priest offers Christ and the others who in the oblation receive him gain merit with God, or that it is an expiatory victim by which they regain the favour of God (Calvin).[2]

Like Luther, the other Reformers made a very clear distinction between Christ's propitiatory sacrifice on the Cross and 'another kind of sacrifice' which is 'made of them that be reconciled by Christ, to testify our duties unto God, and to shew ourselves thankful unto him. And therefore they be called sacrifices of laud, praise and thanksgiving' (Cranmer).[3]

The general agreement between the Reformers over the eucharistic sacrifice makes their disagreement over the eucharistic presence even more striking. Although Luther rejected the medieval insistence that the doctrine of transubstantiation must be accepted as the means of explaining the eucharistic presence of Christ, he was committed to the belief which it sought to express, that is, the real (substantial) presence of Christ's body and blood in strict relation to the eucharistic bread and wine. He was convinced that belief in the real presence was demanded by both Gospel and Bible and therefore was of fundamental theological significance; it could not be relegated to the doctrinal periphery. He argued that you cannot believe that Christ's body was 'given for you' unless you believe that 'this is [his] body'. In answer to the question *why*? he would have responded (primarily) on an exegetical level and (secondarily) on a theological level. Exegetically, the two elements in the Institution Narrative were both said by Christ and are both to be believed. They are both promises; you cannot choose one promise without the other, you choose both or neither. Theologically, the one ('this is my body') is the sign and seal of the other ('given for you'). It was chosen by Christ to be a means of receiving the forgiveness of sins made possible by his death.

As the controversy with Zwingli developed, Luther was forced to indicate why the Sacrament was necessary when the same reception of the Gospel is available, as Luther admitted, through other means:

Thus I can have the Mass daily, nay hourly, since, as often as I will, I can set before myself the words of Christ, and nourish and strengthen my faith in them; and this is in very truth spiritual eating and drinking.[4]

Here we have the classic Protestant tension: if faith is the medium of our relationship with God, why is there need for the Sacrament? Or more specifically, if Christ is received by faith, why the need for a bodily presence in the Eucharist to be received by the mouth? Luther's answer was again primarily an exegetical one: this is what the Word says; our role is not to justify the decisions of God but to respond to them.

On a more theological level, it needs to be said that for Luther the real presence did not in any way undermine the place of faith. The Sacrament is to be approached 'not with any works, or powers, or merits of one's own, but by faith alone',[5] that is, in an attitude in which we know we can do nothing and acknowledge that Christ has done everything. Thus, the offer of God's forgiveness, 'This is my body given for you', is received only by faith. However, this points to a more precise definition of the faith involved in the eucharistic experience than is often assumed in the caricature of Protestant theology: faith is not in itself the medium between the individual and God, it is rather the willingness to acknowledge and accept Christ himself as that medium. Faith is simply the reception of Christ's mediation. It is therefore important to identify the ways Christ has chosen to communicate the benefits of his mediation to us in our faith, and Luther defined these as the appointed contexts of the Word, Baptism, the Eucharist and Absolution.

It is even more important, Luther insisted, to define correctly the character of the mediation as the mediation of Christ *Incarnate*. It is here that we see the root issue in the differences between the Lutheran and Zwinglian sides at the Colloquy of Marburg. During the debate Oecolampadius said to Luther, 'you should not cling to the humanity and flesh of Christ, but rather lift up your mind to his divinity', to which Luther replied: 'I do not know of any God except him who was made flesh, nor do I want to have another. And there is no other God who could save us, besides the God Incarnate.'[6] Luther distinguished between the 'absolute power of God' and his 'ordered power'.[7] He argued that our interest and dealings are with the latter, that is, with the Incarnate Son, the person of Christ, in his divinity and humanity. Christ is the locus of our standing before God and our knowledge of God. In Luther's later thought the Eucharist became not merely a sign and seal of what God has done in Christ but actually a means of union with Christ in the most intimate way. It offers the renewal of our flesh by the life-giving flesh of Christ – the medicine of immortality. At the same time as the physical touching, there is a spiritual touching, for just as with the woman who had an issue of blood and Mary in her conception of Christ, the physical contact with the Son enables a believing, spiritual faith to emerge.

The philosophical category Luther employed to allow for the possibility of the presence of Christ's human body at every Eucharist was that of the ubiquity of Christ's body: Christ's human body is

included in the *communicatio idiomatum* and therefore participates in
the divine omnipresence. Luther's stress on the presence of Christ's
humanity in the Eucharist points to the heart of his theology. He
argued unswervingly that to drive a wedge between the divinity and
humanity of Christ, attributing the power to be present in illocal
ways to one and not the other is to divide the person of Christ and,
therefore, to see the revelatory and redemptive work of God as in
some way 'outside' the work of the Incarnate Son, thus denying the
mediatorial role of Christ and destroying the Gospel.

ULRICH ZWINGLI

Zwingli's thought on the Eucharist developed throughout his life and
it was expressed generally in a highly polemical context, but it would
still be fair to say that, whereas Luther's theological emphasis was on
the objective action of God in the Eucharist, Zwingli's stress fell on
the subjective activity of the participant. This is not to say that
Zwingli intended to deny the initiative of God in the salvific process
but rather that he did not see the Eucharist as involving an essential
and dynamic soteriological function. For Luther the Sacrament
(specifically the elements) was a locus for the reception by faith of the
gift of God and, therefore, was a means of grace. But for Zwingli the
role of the Eucharist (in its whole action) lay in its ability to illustrate
what has taken place by other means and was thus, in Peter
Stephens's words, a 'sign of grace given'[8] rather than a means of
giving a grace.
    Zwingli's concerns were threefold. First, he wished to maintain the
sovereignty of God, rather than tying him to ecclesial activities.
Secondly, he wanted to ensure the freedom of the Spirit, rather than
constraining him to external forms. Thirdly, he desired to protect the
basis of our Christian status as faith in Christ rather than to provide
an alternative meeting with Christ which is in some sense independent of faith. Although this gave an apparently negative thrust
to his statements about the Eucharist, he was also able to mark out
the lines of a much more positive approach, even if he did not have
the opportunity to develop this fully. He saw the value of the
Eucharist lying in its memorial, ethical and corporate functions. It
facilitates 'the contemplation of faith'[9] by its commemoration of the
one sacrifice. It stimulates the will to live the Christian life. It enables

a corporate testimony to be made by those assembled through which they are bound together in common allegiance.

Unfortunately, because of the highly polemical atmosphere in which the debate over the eucharistic presence took place, it was Zwingli's negations rather than his creations which stood in the foreground. He regarded belief in the real presence to be logically incoherent, exegetically unsound and soteriologically destructive. His argument for logical incoherency was based not only on the rational argument that it is 'impossible to understand the words literally',[10] but also on the Christological conviction that, as Christ's body is an authentically human one and, therefore, shares the characteristics of normal human bodies, it can be in only one place at one time (that is, in heaven). On exegetical grounds Zwingli insisted that Scripture must be interpreted consistently. Hence, the words 'This is my body' need to be seen in relation, first, to other sayings of Christ in which he makes use of metaphor and, second, to Christ's warning in John 6: 53 that the interest of the Christian life is in the spiritual realm, not the physical. Therefore, from a soteriological perspective, a belief in the bodily eating of Christ creates a rival method of salvation to that faith in Christ. Eating the body of Christ therefore simply means believing in him:

Whenever he [Christ] speaks of eating his flesh and drinking his blood he simply means believing in the work of that suffering which he bore for our sakes…Therefore to eat his flesh and to believe on him are one and the same, otherwise there are two ways of salvation, the one by eating and drinking the flesh and the other by believing on him.[11]

Hence, the words of Institution cannot be taken in their literal form. They must be seen in their inner meaning, so that they concur with the breadth of Scripture and, correspondingly, with the nature of the Gospel. In this way the bread is designed to signify Christ's body so that it calls to remembrance in the receiver the death of Christ, which is the sole source of his salvation. It is in this sense that Zwingli was able to talk of the presence of the body of Christ: a spiritual presence of the body – which remains essentially circumscribed in heaven – to the believing mind and heart of the individual. He argued that limitation of the presence of the body to this sphere is also demanded by the fact of the ascension. The nature of our relationship with Christ is now necessarily spiritual, not physical, relying on the activity of the Spirit, not the bodily presence of the Incarnate Christ.

In their different attempts to handle the dynamic between Gospel and Eucharist both Luther and Zwingli left a lasting legacy to Evangelical tradition. On the one hand, Luther's adherence to the text of Scripture even when an alternative interpretation would be more compatible with other criteria in the tradition, his appreciation of the mystery of the Eucharist and his attempt to ground the Sacrament in the gracious gift of God remain a challenge. On the other hand, Zwingli's consistent and comparative approach to Scripture, his attempt to ensure that the Spirit's role is not negated by bread and wine, and also his recognition that describing the Eucharist in subjective terms does not deprive it of a dynamic quality, are equally significant. The key question around which the debate revolved was the nature of the person of Christ – human and divine – and the mode of our participation in him. Luther's answer was that of the real presence. But by describing the presence of Christ's humanity in such strict relation to his bodily presence, and then, by describing the bodily presence in such strict relation to the eucharistic elements, he stood perilously close to undermining the non-sacramental relationship and to defining the character of Christ's body in a way which destroyed its human credibility and therefore Christ's solidarity with us. Zwingli's answer involved so distinguishing between the natures that our participation with Christ in his divinity was in danger of being divorced from our participation in his humanity.

JOHN CALVIN

Calvin was critical of Roman, Lutheran and Zwinglian methodology:

> Inquisitive men have wanted to define: How the body of Christ is present in the bread ... But they do not realize that the primary question in fact is: How does the body of Christ, as it was given for us, become ours? In other words, how do we possess the whole Christ crucified and become partakers of all his blessings? Because this primary question has been omitted as unimportant, in fact neglected and almost forgotten, the conflict has raged over the one obscure and difficult question: How is the body eaten by us?[12]

Although Luther did not try to answer the *how* question (the explanation of the body's relation to the bread), he did focus attention so much on the *what* question (the conviction of the body's real relation to the bread), that the *who* question (the relation

between Christ and the believer) became isolated from the general
perspective of the relationship between God and his people in Christ.
The result was to centre attention on the sign rather than on the
fulfilment of the sign. In their own way Zwingli and his colleagues fell
into the same trap:

in taking too great pains to maintain that the bread and wine are called the
body and blood of Christ because they are signs, they took no care to make
the reservation that they are such signs that *the reality is joined to them*; or to
protest that they did not at all intend to obscure the *true communion which our
Lord gives us in his body and blood by the sacrament* (my emphasis).[13]

Calvin was therefore refocusing the debate on the central character of
Christian existence as a real communication with the life and person
of the Incarnate Son. It is neither physical interaction itself nor
spiritual–mental contact alone; it is rather a substantial union[14] with
Christ, a sharing in him, a participation in him; it is about being 'in
Christ'.

To Zwingli, he was saying that the Eucharist offers, through the
appointed signs, the possibility of such communication:

When these absurdities [affixing or enclosing Christ to the bread or
circumscribing him] are discarded, I willingly admit anything which helps
to express the true and substantial communication of the body and blood of
the Lord, as exhibited to believers under the sacred symbols of the Supper,
understanding that they are not received by the imagination or intellect
alone, but are enjoyed in reality as the food of eternal life.[15]

To Luther, Calvin was saying that the substantial communication
present in the Eucharist must be of a kind that is consistent with other
theological considerations deriving from the character of the Gospel.
The eucharistic presence is of a corresponding ontological order to
that presence of Christ made possible by hearing and believing the
Word. It shares in the same characteristics – the objective promise is
received by personal faith, which in turn is evoked by the Holy Spirit.
  It was the role of the Spirit in the faith relationship with Christ
which was the most significant and potentially most positive element
in Zwingli's thought. Calvin went on to make it explicit and central
by arguing that union with Christ is not fixed by sacramental
causality (Rome), or by physical presence (Luther), or by 'the
contemplation of faith' (Zwingli). Instead, 'The bond of connection...is the Spirit of Christ, who unites us to him, and is a kind
of channel by which everything that Christ has is derived to us.'[16]

Calvin thus widened the horizon of the eucharistic presence to a Trinitarian breadth, in which the gift of Christ, as the promise of God, is realized by the activity of the Spirit in the believer, through the use of bread and wine. Therefore, notions of the ubiquity of Christ's body and of its substantial relation to the bread are Christologically demeaning, because they 'detract from his heavenly glory',[17] destructive, because they compromise the true human nature of Christ's body with its given limitations and thereby confuse the natures, and unnecessary, because they deprive the Spirit of his role as the one who 'unites things separated in space'.[18]

Calvin's emphasis on the consistency of the eucharistic experience with the non-sacramental experience meant that he could not identify a specific gift in the Eucharist. However, he did allow a distinct function for the Eucharist, 'whereby Christ reveals himself in a special way':[19]

The Supper too is a special assurance that we are being helped by our God, when we are as it were mid-way along the road that we are being made to go on, striving ever towards our God. Let us note that the Supper is meant to correct and complete the things that are still defective. For our having made a beginning would be nothing unless God continued to make us feel his grace, and of that we have good assurance in the Supper.[20]

The Eucharist is the seal of the promise and it is so not just by a powerful symbolic action but by a real engagement with the person of the promise by the power of the Holy Spirit:

That sacred partaking of his flesh and blood, by which Christ pours his life into us, as if it penetrated into our bones and marrow, he also testifies and seals in the Supper, not by presenting a vain and empty sign, but by manifesting there the effectiveness of his Spirit to fulfil what he promises.[21]

Whereas for Zwingli the Sacrament provided an opportunity merely for the individual to affirm his faith and to confirm his allegiance to the community, for Calvin it strengthened faith, because it actively and effectively, under the power of the Spirit, confirmed faith by realizing the potential available to faith – that is, an ever deeper union with Jesus Christ. It is here that we meet, as we did with Luther, Calvin's definition of faith not as the end result, but as the way of entry to him who is its end:

For, though the Apostle teaches that Christ dwells in our hearts through faith, yet no one would interpret this dwelling to be faith, but all perceive that the splendid result of faith is described, that through it the faithful attain to the possession of Christ abiding in them. After this manner, in calling Himself the Bread of life the Lord willed to teach not only that salvation is laid up for us in faith on His death and resurrection but also that a real communication of Himself brings to pass that His life passes into us and becomes ours, not otherwise than bread when it is taken for nourishment, supplies strength to the body.[22]

To be sure, such participation is available by other means, but this does not detract from the Eucharist's role to confirm and fulfil (assure and seal) the believer's involvement in Christ by an objectively grounded gift of Christ himself, in his body and blood.

Calvin's comments on the sacrificial associations of the Eucharist may help to shed further light on the distinct function which he allowed for the Eucharist. In line with Luther and Zwingli, he rejected any propitiatory character for the Eucharist. Nevertheless, when he was able to escape from the polemic, which was understandably fiercely motivated at this point, he made dynamic use of the memorial context. The assurance provided by the Sacrament is derived precisely from its commemorative character, for it 'sends us to the cross of Christ'.[23] Although absolute efficacy lies in the one, past sacrifice of the Cross alone, in order for it to be effective for us, it needs to make personal contact with us, 'for it would be of no avail to us that the sacrifice was once offered, if we did not now feast on that sacred banquet'.[24] Such is the role of the Eucharist. Calvin went on to develop the covenant language of the Institution Narratives:

He also calls the cup 'the covenant in his blood'. For he in some measure renews or rather continues, the covenant which he once for all ratified with his blood (as far as it pertains to the strengthening of our faith) whenever he proffers that sacred blood for us to taste.[25]

It is here that the two themes of covenant-memorial and union with Christ meet. Through our personal union with Christ continued at the Eucharist we have a personal involvement in his one sacrifice and in his permanent priesthood before the Father. All this, of course, could happen through other means, but again this does not detract from the value of the Eucharist – for it is here, through the meaning attached to the signs, that there is an appointed, specified and promised contact with Christ in his death. And it is a contact with and participation in Christ which is ultimately beyond precise definition:

Now, if anyone should ask me how this presence of Christ in the Eucharist takes place, I shall not be ashamed to confess that it is a secret too lofty for either my mind to comprehend or my words to declare, And to speak more plainly, I rather experience than understand it. Therefore, I here embrace without controversy the truth of God in which I may safely rest.[26]

It is possible that in his experience he sensed that something unique is involved in the Eucharist but, for systematic reasons and out of a genuine recognition of the mystery of God's way in Christ, he would not attempt to define it too closely. Given certain conditions, he was prepared to advise others to be open to the reality of that mystery: 'I therefore freely admit that no man should measure its sublimity by the little measure of my childishness.'[27]

THOMAS CRANMER

The idiosyncrasies of the Reformation in England, Cranmer's liturgical ability to use traditional forms whilst injecting them with new, Reformed, meaning, and the inevitable backcloth of controversy make it difficult to pinpoint Cranmer's mind on the Eucharist. Was he a reluctant Reformer, a Zwinglian radical or, under Bucer's influence, a 'Calvinist stooge'? The first view is generally discounted and so the question revolves around whether his sacramental allegiance was to Calvin or to Zwingli.[28] But perhaps, given the character of the situation in England and the scholarly nature of the man, that is not the right question. It is not an either–or choice, for elements from both men can be found in his teaching. It would be fairer to say that he was not a Zwinglian in that in his desire for a weekly celebration he clearly wanted the sort of centrality for the Sacrament which Zwingli was prepared to do without, and that in his theology he believed that the Eucharist provided a context for a real communication with the ascended Christ. Nevertheless, it could also be said that he was a Zwinglian to the extent that he emphasized the symbolic character of the Eucharist, stressing the priority and mediation of faith to a greater extent than Calvin.

Like Zwingli and Calvin, Cranmer insisted on the consistency of the sacramental with the non-sacramental relationship as determined by the dictates of ascension, Spirit and faith. Hence, attention should be focused not on the bread but on those who use it: 'the change is inward, not in the bread but in the receiver. To have Christ present really here, when I may receive Him in faith, is not available to do me good.'[29] The 'change' is able to happen in the sacramental context not because of what the elements possess in themselves but because they facilitate the faith relationship: 'not that the bread and wine have or can have any holiness in them, but that they be used to an holy work, and represent holy things'.[30]

Cranmer made much use of the physical analogy of the Sacrament – as the bread feeds our bodies, so our souls are to be fed with the body and blood of Christ. Despite the apparent simplicity of the argument, it is actually quite subtle. On the one hand, the Eucharist merely stimulates faith, thus making faith the key ingredient and thereby depriving the sacramental media of any intrinsic value. On the other hand, the spiritual feeding on the body and blood of Christ is, given the condition of worthy reception, simultaneous with and also helped and increased by the physical eating, and thus the Eucharist retains a sacramental function. In other words, the bread helps a job to be done. Thus, in a similar way to Calvin, Cranmer defined the value of the Sacrament in terms of its ability to assure the believer, confirming the word of the Gospel and continuing the believer's growth in the life of Christ.

Nevertheless, there was in Cranmer's thought a greater tendency than in Calvin's for the bread to appear superfluous. Whereas Calvin tried to link the bread and the reality in intimate but not intrinsic connection, Cranmer tended to divide them, so that the function of the Sacrament lay in its affective rather than effective character. This is not to say that Cranmer could not define the Eucharist in effective terms, rather that for him the effective potential of the Sacrament was a product of its affective force: the bread only stimulates faith and thereby facilitates the eating of the body. But for Calvin the signified was so related to the sign that the latter mediates the former to those who have the prerequisite of faith. We are inevitably in the realm of very subtle differences over specifics within the context of general agreement over basics. Calvin did not step into notions of instrumental causality; he still maintained the priority of faith but, whereas he argued that we should view the bread in 'Chalcedonian'[31] terms of neither confounding (as with Rome and Luther) nor dividing (as with Zwingli) the bread from the body, Cranmer veered to the Zwinglian side, of so dislocating the bread from the reality that its sacramental (rather than symbolic, dramatic, analogous) character is undermined. This may be seen by the summary of his eucharistic thought in the words of administration of the 1552 liturgy:

Take and eat this in remembrance that Christ died for thee, and feed on him, in thy heart by faith, with thanksgiving.[32]

The difference in emphasis derives perhaps, as I have indicated, from the way that the role of faith was related to the wider issues of soteriology and spirituality. We have seen that both Luther and Calvin defined faith as the means of entry into union with Christ – a participation which Calvin was prepared to paint in very substantive terms. To be sure, Cranmer too saw personal union with Christ as the point and fact of Christian life, but he so emphasized the merits and righteousness (virtues of Christ) available to the believer through faith that the relationship appears to be an external 'I–Thou' one in which the Christ in heaven shares the benefits he has achieved, rather than an 'I in Thee', 'Thou in Me' union with the present Christ in his incorporative humanity. This influenced the sacramental categories used. In Calvin's words: 'to them eating is faith, to me it rather ensues from faith'.[33] Thus, rather than eating the body having a specific and exclusive relationship to the death, it had for Calvin a more directly personal reference to the whole Christ. Hence, whereas Cranmer placed the focus on the bread's function to facilitate faith in the Atonement, Calvin placed it on the bread's function to cement the union with the Incarnate One made possible by faith in the Atonement.

CONCLUSION

Luther, Zwingli, Calvin and Cranmer were all sacramental in the sense of wanting to retain the Sacrament and to give it a place of honour. Luther, Calvin and Cranmer were also sacramental in the sense of wanting a central place for the Eucharist in the regular life of the Church by a weekly celebration, and in the sense of the reality of their own eucharistic spirituality and devotion. Indeed, their emphasis on communion rather than enactment as the Sacrament's *raison d'être* and their stress on the communal dynamics of the celebration are their lasting gifts not only to the Evangelical sacramental tradition but to all sacramental traditions. Luther's emphasis on communion being with 'Christ and all his saints', Calvin's concern for the discipline and purity of the eucharistic community, Cranmer's liturgical and architectural reordering according to participatory principles, and even Zwingli's definition of a sacrament as an oath of allegiance to a common cause all show how the Reformers were seeking in their different ways to recover and express the truly corporate character of the Eucharist. Furthermore Luther and Calvin were sacramental in the sense of maintaining emphasis on the connection between the elements and the reality. Finally, Luther was sacramental in the sense of attaching an ontological distinctiveness to the Eucharist.

There were two influences of a non-directly systematic kind which influenced their theology. The first was the climate of controversy. Inevitably, polemic influenced their presentation. Even Zwingli was prepared to be more positive after Marburg than he was before or during. And in a different context Calvin might have given less space to the parameters of his 'childishness' and more to the openness to mystery. The defensive mechanism was particularly active in the crucial question of sacrifice with the result that the more creative themes of 'Christ offering us' in Luther, the emphasis on the mediatorial priesthood of Christ in Calvin, and the implications of thanksgiving in Cranmer were not fully developed. The second influence was their own experience of the Eucharist. Their sacramental spirituality clearly influenced at least the esteem in which they held the Eucharist and therefore affected the place they felt it should have and the form it should take in the practice of the Church, and even in the theological scheme itself.

The key theological question which was at stake was simply whether there is a real encounter with the saving reality of Christ in the Eucharist which derives from its specific sacramental character. A further question was whether such an encounter is related as much to the humanity of Christ as it is to his divinity. We have seen that the role of Christ's humanity in the Eucharist was vital for Luther. To be fair, this was also true for the other Reformers. However, by talking in terms of the essential presence of Christ's divinity in the believer compared with the essential presence of Christ's humanity in heaven, Zwingli and Cranmer came close to the danger of dividing Christ's divinity from his humanity which Luther had warned about so passionately. For Luther their approach was disruptive and dangerous because it implied a Nestorian Christ and failed to see that our relation to God is to be defined entirely in terms of the Incarnate Christ. Calvin's way through the dilemma of maintaining both a credible and a present humanity was to emphasize the motifs of union, participation and incorporation by the Spirit who is himself the 'bond of union'.[34] Such language offers the most constructive

possibility for a consistently evangelical understanding of the
Eucharist. However, it is good to be reminded by Nicholas Ridley
that the real issue remains the *who* not the *how* of the Eucharist:

> Both you and I agree herein, that in the Sacrament is the very true and
> natural body and blood of Christ... only we differ *in modo* in the way and
> manner of being: we confess all one thing to be in the Sacrament, and dissent
> in the manner of being there.[35]

Nevertheless, the *how* question of the body's relation to the bread,
though secondary, is still relevant and may influence our apprehension of the reality (the *who* question). Thus, we may still ask, How
sacramental is the Sacrament to be? In liturgical terms, What profile
are the bread and wine to have? Or, in more theological terms, Can
we point to a specific gift and/or special function to the Eucharist
which derives from its sacramental character? How later Evangelical
tradition handled the question and interpreted the answers given by
the Reformers will be considered in subsequent chapters.

useful summary.

CHAPTER 3

The legacy in the Anglican tradition

Revisionist to now show this [handwritten annotation]

The Reformation did not have an easy passage into English life. The radical changes carried out in the short reign of Edward VI were reversed during the reign of Mary. Cranmer, Ridley and Latimer were burnt at the stake for expounding Reformed views of the Eucharist whilst other leaders of the Reformation fled for safety to Geneva and the like. Although the pendulum swung back again when the Protestant Elizabeth became Queen in 1558, the future for the Reformation in England was to be far from smooth. The Settlement of 1559 ended neither the political turbulence nor the polemical disputes which had preceded Elizabeth's reign. Indeed, in many ways it made the situation even more complex. The recreated Protestant establishment found itself fighting a war on two fronts. The battle-lines were drawn not just across the two sides of the Reformation but within the Reformation itself. The integrity of the English Reformation had to be defended on doctrinal grounds against Rome and on practical grounds against the Puritans. The doctrinal limits were set by the Articles and the practical demands were set by an insistence on liturgical and organizational conformity.

The complexities of the age, combined with the movement of history away from the immediate Reformation period, led to the creation (beginning perhaps with Richard Hooker[1] and continued by his successors) of a distinctively Anglican tradition which, whilst committed to the Reformation, was able at the same time to reinterpret it in ways which tentatively rehabilitated certain traditional features of sacramental theology and spirituality. This process began in some ways during the Elizabethan (and generally Calvinist) period, and it also occurred in some form within Puritanism. Hence, it should not be seen as a betrayal of the Reformation but, rather, as a sign that an insufficiency was felt by both traditions with the legacy bequeathed to them by the Reformers.

It is possible to identify three emphases which developed in Anglican thought during this formative period in its history. First, there was a tendency to allow a more prominent liturgical role for the sacramental elements in the eucharistic action. Secondly, there was a concern to concentrate on the experience of the eucharistic presence rather than on the explanations of its mode. Thirdly, there was an attempt to explore the sacrificial dimension of the Eucharist (particularly in relation to the concept of remembrance) in a less inhibited way than that followed by their Reformation Fathers. Of course, all three were intertwined, but for the sake of simplicity they will be considered separately. As there was a definite shift in theological ethos over the period, I shall describe Anglican thought, first, during the reign of Elizabeth, and then briefly refer to developments during the time of the oscillating fortunes of Anglicanism from the reign of James I to Charles II.

THE ELIZABETHAN ERA

Consecration

The 1559 Prayer Book was substantially that of 1552 but the inclusion of the 1549 Words of Administration, though compatible with Cranmer's mature doctrine, related the body to the bread in a much closer way than he ultimately felt necessary. The Johnson case in 1573 centred on the question of supplementary consecration. It is generally agreed that Johnson rightly interpreted Cranmer in his belief that a repetition of the Institution Narrative over any extra bread and wine was not required by the rite. The Commissioners, however, disagreed and insisted that it should be repeated – a conviction that was later enshrined in the Canon Laws of 1603. It was an important decision, first, because it highlighted a shift from the traditional Reformed position and, secondly, because it authorized a higher role for the sacramental elements in themselves and in so doing pointed to a more effective rather than primarily affective sacramental function.

To Johnson's question, 'I pray you tell me one thing whether be the words of Institution spoken for the bread, or for the recyuers?',[2] Zwingli, Calvin and Cranmer would have replied: for the latter. Only Luther would have agreed with the Commissioners that it was for both. Calvin sought to establish an intimate relationship between the sign and the signified and was even prepared to talk of 'sacred food'[3] but (like Zwingli and Cranmer), he had no place for an objective consecration of the elements themselves. In Calvin's mind the Institution Narrative was a warrant for the action and a word to the hearers, not a formula for the bread.[4] For Luther the two could not be separated. The promise to the hearers could be confirmed only if it was substantially present and conveyed by the bread. Hence, in terms of consecration, he remained traditional (and Western). The Johnson case showed that Anglicanism had returned to that same tradition. This is not to say that it adopted or even sought to allow Roman or Lutheran doctrinal beliefs about the effect of consecration, but that an official precedent had been set for seeing the consecration of the elements as a necessary part of the eucharistic action.[5]

Support and authority for the Commissioners' judgement was found in the writings of John Jewel and Richard Hooker. In reply to the contemporary challenge that the Anglican rite lacked a valid consecratory element Jewel maintained that:

We pronounce the same words of consecration that Christ pronounced: we do the same thing that Christ bid us do: we proclaim the death of the Lord: we speak openly in a known tongue; and the people understandeth us; we consecrate for the congregation and not only for ourself: we have the element: we join God's word to it: and so it is made a sacrament.[6]

Three important points emerge from his argument. First, unlike Cranmer he believed that Christ did attach meaning to the elements prior to their distribution. Second and accordingly, he held that the sacramental action not only was related to the moment of reception but was concerned with setting aside the elements for that 'godly use'.[7] Third, his interest was not, therefore, focused exclusively on the hearers and receivers but extended to the elements in their own right (although always with a view to their reception by the people).

With these assumptions Jewel was able to view the sacramental action in effective terms:

We affirm that bread and wine are holy and heavenly mysteries of the body and blood of Christ, and that *by them* Christ himself, being the true bread of eternal life, *is so presently given unto us* that by faith we verily receive his body and blood (my emphasis).[8]

Jewel's interest in consecration, and his corresponding belief in the real reception of the body and blood of Christ by means of the elements, was developed more explicitly by Hooker. He too believed that Christ consecrated the bread and wine prior to their distribution to the disciples, and continues to do so in all our subsequent celebrations – with the result that 'by virtue of his heavenly benediction' these 'mysteries should serve as conducts of life and conveyances of his body and blood unto them'.[9] Hence, consecration is an essential prerequisite to reception, for it is by the 'solemn benediction'[10] that Christ 'doth by his own divine power add to the natural substance thereof supernatural efficacy'.[11] The elements are changed in use so that they become 'causes instrumental upon the receipt whereof the *participation* of his body and blood ensueth'.[12]

By reclaiming the concept of consecration and by their consequential effective emphasis, Jewel and (in particular) Hooker made a clear break with Cranmer and, in one sense, even one with Calvin. The elements do not just help a job to be done, as with Cranmer, but – given certain conditions – they are actually used by God to do a job. In essence this is very close to Calvin's view of the Eucharist for, as we have seen, he did describe it in instrumental ways. Nevertheless, Calvin's concept of the identity between the bread and the body also involved their disjunction. When combined with his Reformation definition of a sacrament as a seal of the Word, this led to his concentrating liturgical attention on the hearers and not on the means. The result was to leave the door open to the basic Protestant dilemma, which is: if we are to 'preach' to the people in the Sacrament and not to the bread, and if they hear and believe that Word, what need is there for the bread? It also left room for the dualism and subjectivism of Zwingli's approach, to the detriment of Calvin's own stress on the objectivity of the Sacrament and his awareness of the Spirit's ability to use the physical in the spiritual life.

Presence

Whilst denying both transubstantiation and bare symbolism, the Elizabethan theology of the eucharistic presence directed its attention towards the *reality* of communion with Christ and away from precise attempts to define its mode. This approach can be seen in the omission of the Black Rubric from the 1559 Prayer Book and in the replacement of the denial of the 'bodily presence of Christ's flesh and blood' in the 1553 Articles, with the following statement in the Articles of 1563 and 1571:

The Body of Christ is given, taken, and eaten, in the Supper, only after an heavenly and spiritual manner. And the mean whereby the Body of Christ is received and eaten in the Supper is faith.[13]

The doctrinal position was not necessarily altered. Both Articles held a middle position between transubstantiation and bare symbolism. However, whereas in 1553 attention was focused on the negative (that is, what is not involved), in 1563 and 1571 it was fixed on the positive (that is, affirmation of the real gift of the Eucharist). The change may have been a small one but it was important. It was reflected in the Second Book of Homilies of 1562 and in the Revised Catechism,[14] and can be found in the writings of the period, including those of Jewel and Hooker. Jewel may be seen as representative of the Protestant establishment as it sought to defend its integrity, and Hooker may be seen as the pioneer of the more explorative reinterpretation of the Reformed tradition which became characteristic of Anglicanism in the subsequent period and beyond.

John Jewel

Jewel was locked in debate with the Roman Catholic Thomas Harding, hence his writings have a strong stamp of the polemic. However, the nature of the polemic at this stage generated a clear affirmation of the reality of the eucharistic experience: 'That we verily and undoubtedly receive Christ's body in the sacrament, it is neither denied, nor in question.'[15]

This conviction was expressed within the framework of Reformed theology: he differentiated between the sign and the signified, located the body of Christ in heaven, and emphasized the role of faith as the mode of eating. Further, he appealed to the comparison with Baptism, argued that in the Eucharist we are lifted up to the ascended presence of Christ, and stressed the consistency of the eucharistic participation in Christ with that available through other means. However, it was as Jewel and Harding argued over the meaning of 'union with Christ'[16] that the real difference between them became clear. Accused of denying a bodily participation in Christ, Jewel replied that far from deincarnating our experience of Christ he held that the various means of participation with Christ all involve a bodily relationship. For Jewel the Eucharist was not the only setting for such a meeting but rather the means 'to grow deeper into him'.[17] The real difference between them lay in their understanding of bodily participation. Like Calvin, Jewel tried to steer a course between concepts of mental assimilation and categories of substantive, material indwelling, in an attempt to replace them with personal, soteriological terms of involvement with the whole Christ. He maintained, therefore, that we have a 'full perfect spiritual conjunction, excluding all manner of imagination or fantasy: not a gross and fleshly being of Christ's body and our bodies, according to the appearance of the letter'.[18]

Thus Jewel was able to say, on the one hand, that 'Christ's body is not naturally or corporally present within us'[19] and, on the other hand, that in the Sacrament 'Christ is joined unto us corporally, as being man, because we are fed indeed and verily with his flesh'.[20] He meant that Christ, in his body, is not present *in* us (and therefore is not present bodily *in* the Sacrament), but is rather present *to* us and *united with* us, in the power of his flesh to save. In other words, Christ is in us and we are in him 'not by a natural but by a spiritual mean of being'.[21]

Throughout his sacramental theology Jewel was anxious to maintain the integrity of the faith relationship and the activity of the Spirit, and so did not posit a distinct gift to the Eucharist. But as we have seen in his concept of consecration he did allow an active part for the sacramental elements. It is in the 'holy mystery of the sacrament'[22] that 'by them'[23] Christ gives to us his body and his blood to be received by faith.

Richard Hooker

Hooker concentrated his attention on the primary content of eucharistic theology and experience, which is (so he defined) 'the *real participation* of Christ and of life in his body and blood *by means of this sacrament*'.[24] The 'union with Christ' motif was therefore central to his eucharistic thought and to his theology in general. Indeed, he set his whole sacramental analysis within an incarnational and soteriological framework. Before trying to answer 'how the sacraments do serve to make us partakers of Christ?', he first considered 'how God is in Christ' and 'how Christ is in us'.[25] This enabled him to establish the ground rules for the Eucharist. He argued that although Christ's human nature has become God's 'inseparable habitation', its human properties, such as localized presence, are not affected. Nevertheless, this does not mean that we can find God beyond or behind the Incarnation, for 'wherever the Word is it hath with it manhood else the Word be in part or somewhere God only and not man, which is impossible'.[26]

Here Hooker was being sensitive to Luther's concern that our relationship with God must be defined solely in terms of the Incarnation. However, he did not find Luther's insistence on the presence of the manhood in the same way as the divinity to be valid or necessary. The presence of the manhood is derived from and dependent upon the nature of the deity and differs, not in the reality of its presence, but in its mode and effect. Thus, Hooker was able to say, on the one hand (in a way reminiscent of Zwingli), that 'Christ is essentially present with all things in that he is very God, but not present with all things as man',[27] and on the other (in a way reminiscent of Luther), that his humanity is '*nowhere severed* from that which is everywhere present'.[28] Hence, Christ's divinity is present because of the characteristics of divine nature to be present everywhere, whilst his humanity is present for the very reason that it was joined to the divinity in the Incarnation, that is to save. But that soteriological presence involves the closest form of personal presence: 'His body crucified and his blood shed for the life of the world, are the true elements of that heavenly being, which maketh us such as himself is of whom we come.'[29] Thus, our participation in Christ is 'that mutual inward hold which Christ hath of us and we of him, in such sort that each possesseth other by way of special interest, property and inherent copulation'.[30]

Hooker distinguished between an imputed participation, by which we are justified by the righteousness of Christ through faith, and an imparted righteousness through which our 'souls and bodies are made more like him in glory'.[31] Both involve a personal presence of Christ to the believer, but whereas the first is a state which is applied whole, the second involves an 'infusion of grace'[32] in degrees of intensity and by different means. Behind Hooker's distinction lay not only the Protestant separation of justification from sanctification but also an attempt to hold together the best of Protestant and Catholic concepts of salvation.[33] He was clear in his rejection of an imparted, justifying righteousness which he believed undermined the basis of the Gospel. He was adamant that the edifice of salvation by grace can be protected only by a doctrine of imputed righteousness through faith in Christ. This, he maintained, involves a true presence of Christ to the believer and a real incorporation into him.

Nevertheless, in answer to the fundamental question of the real value of the Eucharist – given that God saves us or, to say the same thing, gives us Christ, through faith – he would have argued that such justifying faith marks only the beginning of the life of Christ. Indeed, he would question whether that life is actually present if the evidence of a changed life – that is, sanctifying righteousness – is absent. And it is here that the Eucharist has its part to play, for whereas faith in Christ puts us right before God, the Sacrament goes on to create the righteousness of Christ in the moral, spiritual and bodily life of the individual as the believer is united more deeply and more really in the life of Christ by means of the elements through the activity of the Spirit.

Hence, the Sacrament is not just a duplicate of the Word. Its purpose is not '*to teach* the mind, by other senses, that which the Word doth teach by hearing'.[34] It is rather to be a physical 'mark'[35] and a 'means effectual'[36] of God's communication of the grace of Christ, 'because it pleaseth the Almighty God to communicate by sensible means those blessings which are incomprehensible'.[37] Thus, rather than defining the Sacrament as a seal of the Word, Hooker was prepared to propose a distinct function for the Eucharist which, though ultimately dependent on the Word, had its own limited autonomy. Here was another example of the subtle but significant break which Anglicanism was making with the Reformed tradition. Although faith was still seen as the prerequisite for the Sacrament, and although the Sacrament was still not defined in causal terms *per se*, a higher emphasis was placed on the sacramental media as the means and instruments of God's activity. Whereas in Calvin the grace, in the last analysis, was separate from the elements – allowing the implication that they are in effect unnecessary – in Hooker the grace was *tied* to the elements (but not subsumed in them) because they have been designated by God to communicate that grace.

In analysing Hooker's understanding of the eucharistic presence it must be remembered that he was clearly influenced by his own deep experience of the eucharistic mystery. He claimed that precise and speculative theories on the relation of the body to the bread are redundant and damaging. They are redundant because 'the real presence of Christ's most blessed body and blood is not therefore to be sought for in the sacrament, but in the worthy receiver of the sacrament'.[38] They are damaging because they distract from the delight and joy of the eucharistic experience, which is able to discern in the elements 'more than the substance which our eyes behold'.[39]

Sacrifice

We have seen that the polemic with Rome worked positively in the areas of consecration and presence because it concentrated attention on the reality of eucharistic experience. However, with regard to the theme of sacrifice, the need to deny the propitiatory value of the Eucharist meant that little headway was made in moving the debate beyond the parameters of the immediate Reformation period. Nevertheless, positive attention to the sacrificial dimension of the Eucharist was not entirely absent. The Eucharist was seen to involve a real (albeit subjective) engagement with the one, sufficient sacrifice of Christ, by providing a context for encountering its saving significance. The sacrifice, though past and complete, makes contact with the present through the memorial action of the Eucharist, culminating in its worthy reception.

This was, of course, merely a reiteration of the sacrificial aspect of the Eucharist with which all the Reformers agreed. However, there were hints of a more explorative consideration of the relationship between the Eucharist and the sacrifice of Christ. For example, Jewel was prepared to see in the eucharistic memorial of the one sacrifice a Godward as well as a manward aspect: 'We offer up Christ, that is to say, an example, a commemoration, a remembrance of the death of Christ.'[40] Here he was maintaining – as he was in his concept of consecration – that the Eucharist is, in some sense, something which the Church *does* as well as receives. But the sacrificial content which this involves was seen to be on the same essential level as the activities of 'prayers', 'praises' and 'thanksgiving' which, of course, are not limited to the Eucharist. Likewise, when Jewel criticized the Roman Canon for offering and presenting Christ to the Father on the grounds that 'contariwise, Christ presents up us, and maketh us a sweet oblation in the sight of the Father',[41] he would not have restricted this to the sacramental event. Nevertheless, his use of such language marked a beginning of developments which were to become more prominent later.

Reflecting a similarly active understanding of the Eucharist, Hooker held that the elements 'serveth as well for a medicine to heal our infirmities and purge our sins as for a sacrifice of thanksgiving'.[42] Just as the elements are the means of the gift of God to us, so they enable the gift of our thanksgiving to be made to God.

The accommodation of certain traditional features within Reformed doctrine, which had begun in the previous period, became more explicit (particularly in the Laudian school) during the post-Elizabethan period.[43] However, it should be said that Roman sacramental teaching was still seen to be in serious error.[44] The divines did not want to revive *ex opere operato* theories, or the doctrine of transubstantiation, or the Sacrifice of the Mass, but they did want to affirm and develop the interpretation of the Protestant legacy begun by their immediate predecessors in the general areas of consecration, presence and commemorative sacrifice.

Consecration

Theories on what actually constituted consecration were varied. They ranged from recital of the Institution Narrative to a general repetition of Christ's action; and from a prayer for the effects of consecration to a blessing of the elements or an invocation of the Spirit upon them. However, all were agreed that a liturgical consecration was necessary in order for the bread and wine to be able to fulfil Christ's intention for them[45] – and this received official Anglican acceptance in the liturgy of 1662. Through such action the elements are changed in use so that they both represent and convey the body and blood of Christ:

Neither are [the elements] to be accounted barely significative, but truly exhibitive also, of those heavenly things whereto they have relation, as being appointed by God to be a means of conveying the same unto us, and putting us in actual possession thereof.[46]

Presence

There emerged a consensus of belief in a 'real presence' of Christ through the reception of the consecrated elements. The argument with Rome was seen not in terms of a denial of the fact of the presence but of its mode and meaning: 'our difference is not about the truth or reality of the presence, but about the true manner of the being and receiving thereof'.[47]

For the most part, the complexity of the difference between the pervading Anglican concept of a real presence to the receiver and the doctrines of a substantial change in the elements was acknowledged. Hence, generally the divines defined the real presence in terms of real relationship between the communicant and the saving reality of Christ through the use of the consecrated elements. In John Cosin's words, 'the Body and Blood are sacramentally united to the bread and wine so that Christ is truly given to believers'.[48]

The divines repeatedly emphasized that Christ is given 'mystically and after an ineffable manner'. This reluctance to define the dynamics of the eucharistic presence in a precise way stemmed not only from their recognition of the theological mystery of the Eucharist but also from their sensitivity to the experiential reality of the event. Richard Montague charged his readers to 'Be content *That it is*, and do not seek nor define *How it is so*'.[49] Christopher Sutton gave similar advice in his highly influential devotional work: 'Do not say with the Capernaites, Master, how cometh Thou hither? but with the disciples asking no question be glad thou dost enjoy him.'[50] Laud's embellishment of churches, Andrewes' engraved chalices, Herbert's poetry, the general defence of kneeling for communion and the tendency to adore 'at the Sacrament',[51] if not the Sacrament itself, should be seen as expressions of a sacramental encounter, in which the believer, through the use made of bread and wine, is united with the full reality of Christ with such intensity that it is beyond the power of mind and words to explain.

Sacrifice

This period was a formative one for the development of Anglican thinking on the eucharistic sacrifice. Existing alongside the affirmation of basic Protestant principles were various attempts to revive a more operative level of cultic activity which were to become recurring themes in later Anglican thought. For example, although the Protestant concern to maintain the once-for-all character of the Cross and its all-sufficient efficacy remained central to the divines, they still explored ways of giving a fuller content to the eucharistic commemoration.

Andrewes began from the understanding that the Church is under command to *do* something in remembrance of Christ in the Eucharist. Therefore, the Eucharist has an objective quality not by repeating the sacrifice, but by repeating the 'memory' of the sacrifice. The result, he argued, is that we are 'carried back to Christ' so that 'by the incomprehensible power of his eternal Spirit not He alone, but the very act of His offering is made present to us, and we incorporated into His death and invested with the benefits of it'.[51]

Laud repeated the concept of a representation in memory but directed the act of commemoration to God as well as to the Church.[52] The same theme can be found in various writers, including Thomas Morton, who said that 'we offer (commemoratively) the … very same body and blood of Christ His all sufficient sacrifice on the cross, although not as the subject of his proper sacrifice, but yet as the only adequate object of our commemoration'.[53]

Jeremy Taylor described the commemorative offering in a qualified sense as an offering of Christ, and made a strong link between the commemoration of the sacrifice, through representation, and its application:

He is offered to God, that is, He is by prayers and the Sacrament represented or 'offered up to God as sacrificed' which in effect is a celebration of His death… It follows, then, that the celebration of this sacrifice be in its proportion an instrument of applying the proper sacrifice to all the purposes which it first designed.[54]

Others joined him in seeing the commemorative sacrifice as impetratory. For Cosin the sacrificial representation and commemoration before God of the past sacrifice pleads its effect in the present.

In addition to developing the commemorative aspect of the Eucharist, several writers introduced the motif of the eternal offering of Christ as a way of relating the past sacrifice of Calvary to the present moment. They did not mean that the sacrifice itself continues but rather that it is permanently effective (because, in Christ's presence before the Father, he 'setteth it before his eyes'[55]), and that it is continually applied through the intercession of the risen Christ whose priesthood is one of 'blessing not sacrifice'.[56] The Eucharist was therefore seen as a representation of the heavenly activity of Christ and as a means through which that eternal ministry is received by the Church.

CONCLUSION

The sources reviewed in this chapter – particularly those of the post-Elizabethan period – are not normally drawn upon by those attempting to trace and develop a distinctively Evangelical position. But the theologians of this period should not be so quickly discarded. Their intention to remain faithful to the wind which had blown through the

Church at the Reformation, coupled with their increasing distance from the centre of the storm itself, enabled them gently to shift some of the surrounding sands that were threatening to smother the sacramental life of the Church. We shall see in later chapters that their developments in the areas of liturgical consecration, the reality of the gift of Christ's eucharistic presence, and the contiguous relationship between Calvary, the Eucharist and the ministry of the ascended Christ were duplicated and, at times, extended in more specifically Evangelical contexts. These themes will be used as a basis for the theological analysis in part 3, as we continue the search for an authentically Evangelical expression of eucharistic theology and spirituality.

A very astute summary.

CHAPTER 4

The legacy in the Puritan tradition

Existing alongside and within the late sixteenth- and seventeenth-century Anglican tradition which we have been examining was the Puritan tradition. Definitions of Puritanism are notoriously difficult.[1] They are either so broad that they slip into vagueness and inaccuracy or so narrow that they fail to do justice to the character and influence of the movement. For the purpose of informed theological selectivity rather than exhaustive historical analysis, I shall risk the former danger and identify with the Elizabethan pamphleteer who said that 'the hotter sort of protestants are called puritans'.[2] The Puritans were those who showed a more radical commitment to the logical intentions of Protestantism as they found expression in Geneva and the other cities of the Continental Reformation. Specifically, the tradition tended to an ecclesiology of the elect and converted rather than the born and baptized; a ministry based more on preaching and teaching than on sacraments and worship; an authority in which the Bible was regulative for all of the Church's life and not just its doctrines; and a piety of consuming zeal pervading the household rather than a beatific vision enshrined in the 'sanctuary'.

The Puritans ranged from those who were satisfied with the episcopal organization of the Church and its existing liturgy but were anxious to develop features of Puritan theology and spirituality, to those who were dissatisfied and therefore aimed for a more far-reaching political and liturgical reform of the Church, to those who were disaffected and thus sought a complete break with the Established Church, regarding it as not only beyond repair but seeing the very concept of a national Church as unbiblical. In connection with the latter brief reference will be made to those who departed from certain Puritan principles in favour of other, more charismatic ideas. Such an inclusion may be justified on the grounds, first, that despite the differences in their presented theology, there were significant implicit links between the two and, second, because some of the sacramental attitudes of the more charismatic groups, such as the Quakers, had been anticipated in an incipient form within mainstream Puritanism.[3]

THEMATIC LITURGICAL ANALYSIS

Consecration

The Forme of Prayers (1556), or as it is known more commonly, the Genevan Service Book, was the English liturgy compiled by John Knox and others for the needs of the Marian exiles in Geneva.[4] Substantially similar to Calvin's Strasburg liturgy, it became the basis of the Scottish Book of Common Order (1564) and the liturgies of English congregations in Waldegrave (1584) and Middleburgh (1586).[5] It provided English Puritan ministers with inspiration for their adaptations of the Book of Common Prayer and although, as Bryan Spinks has shown, it was by no means the only credible Puritan alternative to the Prayer Book, it none the less exerted considerable appeal and influence.[6] Its major structural differences from the Anglican order lay in the more prominent place it gave to preaching, the encouragement it gave to individual ministers to amend the form as they felt necessary, and the specific emphasis it gave to the fraction.

The Forme of Prayers did not contain a consecration of the elements; neither did its immediate descendants. It would seem that this was felt to be a deficiency certainly in Scotland and most probably in England. There is considerable evidence and some consensus of opinion that advantage was taken of the permission to vary the rite at this point by introducing a blessing for the elements.[7]

Although the Separatist traditions rejected set liturgical forms, they did provide description and direction on how the Eucharist should be celebrated. Again, the general impression is that a blessing of the elements was required as well as a statement that, as a result of the blessing in the context of the whole action, they have taken on a sacramental significance.[8]

Puritans were not convinced by the claims of Anglican theologians that Cranmer's liturgy included a valid consecration. Before, during and after the Westminster Conference they repeatedly objected to the

Prayer Book on the grounds (amongst others) that it lacked a specific
consecration of the elements. Hence, whilst of course the Confession
rejected any implication of a 'change of the substance of bread and
wine',[9] its liturgical, or rather rubrical expression, the Directory,
ordered that the elements should be 'set apart and sanctified to this
holy use, by the Word of Institution and Prayer'.[10] Hence, whereas
the Forme of Prayers followed Calvin in seeing the words as a
warrant for the action and as a message for the participant, and
therefore placed them in the exhortation, the Directory transferred
them to the Prayer of Thanksgiving. The suggested petition for
'sanctifying and blessing' the elements directed the minister to ask
'the Father of all mercies and God of all consolation' for the
'effectual working of his Spirit in us; and to sanctify these Elements
both of Bread and Wine'.[11] It is worth remembering that the
Directory was highly influential not only amongst specifically Puritan
congregations but throughout the whole country. During the
Commonwealth period, when use of the Prayer Book was forbidden,
the Directory was *the* authorized liturgical form and its use was
mandatory.

Despite the ecclesiological differences between the Presbyterians
and the Independents, which in the end led to the political failure of
the Commonwealth, the Savoy Declaration of 1658 (the Independents' statement of faith) showed almost complete agreement
with the Westminster Confession's sacramental teaching. It too
regarded some form of consecration to be necessary: 'The Lord Jesus
hath in this Ordinance appointed his Ministers to pray and bless the
Elements of Bread and Wine, and thereby to set them apart from a
common to an holy use.'[12]

The Savoy Conference of 1661 was convened after the restoration
of the monarchy and episcopacy under the charge, on the one hand,
to revise the Prayer Book and, on the other, to provide scriptural
alternatives for consideration. Amongst the amendments suggested
by the Presbyterians was their call for the addition of a petition for
consecration and for direction to be given concerning the fraction.[13]
The Presbyterian alternative to the Prayer Book was provided by
Richard Baxter's Reformed Liturgy. His eucharistic rite included the
following petition:

sanctify these thy creatures of bread and wine, which, according to thy
institution and command, we set apart to this holy use, that they be
sacramentally the body and blood of Christ.[14]

The prayer was followed by the reading of the Institution Narrative at the end of which 'the minister says':

This bread and wine, being set apart, and consecrated to this holy use by God's appointment, are now no common bread and wine, but sacramentally the body and blood of Christ.[15]

Baxter regarded all three elements – Words of Institution, prayer for blessing, and declaration of sacramental status – to be necessary for consecration to be complete.

Although Baxter's liturgy was rejected by the Bishops, the Puritan concern for a definite consecration and a clearer fraction was taken up and, at least partially, met by the following decision:

That the manner of consecrating the elements may be made more explicit and express, and to that purpose these words be put into the rubric, 'Then shall he put his hand upon the bread and break it', 'then shall he put his hand unto the cup'.[16]

Rather than being an irenic concession, this was simply evidence of the agreement between the two traditions on the necessity of a consecration to the performance of the sacramental function.

Presence

There was also a large measure of agreement between Anglicans and Puritans over the nature of the sacramental function. Whilst maintaining the Reformed distinction between the sign and the signified, the Puritans affirmed the reality of their sacramental relationship: 'the sacramental union, is not a physical or local, but a spiritual conjunction of the earthly signs, which are bread and wine, with the heavenly graces, which are the body and blood of Christ in the act of receiving, as if by mutual relation they were one and the same thing'.[17] Lewis Bayly went on to make clear that the believer receives the body and blood with 'the mouth of faith',[18] but this too was not a party emphasis. Neither Anglican nor Puritan saw any conflict between belief in the real gift by the means of the Sacrament and a real reception of it by the faith of the participant. Both dimensions were demanded by the sovereignty of God, a God whose objective work includes requiring and enabling authentic response to him in the subjectivity of the individual.

For example, Baxter could describe the Sacrament in effective terms whilst at the same time allowing for the characteristics of the faith relationship: 'the giving of Christ himself really for life, as with his covenant benefits, to the believing receiver, in the investing sacrament of the bread and wine, ministerially delivered by the pastor in Christ's name, together with the acceptance of the receiver'.[19] Similarly, the confession of Barrows' Separatist Church in Amsterdam described the consecrated elements in these terms: 'They are in the ordinance of God, signs and seals of God's everlasting covenant, representing and offering to all the receivers, but exhibiting only to true believers, the Lord Jesus Christ, and all his benefits unto righteousness, sanctification and eternal life, through faith in his name, to the glory and praise of God.'[20] Bayly emphasized the objectivity of the Sacrament and stressed that it involves the believer in the whole Christ, which includes his full corporeal humanity as well as his divinity: 'The Sacramental bread and wine therefore are not bare signifying signs but such as where-with Christ doth indeed exhibit not only his Divine virtue and efficacy, but also his very Body and Blood.'[21]

As Baxter, 'Barrows' Confession' and Bayly make clear, the Puritans regarded the gift of the Eucharist as not merely the appropriation of the saving benefits of Christ's work but as a real reception of Christ in his person. John Preston identified the difference between the Reformed and the Roman positions in terms of description rather than of denial of the eucharistic presence: 'We say Christ is communicated to us in the sacrament as truly and readily as they, only there is a difference in the manner, we say it is spiritually, they say it is corporally.'[22] Elsewhere he defined the purpose of the Eucharist as 'to knit the knot stronger between Christ and us'.[23] For John Owen the category which most fully explained the sacramental experience was that of participation in Christ: 'It is a universal unimpeachable persuasion among all Christians that there is a near intimate communion and participation of him in the supper of the Lord. He is no Christian who is otherwise minded.'[24]

Thus, as with Calvin and those within the Anglican tradition, the Eucharist was seen as a means of furthering the believer's union with Christ. But, as with Calvin and most of the Anglicans, this was presented in ways which admitted the eschatological characteristics of the Church's relation with Christ in the time between ascension and *parousia*, and also allowed for the positive role of the Spirit which this involved. Rather than compensation for the absence of Christ on earth, the Spirit brings his presence to the life of the believer: 'Though Christ be in Heaven and we on Earth, yet he can join our Souls and Bodies to his at such a distance, without any substantial change in either, by the same infinite Spirit dwelling in him and us.'[25]

Sacrifice

The Puritans on the whole may have been somewhat more reluctant to apply explicitly sacrificial characteristics to the Eucharist than were their Anglican peers, but for the most part, the motifs and elements which were developing in Anglicanism over the period can also be found in Puritanism. In particular, Puritans were also exploring the commemorative aspect of the Sacrament. William Perkins argued for a frequent celebration on the grounds that 'it is nothing but the shewing forth of the Lord's death till he come; which is not once or twice in the yeare, but often yea, continually to bee remembered'.[26] Owen identified the Sacrament's power to concentrate the faith as its great merit and purpose: 'Our minds are apt to be distracted: the ordinance is to fix them; and if we act faith in an especial manner in this ordinance God will be glorified.'[27] The Prayer of Thanksgiving in the Forme of Prayers commemorated Christ's passion by describing the meaning of his sacrificial death and then by rejoicing that, on account of his death, God 'doth acknowledge us [his] children and heirs'.[28] In Scotland the minister, following the Book of Common Order, would kneel as he thankfully proclaimed the Lord's death – an indication of the solemnity of the remembrance.[29] The Westminister Confession defined 'the perpetual remembrance of the Sacrifice of himself in death'[30] as one of the reasons for the institution and observance of the Eucharist. This was heightened in the Savoy Declaration, which saw the Sacrament as for 'the perpetual remembrance, and shewing forth of the Sacrifice of Himself'.[31]

Baxter regarded the commemoration as one of the three structural elements in the eucharistic action, the other two being the consecration and the communion. He defined the content of the commemoration in the following way:

For he hath ordained, that...as it were, in effigy, in representation, he might be still crucified before the church's eyes; and they might be affected, as if

they had seen him on the cross. And by faith and prayer, they might, as it
were, offer him to God; that is, might shew the Father that sacrifice, once
made for sin, in which they trust, and for which it is they expect all
acceptance of their persons with God, and hope audience when they beg for
mercy, and offer up prayer or praises to him.[32]

Baxter was clearly juggling with the three-piece puzzle which, as
we have seen, dominated the thought of many Anglican writers – the
past, completed act of Calvary, its eternal efficacy, and the Church's
involvement in its application, particularly in the context of its
sacramental remembrance. He delicately fitted them together in the
Christological section of his Prayer of Consecration. The prayer
affirmed Christ's past death as the atoning sacrifice for our sins, but
allowed for a contact between its commemoration in the Eucharist
and Christ's 'intercession with the Father'. The plea that Christ will
'Reconcile us to the Father' has, therefore, a threefold aspect.[33] It is
based on the sacrificial death of Christ, effective in his ongoing prayer
and engaged by the Church's involvement with that prayer through
its remembrance of the death.

The seriousness with which the Puritans stressed the remembrance
function of the Eucharist led them to develop a novel concentration
on the symbolic value of the fraction. As Bryan Spinks has shown, it
was given increasing degrees of emphasis in Puritan liturgy from the
Forme of Prayers to the Reformed Liturgy[34] and, as we have seen, the
Prayer Book's omission of a liturgical fraction was a constant Puritan
complaint. Baxter's rite contained a libation as well as a fraction, and
both were placed in the Prayer of Consecration rather than before the
distribution. The accompanying words were climactic:

The body of Christ was broken for us, and offered once for all to sanctify us:
behold the sacrificed Lamb of God that taketh away the sin of the world.
We were redeemed in the precious blood of Christ, as of a Lamb without
blemish or spot.[35]

And it was the 'Bread thus consecrated and broken'[36] that was to be
distributed – the fraction was as necessary as the consecration.

Similarly, Owen saw the fraction and libation as integral to the
eucharistic action. He defined the Eucharist as 'A holy action,
instituted and appointed by Christ, to set forth his death and
communicate unto us spiritually his body and blood by faith, being
represented by bread and wine, blessed by his word and prayer,
broken, poured out, and received by believers'.[37] The liturgical

emphasis clearly cohered with the attitude of piety, for even John Bunyan found that in the Sacrament he 'discerned the Lord's body as broken for [his] sins, and that his precious blood hath been shed for [his] transgressions'.[38]

UNDERLYING THEOLOGICAL THEMES

History – theology – piety

Thus on the explicit level of eucharistic theology the Puritan tradition was in substantial agreement with the Anglican tradition.[39] However, on the implicit level of theological and experiential expectation they showed significant differences. The causes of the divergence can be seen in terms of, first, the influence of historical and sociological factors and, secondly, the underlying theological and pastoral attitudes of the two traditions.

The Anglican establishment in the seventeenth century was Protestant and almost all the divines were anxious to distinguish themselves from Roman theology and practice, but generally they approved of the received organization and liturgy of the Church, both of which showed visible links with the papal past. However, for the Puritans these links represented tangible evidence of the need for a more radical reformation. Behind their persistent attack on the external arrangements of order and worship lay the Puritan concern that the continuation of the Reformation faith was under serious threat. They feared that without effective discipline the Church would lose its purity, and without New Testament ordered worship the Church would lose its faith. The result would be a return to its immediate and sinister past. Even for those Puritans content with the existing polity and liturgy there was a zeal for the nurture of that purity which distinguished the covenanted community from its 'comprehensive' neighbour and of the faith which marked the 'godly' from the 'common sort of Christians'.[40]

In short, the threat of Rome, or rather, of the unreformed, was perceived as more immediate and hostile by Puritans than by Anglicans. Indeed, it was perceived as present in the English Church itself, and therefore was not just on the doorstep but still in the house. Thus, the tirade of insult and objection directed towards the Prayer Book and the absolute antipathy engendered by the Scottish liturgy of 1637 – despite the large measure of doctrinal agreement between the two schools – can be understood only in the context of the historical setting.[41] From the Prayer Book's use of the surplice to its prescription for kneeling, from the Elizabethan vestments to Laudian altars, and from private administrations for the sick to attitudes of eucharistic devotion, the Puritan charge was popery.

The objections which were to have the most far-reaching impact on Puritanism, and which inculcated it with a subliminal suspicion of the Eucharist, were directed towards the indiscriminate giving of communion and to the Prayer Book's structural weighting against preaching. The First Admonition to Parliament contrasted the apostolic with the Anglican practice: 'they shut men out by reason of their sins from the Lord's Supper. We thrust them in sin to the Lord's Supper.'[42] And in debate with Whitgift, Cartwright pronounced:

This I say, that, when as the life of the sacraments dependeth on the preaching of the Word of God, there must of necessity the Word of God be, not read, but preached unto the people, amongst whom the sacraments are ministered.[43]

Concern for the purity of the Eucharist was a product of the Puritan passion for the purity of the Church. It led first to an increasing tendency to 'fence off the table'. The corollary of this was a greater emphasis on the danger of a sinful approach to the Sacrament than on the grace it made available. It fostered a tendency to define the true Church not in terms of its authentic proclamation of the Word and its right celebration of the sacraments, but by the effectiveness of its discipline and even the discernible presence of the Spirit. In its extreme form it led to a rejection of the need for sacraments at all on the grounds that the immediacy of the Spirit negates the need for the sacramental institutionalization of his activity.

The passion for preaching was a product of the Puritan zeal for authentic faith. It led at first to a healthy emphasis on the unity of Word and Sacrament. However, in time it tended to create such an emphasis on the priority of preaching that the Sacrament came to be seen as dependent on the presence of a preacher and power of his message. In effect, it encouraged a spirituality divorced from sacramental anticipation.

I have deliberately encroached on the underlying theological and experiential emphases in order to demonstrate the link between the historical climate in which Puritanism found itself and the life of faith which evolved within that context. However, we must now develop a more detailed analysis of the theological position.

The doctrine of prevenient grace and sacramental spirituality

In his comparison of Anglicans and Puritans, John New has argued forcibly that although both regarded the sacraments as means of grace and though they were doctrinally almost indistinguishable, Puritans actually approached the sacraments with a lower expectation of their practical efficacy. This, he claims, was because they stressed the concept of prevenient grace more rigorously than their Anglican counterparts.[44] The Puritan merely expected the sacraments to authenticate that grace *previously* given by God in the decision of his sovereign will, whereas for the Anglican they were, in Hooker's words, 'an instrument or means whereby we receive grace'.[45]

Although New may have somewhat overstated his case and given an over-negative impression of Puritan sacramental experience (and, indeed, any sacramental theology deriving from Calvin's theology), his thesis is helpful in highlighting a tendency present germinally in Calvinism, which was taking root in Puritanism – particularly in its more radical developments – and which has often been just below the surface in later expressions of Evangelical spirituality. This tends to divorce the activity of God from the sacramental life of the Church by stressing either the prior will of God or (ironically, as in later Arminian types of Evangelicalism) the response and decision of man. Either emphasis tends to forget that both God's will and our response are linked by him to places and means, which include the sacraments. Rather than God's prevenient grace, which is actively sealed by him in the sacraments, we are left with a precarious grace which is sealed – it is hoped – in subjectivity. The flowering of this propensity can be seen in much of the Puritan teaching on assurance. The doctrine of assurance was the subjective counterpart to the Puritan emphasis on the sovereign will of God. Thomas Brooks described it in this way:

It is one thing for me to have grace, it is another thing for me to see my grace; it is one thing for me to believe, and another thing for me to believe that I do believe; it is one thing for me to have faith, and another thing for me to know that I have faith. Now assurance flows from a clear, certain, evident knowledge that I have grace, and that I do believe.[46]

[handwritten marginal note:] The dichotomy between 'Anglican' & 'Puritan' always seem unfortunate since most Puritans were 'Anglican'.

However, although he spoke highly of the Lord's Supper as an appointed means of communicating that assurance to the believer, and though clearly he had experienced it doing so, it plays only a very small part in his whole treatise on the character and means of assurance. It is present but it is peripheral. The real sources for the believer's assurance are to be found in a variety of other spiritual exercises, the success of which may be seen in certain experiential signs. The tendency to stress a direct and unmediated relationship between God and humanity to the exclusion of sacramental activity can be seen in its extreme form amongst the Seekers, Ranters and Quakers. George Fox dismissed the Eucharist on the grounds that it appeared to achieve nothing in the lives of the participants and could not be compared to the mystical identity experienced through the Christ created by the direct movement of the Spirit:

For after you have eaten in remembrance of his death then you must come into his death and die with him if you will live with him as the Apostles did: and yet it is a nearer and further state to be with him in his death than to take bread and wine in remembrance of his death.[47]

Geoffrey Nuttall has argued that 'there was considerable precedent within Puritanism for the neglect of the Sacraments by Fox and the Quakers'.[48] He refers to the various circumstances which led the Puritans, Separatists and the Pilgrim Fathers to live without the ordinances and to imply that it was possible for the Church to exist and Christian life to operate effectively without them. Such practices stemmed from causes which sought to maintain the highest integrity and honour for the Sacrament. However, in reality, the refusal of some Puritans to communicate from a non-preaching minister or in the posture of kneeling, the refusal of some Independents to administer the Eucharist if the purity of the congregation could not be established, and the neglect by the Pilgrim Fathers of the Sacrament because of the absence of an acknowledged minister all tended to push the Eucharist to the outside of ecclesial life. Indeed, even the English monthly and Scottish quarterly celebrations, which, despite pressures for greater frequency, became the norm in Puritan and Presbyterian circles, perpetuated the Continental practice of a 'Zwinglian liturgy' for a Calvinistic theology, in which the Sacrament, though important, was not central.[49]

Another discernible feature which emerged certainly in Separatism and probably in mainstream Puritanism was a heightening of the communal dimension of the Eucharist in which the believers are together joined in the life of Christ. Robert Browne define the Sacrament as:

a mark of the apparent church, sealing unto us the breaking and eating of bread and drinking the cup in one holy communion, and by the word preached, that we are happily redeemed by the breaking of the body and the shedding of the blood of Christ Jesus, and we thereby grow into one body, the church, in one communion of graces whereof Christ is the head.[50]

This heightening of the communal dimension helped to fuel both the Separatist charge to the Puritans not to participate in Anglican communions and also the Puritan charge to Anglicans that the sacraments should always be administered in a corporate setting. However, despite important correctives to individualistic understandings of the Sacrament, this emphasis held within it the danger of so defining the Eucharist in the horizontal terms of the relation between believers that the vertical dimension of their relation to Christ could be excluded. Rather than the Eucharist being seen in Lutheran terms of communion 'with Christ and all his saints' it stood close to becoming merely a Zwinglian badge of membership. Movement along such a road was encouraged by strong concepts of the gathered and covenanted Church which in turn were sacramentally expressed in the emphasis on disciplined self-examination and by 'fencing off the table'.

The preaching of the word and sacramental spirituality

A tendency to undermine the significance of the sacraments has been detected in the Puritan's doctrine of prevenient grace, which located divine activity in the decision of God and saw the sacraments as occasions when that will was confirmed in a static rather than an active way. A parallel and related propensity can be found in relation to the Puritan emphasis on the doctrine of original sin. The doctrine stresses the depravity of humanity in order to show our utter dependence on the gracious movement of God to us. Such a movement found its outlet in God's Word – and God's Word, as Puritans tirelessly maintained, required exposition and application: 'It is not the letter of the Word that ordinarily doth convert, but the spiritual meaning of it, as revealed and expounded.'[51]

The supreme point of encounter between God and his people was considered to be the presentation of his Word in the mode of preaching. Thus, the need for a liturgical consecration, which, as we have seen, Puritans, like Anglicans, were emphasizing, needs to be seen in the light of, and to some extent qualified by, their overriding emphasis on the activity of preaching. Thomas Cartwright described preaching as God's 'most excellent and most ordinary means to work in the hearts of believers'.[52] And later the Directory defined 'Preaching of the Word' as 'being the power of God unto salvation, and one of the greatest and most excellent works belonging to the ministry of the Gospel'.[53] The sacraments had an important but subordinate place. They were to support the Word as it was preached and could not work independently.

The temptation within Puritanism was to define the sacraments' efficacy in relation to the immediate presentation of the Word in preaching. Cartwright himself managed to resist the impulse. In debate with the Separatist Robert Harrison he allowed an independent validity to the sacraments by refusing to dismiss those administered by 'dumb ministers' as meaningless rituals. His concern, therefore, was not ultimately to fix the sacraments to the sermon but to tie the sacraments and the Gospel together. Similarly, John Preston described the Eucharist as:

nothing else but the Seal of the Gospel of the New Covenant. The Gospel is that an offer of Christ to all that will take him for the remission of sins. In the sacrament there is an offer of Christ to us. The Gospel presents it to us under audible words, and the sacrament presents it to us under visible figures; this is all the difference. If we would know what the sacrament is, consider what the Gospel is and the covenant, and you shall know what it is, for it is but a seal, but a memorial of the Gospel.[54]

This was the evangelical essential they were anxious to defend: that the Sacrament is to be defined in terms of the Gospel and therefore must be integrally related to the proclamation of the *kerygma* – an activity which the Puritans felt was not adequately fulfilled in a good deal of contemporary Anglican practice.

However, as hinted at earlier, alongside the theological concern for the unity of Word and Sacrament, a practical spirituality developed which tended to divorce them. The growth of roving Puritan preachers, the Puritan lectureships, the catechizing classes and the 'prophesying' meetings all diverted Puritan ministry from the regular round of worship and pastoral care, and created a rival, unofficial, non-liturgical and non-sacramental setting to the official

Is this still *anachronistic?*

Sunday worship. This was reinforced by Puritan Sunday worship itself, which centralized the activity of preaching as clearly as the architecture of its buildings focused attention on the pulpit and Bible rather than the table and Sacrament. Indeed, as we have seen, the very validity of the Sacrament began to be defined by whether the minister qualified as a 'preaching minister'.

The shift in spirituality was further developed in the experience of the hearers. Congregations were to have the highest expectations for a sermon, for here they were to listen to the actualization of the very Word of God. Puritans gave priority to preaching over liturgical prayer and worship because here they found their hearts being 'warmed'. It was through preaching that they would be moved to pray privately and within their households. It was through preaching that they found their hearts lifted to heaven – the seat, as Owen said, of authentic worship. It was through preaching, with its facility for practical, spiritual advice, that the Puritans were able to identify the work of Christ within them and discover the ways it could be continued. Puritan literature is packed with rich and experiential devotion, but to a large extent reference to the Eucharist is minimal. One is left to conclude that the strength of personal piety stemmed more from the impact of powerful preaching and the devoted fellowship of the covenanted Church and from the enjoyment of personal and family prayer and Bible reading than from experience of the Eucharist.

CONCLUSION

The negative undercurrent was not, however, the whole story. I have been pointing to implicit tendencies rather than providing definitive description. These were seeds which would bear the weight of their fruit in later Evangelical tradition. Indeed, it is testimony to the experiential effect of the celebration of the Eucharist that despite the theological influences and historical circumstances working towards its minimization, such leading divines – and brilliant preachers – as Goodwin and Owen should seek to express a unique function for the Sacrament. Goodwin compared the Supper to the Word and concluded that whereas in the Word Christ is displayed in an indirect and piecemeal way, in the Supper 'we have to do with Christ himself, his person, &c. We are put upon him, let into him immediately and directly, and are to converse with him, as a spouse with her husband, in the nearest intimacies.'[55]

Likewise, Owen was definite in his delineation of a specific eucharistic 'way of participation of Christ':[56]

The communication of Christ herein, and our participation of him, are expressed in such a manner as to demonstrate them to be peculiar; such as are not to be obtained in any other way, or divine ordinance whatever; not in praying, not in preaching, not in any other exercise of faith or the word or promises. There is in it an eating and drinking of the body and blood of Christ, with a spiritual incorporation ensuing, which are peculiar unto this ordinance.[57]

Perhaps the most poignant references in Puritan liturgy and sacramental writing are when the joy and privilege of sharing in the Eucharist are given expression. Following the Forme of Prayers, the minister, after acknowledging our unworthiness, went on to say: 'yet nevertheless at the commandment of Jesus Christ our Lord, we present ourselves to his table'.[58] Echoing the Forme of Prayers, the Directory called upon the minister to 'profess' that by 'the Name of Jesus' we are 'admitted to eat and drink at his own Table'.[59] John Owen unpacked the symbolism by further imagery:

faith is so to receive him as to enable us to sit down at God's table as those that are the Lord's friends – as those invited to feast upon the sacrifice. The sacrifice is offered; Christ – God's Passover; God makes a feast upon it, and invites his friends to sit down at his table there being now no difference between him and us.[60]

Here we have touched upon the essence of the authentically Evangelical experience of the Eucharist: we present ourselves to receive, we accept the invitation to 'eat and drink at [Christ's] table'[61] that 'we may possess His body and blood, yea, Jesus Christ Himself, very God and very man, Who is that Heavenly bread which giveth life unto the world'.[62]

a Reasonable summary. There are problems / difficulties not entirely solved.

CHAPTER 5

The traditions in the Revival

THE RECEIVED TRADITION

Those who discuss the quality of the Church's life in the late seventeenth and early eighteenth centuries argue over the extent of its deficiency, not the fact of its decline. It is accepted that the passion and power of religion in the sixteenth century and for most of the seventeenth century had by now generally given way to a more sober and privatized form of faith in which the instruction of the individual conscience, rather than the public debate of doctrine, became the focus of religious attention. Nevertheless, preserved amidst the pervasive latitudinarian ethos were pockets of piety which refused to reduce doctrine to belief in the Supreme Beneficent; and which never could be content with a shallow and lifeless form of worship or an understanding of Christian life-style more in terms of moral duty than of personal commitment.

Anglican eucharistic thought and devotion reflected the ethos – although it showed a similarly pervasive malaise, it also contained signs of energy and depth. For the most part the Eucharist was infrequently celebrated – four or five times a year – and, just as the fashionable white-washed walls of the churches spoke to the worshipper of the light of reason, so the increasingly dominant theology tended to shave the rite of its mystery (as sensed by the Laudians) and its statement of the Gospel's objective reality (as appreciated by the Puritans). The tendency came to a head in 1735 with the publication, most probably written by Benjamin Hoadley, *Hoadly.* of *A Plain Account of the Nature and End of the Sacrament of the Lord's Supper*. Hoadley's thought was based on the most negative elements in Zwingli's thought, placed in the framework of a weakened Christology and soteriology. He saw the Sacrament as designed to be a bare remembrance of the Christ who is necessarily absent. It functions by

61

an entirely affective role: 'the bread and wine...lead us by their peculiar tendency to all such thoughts and practices as are indeed the improvement and health of our souls'.[1] The elements were seen as tokens which point our minds to a belief that we are in God's favour, providing that, as we receive them, we believe and receive 'the whole doctrine of Christ' and are 'not wanting to ourselves in other parts of our duty'.[2]

However, this was not the whole story. First, there were repeated calls from bishops and High Churchmen for more frequent cele-brations. Second, there was a tradition going back to Bishop Ken's *Manual of Prayers for the Use of Winchester Scholars*, of devotional manuals which encouraged a more serious sacramental life. These manuals, which had a large circulation, reflect the survival of eucharistic spirituality. Third, the publication of *A Plain Account* provoked a sustained war of pamphlets in which Hoadley and his defenders were strenuously attacked.

Richard Buxton's analysis of the period has identified two distinct streams of positive eucharistic thought which he has labelled the '1662 tradition' and the '1718–1764 tradition'.[3] The former was a somewhat amorphous theological ethos which emerged from the use of the 1662 Prayer Book, while the latter was a more precise theological position which developed mainly amongst the Nonjurors and found liturgical expression in the Nonjuring rites of 1718, 1734 and the Scottish Communion Office of 1764.[4] The 1662 tradition was certainly the more dominant and popular of the two, and it can be seen doctrinally systematized in the writings of Daniel Waterland.[5] Waterland's moderate sacramentalism carefully codified the mix of Reformed faith and traditional eucharistic motifs which had already evolved within both Anglicanism and Puritanism.

The 1718–64 tradition was a minority position, but it was a significant and influential one. Its clearest expression can be found in John Johnson's *The Unbloody Sacrifice and Altar*.[6] Although there was much within the theological and liturgical experimentation which was alien to the Evangelical mind, the 1718–64 tradition nevertheless had an important bearing on the Revival. The early Evangelicals were indebted to the inspiration provided by the spirituality and morality of the Nonjurors. John Wesley was influenced at home by Thomas Deacon and in the Holy Club by John Clayton. He was deeply affected by his personal contact with William Law, and his eucharistic theology is difficult to distinguish from that of Dean

Brevint. George Whitefield, Henry Venn and Thomas Scott were also influenced by Law in their formative periods. And Thomas Wilson's *A Short and Plain Instruction for the Better Understanding of the Lord's Supper* played a key part in Charles Simeon's conversion.[7] The Evangelicals did not limit the saving encounter with God to the cult as implied by John Johnson, and they tried to cut the connection between devotion to God and acceptance by him as implied by William Law but, as we shall see in the next two sections, they were just as adamant to channel the celebration of the Gospel to the eucharistic commemoration of its source. I shall deal first with the eucharistic theology and spirituality of John Wesley, and then move on to consider the thoughts and experience of some key Evangelical leaders who remained within the Church of England.

JOHN WESLEY AND THE EUCHARIST

John Wesley was not a speculative theologian.[8] This theology was driven not by the pursuit of the truth of God in itself but a yearning for both the love of God and the loving of God in the life of faith. This is seen clearly in his theology of the Eucharist – it is grounded in the dilemmas and didactic of practice. Hence, the most appropriate method of entering into his sacramental thinking is not by a simple identification of traditional eucharistic themes – for this would merely give the co-ordinates of his thought, not the collage of his experience – but rather by an examination of the outworking of his teaching in the twin thrusts of his theological practice: the presentation of the Gospel and the call to holiness.

Wesley had been profoundly affected by his contact with the Moravians. Struck by the vibrance and confidence of their faith and challenged by discussion with Peter Böhler, Wesley concluded that his devout 'method', inspired by Kempis, Taylor and Law, was a misplaced attempt to win his salvation by his 'own works or righteousness'.[9] After a period in which he deliberately sought an experience of saving faith, he received it as a conviction enabling 'a full reliance on the blood of Christ shed for *me*'.[10] Nevertheless, within less than fourteen months of his Aldersgate experience he had broken from the Moravian Fetter Lane Society on grounds which, though complex, centred on their neglect, even dismissal, of the Lord's Supper.[11]

Under the influence of Mölther, the Fetter Lane Society combined a radical interpretation of Luther's principle of salvation by faith alone with a Quietist spirituality reminiscent of the Quakers. They excluded all religious activities and replaced them with a doctrine of stillness. Their reasoning was that the only human involvement in the work of salvation is to be still and receive the gift of faith, which will come complete and unmistakably – the recipient would become instantly righteous and without sin. The underlying assumption was that any personal or ecclesial action, whether in terms of devotion or of ministry, implied a co-operation with the work of God and therefore created a salvation by works rather than by grace. The equation was extended to the traditional Protestant distinction between justification and sanctification. If sanctification was seen as a process apart from the state of justification, then the principles of grace and faith would be betrayed, and holiness would become, in some way, dependent upon human effort. Therefore, rather than being two separable movements, they must be seen as the product of one momentous event.[12]

Wesley's response was on two levels. He argued, first, that there are degrees of faith, and second, that God has chosen certain methods to create and continue that faith: 'By "means of grace", I understand outward signs, words, or actions, ordained of God, and appointed for this end, to be the ordinary channels whereby he might convey to man, preventing, justifying, or sanctifying grace.'[13]

In contrast to the Moravians, he delineated phases of salvation and maintained that the means of grace – principally, prayer, Scripture and the Lord's Supper – were designed to meet the different needs at each stage. Wesley's understanding of the universality of grace led him to the belief that the grace of God is present in a person before justification, creating – given the right conditions – a faith which seeks God. If pursued, this seeking faith will lead to repentance and justifying faith which, if authentic, will in turn be accompanied by the distinct but complementary gift of new birth.[14] The new birth involves a real change in the believer's moral and spiritual depths which may, at some stage, result in 'a total death to sin, and an entire renewal in the love and image of God'.[15]

Hence, the Wesleyan understanding of salvation may be seen in terms of an anticipation in the predisposition to justification, an inauguration in the moment of belief and experience of new birth (both of which are sustained in the life of faith) and an eschatological consummation, which is possible now in a provisional form in the 'renewal in love' but is not complete until heaven.

Wesley's defence of the means of grace concentrated on the Lord's Supper. The controversy had taken the classic Protestant sacramental problem of identifying the real value of the Sacrament over and against that of hearing and receiving the Word, and pushed it one stage further back and, therefore, heightened it into a crisis by the logic, Why the need for the Sacrament – and, indeed, the Word – if Christ, in his death, is received through faith? Wesley's answer to the harder, Moravian, form of the dilemma also met its softer, Protestant, form. His first appeal was to Scripture and his second to experience:

> Why did my dying Lord ordain
> This dear memorial of His Love?
> Might we not all by faith obtain,
> By faith the mountain sin remove,
> Enjoy the sense of sins forgiven,
> And holiness, the taste of heaven?
> It seem'd to my Redeemer good
> That faith should *here* His coming wait.
> The prayer, the fast, the word conveys,
> When mixed with faith, The life to me;
> In all the channels of thy grace
> I still have fellowship with Thee:
> But chiefly here my soul is fed
> With fulness of immortal bread.
> Communion closer far I feel,
> And deeper drink the'atoning blood.[16]

His approach was thus neither to 'neglect' the means nor to 'rest' in them. It was rather to 'wait' in them as appointed places of God's activity.[17] Wesley knew from his pre-conversion experience that the temptation to formality is real:

> But I of means have made my boast,
> Of means an idol made;
> The spirit in the letter lost,
> The substance in the shade.[18]

Nevertheless, the solution is not to dispense with the means but to find Christ through them: 'I use, but *trust* the means no more.'[19]

For Wesley the Eucharist fitted into this scheme on an equal ontological footing. The sacramental grace is not bestowed *ex opere operato*. As in prayer and preaching, it is always subject to the dynamics of the faith relationship. Further, as we shall see, there is not a presence of the person or death of Christ in the Eucharist which is different in ontological category from that available through preaching and received through faith. But for Wesley such equality worked both ways. His roots in post-Calvinist Anglican theology allowed him to view the Sacrament independently of the Word as preaching. Its role was not merely to confirm the Word, for it could actually be the Word. It could, and quite clearly did, present and convey the *kerygma* to those with willing hearts and seeing eyes:

> Come to the Supper come,
> Sinners, there still is room;
> Every soul may be his guest,
> Christ revives his sufferings here,
> Still exposes them to view
> See the Crucified appear,
> Now believe He died for you.[20]

These are remarkable words when one considers the extraordinary results the Wesleys were seeing from their preaching ministries, but they are overshadowed by the claim that the Eucharist has a functional superiority to the other means of grace, including the Word. The Eucharist is the 'grand channel'[21] of his grace, his 'kindest word'.[22] indeed, his 'dearest dying word,'[23] where 'chiefly my soul is fed'[24] and at which we 'never can on earth be higher, or more completely blest'.[25]

Clearly, Wesley did not fall into the trap to which, as we saw, some Puritans were prone: he did not make the Sacrament a parasite of the sermon. In line with Hooker and in contrast with Calvin, he did allow a limited autonomy to the Eucharist. However, the underlying evangelical concern of Calvin and the Puritans – to tie the Sacrament to the Gospel – was maintained by him, as indeed it was by Hooker. Participation in the correct liturgical enactment of the Sacrament is not a sufficient guarantee of its efficacy. This depended on the presentation and the response to the reality of the Gospel. Wesley's passionate belief was that the Eucharist is a context – in fact, a peculiarly appropriate context – in which this could happen:

> Sinner, believe, and find Him here;
> Believe, and feel He died for you.[26]

We must now move on to consider Wesley's understanding of the inner working of the Eucharist in order to see why and how he believed that the Sacrament operated as an intensified context for the initiative of grace and the response of faith in the processes of justification, sanctification and even the renewal in love. On a technical level, Wesley would have dismissed this as an invalid procedure. The motive for sacramental participation is not to be found in the dissemination of its mechanics but in the obedience to the command and in the verification of experience:

> I cannot the way decry,
> Need not know the mystery;
> Only this I know – that I
> Was blind, but now I see.[27]

Nevertheless, on another level, the reality of the experience provoked a theology which was at points quite specific. Wesley drew consciously and directly from high Anglican sources – most notably from the Nonjuror Dean Brevint – but infused the tradition with the criteria of his Evangelical experience.

Consecration

Wesley believed in an objective consecration. The Pauline description of the cup as 'the cup...which we bless' means 'setting it apart to a sacred use, and solemnly invoking the blessing of God upon it'.[28] In line with Brevint and the Nonjurors, he identified the Spirit as the agent of consecration:

> Come, Holy Ghost, Thine influence shed,
> And realize the sign;
> Thy power into the bread,
> Thy power into the wine.[29]

The result of the Spirit's work in the action of the Church is to 'raise' the 'creatures'[30] of bread and wine so that they may 'convey His grace' and become 'glorious instruments Divine':[31]

> The outward sign of inward grace
> Ordained by Christ Himself receive:
> The sign transmits the Signified
> The grace is by the means applied.[32]

There is a 'mystical relation' rather than a substantial identity between the elements and the reality.[33] However, the relation is such as to allow a real role for them. The source of the blessing is in the promise of God and its end is in the receiving faith of the participant, but the elements play an objective and effective part in its communication – 'Thy blessing in Thy means convey.'[34]

In order to determine what Wesley believed to be the content of the blessing we must approach his doctrines of the eucharistic presence of Christ and the eucharistic sacrifice together.

Presence and sacrifice

On one level (generally corresponding with his writings), Wesley's doctrine may be stated quite precisely. However, on another level (generally corresponding with the hymns), the reality of the eucharistic mystery cannot be fully known simply by a spotlight on one or two systematic points; it is too diverse and complex – like a beam refracted through a prism into several colourful rays. The richness of Wesley's images can be glimpsed by focusing on the role of the Eucharist in the presentation of the Gospel and in the life of holiness.

Wesley saw the essence of conversion as the acknowledgement of the sole sufficiency of Christ's atoning work. It is faith in Christ crucified that saves. In the Sacrament 'this sacrifice, once offered, is still represented in remembrance of the remission of sins'.[35] Hence, the *anamnesis* creates the possibility of an encounter with the meaning of the Cross:

> The Lamb as crucified afresh
> Is here held out to man.[36]

As we have seen, this process is not different in category from the activity of preaching, the purpose of which is also to

> ...show poor souls the dying Lamb
> And point them to his blood.[37]

However, its unique functional force and specific degree of significance is derived not merely from its mandate to 'recall' but its charge to do so in sacramental form. Here Wesley combined a subtle blending of the affective and effective emphases. The bread and wine are real 'tokens'[38] of his body and blood – their value is acquired from the Spirit's activity, not the attitude of the individual – but their role is to affect the faith of the participant so that he is carried back to the historical event of the Cross to stand convinced of its significance. The elements within the liturgical event may therefore

create, or at least facilitate, faith and then convey the Gospel's gift to
faith. The result is not just a return to a historical event and a
theological appreciation of its significance, but an eschatological
breakthrough in which the Christ who is substantially in heaven

> ...dost even now [His] banquet crown
> To every faithful soul appear
> And show [His] real presence here.[39]

Behind the possibility of a converting-faith encounter in the
Eucharist lies a complex matrix of relationships between the Cross,
the ascended Christ, the Church and the individual. The sacrifice is
past and complete: "'Tis done, the atoning work is done',[40] but
despite this, 'His death is ever new',[41] because it 'subsists eternal in
the lamb'.[42] The sacrifice is thus eternal, not through repetition by
Christ or, still less, by the Church,[43] but through the eternal presence
of the Victim–Priest before the eyes of the Father. Thus as once 'He
gasp[ed] in death – Forgive',[44] so, on the basis of his death, he
permanently prays:

> '...Forgive them.
> All their sins were purged by Me'.
> Still our advocate in heaven
> Prays the prayer on earth begun,
> 'Father, show their sins forgiven,
> Father glorify Thy Son'.[45]

Wesley emphasized the universal validity and inclusive character
of Christ's death:

> Would the Saviour of mankind
> Without His people die?
> No, to Him we all are join'd
> As more than standers by.[46]

However, he also made clear that the relationship which all people
have with the death of Christ in principle must become a practical
and personal one. The process by which this is envisaged is a typically
Wesleyan fusion of divine initiative and human activity. The drama
of heaven involves the directing of the one sacrifice made for all to its
particularization in the life of the individual, so that the blood 'which
cancels sin' becomes the 'sprinkled blood' of reconciliation.[47] And
the Church's script is to echo the prayer which the wounds of Christ
speak to the Father by its own symbolic performance:

> Yet may we celebrate below,
> And daily thus Thine offering show
> Exposed before Thy Father's eyes;
> In this tremendous mystery
> Present thee bleeding on a tree
> Our everlasting sacrifice.[48]

Wesley was adamant that conversion is only the beginning of Christian life. It seems that his expectations of justifying faith were not fully realized in his subsequent experience.[49] Although holiness had been imputed to his soul, it had not transformed his life. He was thrown back on his earlier sources of Kempis, Taylor and Law to sustain his vision of a realized holiness, though now his criteria for the quest were more objectively centred. His method was now the replacement of his mind of flesh with the 'mind which was in Christ',[50] and which, by grace through faith, he possessed in principle already. It was the translation of status into state rather than the striving for status by imitating the state.

He believed that the Eucharist provided a vital context for this process primarily because it allows the imputed but relative – essentially juridical – identity with Christ, to become a real – increasingly moral and personal – identity by continually exposing us to the grace of the Cross (the grace which not only justifies but also sanctifies). The Eucharist thus draws us into an ever deeper communion with Christ:

> Saviour, Thou didst the mystery give,
> That I Thy nature might partake;
> Thou bidd'st me outward signs receive,
> My body, soul, and spirit to join
> Inseparably one with Thine.[51]

And, by its effective proclamation of the Cross as something done for us, the Eucharist sets the scene for an ever closer union with the Cross as something done in us:

> Hallow'd by the streaming blood,
> Blood whose virtue all may know,
> Sharers with the dying God,
> And crucified below.
> Jesu, Lord whose cross we bear,
> Let thy death our sins destroy,
> Make us who Thy sorrows share
> Partakers of Thy joy.[52]

The life of holiness is, then, 'one inwardly and outwardly devoted to God'.[53] It involves obedience, offering and consecration, all of which have no independent value and, therefore, must be 'joined'[54] with the one oblation of Christ:

> Our mean imperfect sacrifice
> On Thine is as a burden thrown;
> Both in a common flame arise,
> And both in God's account are one.[55]

The 'conformity'[56] which the believer seeks with Christ includes a moral as well as a legal identification with his death. Both find a liturgical voice in the eucharistic presence of the historical and eternal work of Christ:

> Thou art with all Thy members here,
> In this tremendous mystery
> We jointly before God appear,
> To offer up ourselves with thee.[57]

The result of the dedication to obedience will be a lessening of the propensity to sin, which may culminate in an experience of the 'renewal in love' which he defined as 'pure love, filling the heart, and governing all the words and actions'.[58]

It may be justifiably argued that in his concept of Christian perfection Wesley upset the balance between the now and the not yet by positing a moral identity with Christ which belongs to the Eschaton alone. But this criticism highlights the complexity and genius of Wesley's thought. He refused to limit the hope to heaven. His expectation of perfection was a statement of a spirituality in eschatological yearning. We can see, therefore, that there was a very close connection between his doctrine of the Eucharist and his doctrine of Christian perfection. Just as the renewal in love is a qualified but genuinely eschatological experience, so the Eucharist provides a partial but real experience of the eschatological reality, for 'Ev'n now the marriage feast we share':

> Here He gives our souls a taste
> Heaven into our heart He pours.
> That, that is the fulness;
> But this is the taste.[59]

EIGHTEENTH- AND EARLY NINETEENTH-CENTURY EVANGELICALS

In order to examine the eucharistic thought of the Evangelicals who remained in the Church of England, I shall adopt a similar scheme to that followed in the analysis of Wesley and identify the part they saw the Eucharist playing in conversion and in the life of faith.

When reviewing his perplexed, even desperate search for salvation, George Whitefield saw his Holy Club Eucharists as important stages. In them he 'found grace in a very affecting manner, and in abundant measure, sometimes imparted to [his] soul'.[60] Edward Bickersteth claimed that his 'spiritual faculties' were first awakened in a Communion service.[61] As has already been indicated, it was Thomas Wilson's communion manual that first revealed the reality of the Gospel to Charles Simeon. He received a consciousness of saving faith a few days afterwards – an experience which was sustained and intensified the same morning through the Sacrament: 'at the Lord's table I had the sweetest access to God through my blessed Saviour'.[62]

Daniel Wilson's conversion was even more closely connected with the Eucharist. After an intense personal struggle in which, though convicted of his own sin, he found it impossible to make the step of faith, he concluded that 'the hearing of the Gospel, and the reading of God's word produce no effect in my obdurate heart'.[63] It seems possible that soon after this he underwent an intellectual conversion – a conversion of his mind to the truth of Christ. But this did not reach his personal and existential depths until the time of his first communion, which he described in the following way:

on last Sunday morning [i.e. yesterday], I took that solemn and important step, and the Lord was with me. Never did I enjoy so much the presence of my dear Redeemer, as I have since that time... *Yesterday and today have been, I think, the happiest days I ever remember.*[64]

These Evangelicals did not systematize their experience by formally stating with Wesley that the Sacrament could be a 'converting ordinance'. Nevertheless, they did have a vision in general terms for the Eucharist's evangelistic potential. Some were prepared to relate this specifically to the actual celebration and even to the moment of reception. Their general vision may be seen in the character of their sacramental manuals and in their sermons and addresses on the Lord's Supper. The manuals provide a visible example of the unity of Sacrament and Gospel for which many of the Evangelicals were striving – they were combinations of Gospel tract and communion meditation.[65]

The Evangelicals were concerned to show that the Sacrament is not effective *ex opere operato*, but their motivation was pastoral rather than polemic. The enemy was seen not as Rome, still less as High Church devotion, but as 'formality [which] is the most dangerous of all states'.[66] Wilson argued that 'the Sacrament of Christ's body and blood is profitable only to the faithful. It does not operate necessarily. It is merely an instrument in the hands of God communicating grace to the heart.'[67]

The Evangelicals defined 'faithful reception' in a much more active sense than was common in contemporary Anglicanism. For them it involved evangelical faith, that is, a dynamic apprehension of the Gospel. Indeed, their Reformation definition of faith actually fuelled their passion for the Sacrament: they recognized that the themes of the Eucharist are the essential themes of the Gospel: 'The Sacrament does eminent honour to this foundational doctrine of Christianity [the Atonement]. It sets forth the Lord's death, it bears witness to the Lamb of God who was slain to take away the sin of the world.'[68] Therefore the preparation outlined in the manuals and in the sermons consisted to a large extent in engendering a correct understanding of Christ's death which, if successful, would itself be converting.

Haweis would allow only those with experiential evidence of conversion to receive the Sacrament, but others adopted a more open approach. Wilson and Bickersteth tried to strike a balance between, on the one hand, advising adequate preparation on the meaning of the Eucharist – a process which would normally involve some form of acknowledgement of the Gospel – and, on the other, so emphasizing the need for self-examination that all but the most pious and self-confident would be discouraged from participating. Thus, although Bickersteth limited participation to the 'sincere Christian',[69] he was also concerned to make clear that the 'ordinance requires not perfecting in any grace in those who come. If a man have but the beginnings of holy dispositions let him come to have them strengthened.'[70]

Simeon, characteristically, was clearer in his acknowledgement of the ambiguities of Christian existence and, perhaps reflecting on his own experience, he was more willing to admit the possibility of

conversion occurring through the Sacrament: 'Christ sometimes
reveals himself in the breaking of bread, to those who had not so fully
discovered him in the ministration of the word.'[71]

Romaine, writing some decades earlier, was unabashed in his call
of all those who have 'been led to seek a life from the free grace of
God'[72] to communicate:

> If this be thy state, thou art safe. Thou art invited, and thou wilt be a
> welcome guest at the Lord's table... Lift up thine heart to God in prayer,
> and desire thou mayest find his presence in his own ordinance. Be
> encouraged by the experience of others.[73]

Although the Evangelicals saw a significant role for the Eucharist
in the process of communicating the Gospel, they reserved their
energies for the part it should play in the life of faith. Whitefield found
the period between his deaconing and his priesting a difficult time. As
a missionary deacon unauthorized to minister the Sacrament, he not
only felt that his work was being hampered[74] but that his personal
spirituality was being deprived through very infrequent participation. He found a welcome respite in Gibraltar during the crossing
to Georgia: 'I received (what my soul longed after) the Sacrament of
Christ's Most Blessed Body and Blood.'[75] Wilson was beset by a heavy
sense of his own sin throughout his life but he clearly experienced a
high degree of comfort and relief in the Eucharist: 'I have just come
from the blessed sacrament. I have found it good for my soul. I have
had some views of the grace and glory of Christ.'[76]

 The manuals were written to encourage Evangelicals towards a
more frequent participation in the Sacrament. Detailed arguments
were used to meet objections – usually from fear of unworthy
reception – to regular sacramental involvement. The manuals and
sermons were severe on those who remained unconvinced and
deliberately avoided the Eucharist:

> they confirm that they have no friendship for [Christ].[77]
> No-one properly speaking, continues a member, even of the visible body of
> Christ, who does not habitually join in celebrations of this holy mystery.[78]

As the testimonies of Whitefield and Wilson indicate, their
motivation for frequent celebrations did not derive merely from an
obedience to 'the words of a friend', even 'his dying words',[79] but
stemmed from their rich experience of the Eucharist which, for some,
involved a conviction that the Sacrament involved a unique spiritual

encounter; 'There takes place at the Lord's Table that peculiar union with Christ which no other means of grace is designed to convey. And who can estimate the value of this blessing?'[80]

Although the Evangelicals did not define this sense of specificity systematically, it is possible to trace a logical line from their understanding of the Eucharist's relation, first, to Christ's sacrifice, second, to the believer's faith and, third, to Christ's presence. This nexus of thought may account for such unselfconscious statements as Bickersteth's crescendo: 'Here we may have the nearest approaches to the Divine Presence, that our state in this world admits... There is a blessed manifestation of the Divine Presence, to the soul to be here expected.'[81]

It has been shown in chapter 1 that the fundamental Evangelical experience is based on the recognition of the absolute salvific sufficiency of Christ's Atonement. As we have just seen, the fundamental merit of the Eucharist for the eighteenth- and early nineteenth-century Evangelicals was that it concentrated almost exclusively on this central reality.[82] It did not do so merely as a past event but as an eternally effective one which is powerfully present – to the eye of faith – in the dynamic symbolism of the sacramental event: 'Here we are taught to look upon him as bleeding for us on the accursed tree. Here the Lamb of God, as if he had been newly slain, is in the ordinance set forth as crucified.'[83]

The unique experience of the Eucharist was, therefore, seen as deriving from its function of representing and commemorating Christ's one sacrifice in a unique way. Bickersteth was even prepared to allow a Godward direction to the commemoration which, though not exclusive to the Eucharist, involved a special degree of intensity:

This is done for our own edification, as a testimony to the world, and as a prevailing mode of pleading merits before God. It has been observed that 'What we more compendiously express in that general conclusion of our prayers, *through Jesus Christ our Lord*, we more fully and forcibly represent in the celebration of the Holy Eucharist, wherein we plead the virtue and merits of the same sacrifice here, that our Great High Priest is continually urging for us in heaven.'[84]

However, it is the ability of the Eucharist to increase 'our own edification' which most excited the Evangelicals and explains their willingness to attach a specificity to the Eucharist. Because of its dramatic power, 'the Lord's Supper is peculiarly calculated to increase faith'.[85]

The use made of bread and wine in the sacramental action culminating in reception so strongly affects our faith in the Atonement achieved by Christ's death that we are in a peculiarly open state to enjoy the presence of Christ, which is then conveyed to us by 'these holy mysteries of God' whereby the Father 'gives us the children's bread'[86] and through which 'Jesus Christ makes over his whole self to every believer'.[87]

Thus, the commemoration 'touch[es] the most sacred sympathies of our souls' – that is, it awakens a heightened context of faith. The context should be further stimulated by an expectation of grace – 'we should prepare for large accessions of spiritual strength'.[88] But, although it is faith which 'realizes the sign',[89] the sign, 'to the eye of faith',[90] coincides with the reality:

we see him present with us in the symbols of Bread and wine.[91]

Christ is also the substance of the bread.[92]

the nearest approach to God of which our present state admits...[is involved in the] partaking of the consecrated emblems of the body and blood of Christ, [and] celebrating the mysteries where the Saviour is peculiarly and really present.[93]

Despite the undefensiveness of the Evangelicals' comments, they should not be seen as defining a unique ontological category of presence, for all affirmed the Sacrament's essential unity with the Word and with prayer.[94] Their point was not that something different is given in the Eucharist but that the same thing, or rather the same One, is given in special degree by the functional force of the Sacrament. Thus, although Simeon was prepared to talk of a 'peculiar presence',[95] he clarifies his meaning as follows: 'And, though I am not aware of any express promise of a more than ordinary manifestation of the Saviour's presence in that most sacred ordinance, yet I believe that he does seal it with a peculiar blessing.'[96]

In the minds of the Evangelicals the reality of the 'peculiar blessing' was also derived from three other dimensions of experience made possible by the sacramental commemoration of Christ's death. First, the Sacrament 'is our Eucharist, or festival of praise and triumph'.[97] As shown by Max Warren,[98] the theme of *Christus Victor*, or the celebration, in Haweis's phrase, of Christ's 'glorious victory',[99] permeated the Evangelicals' view of the Sacrament. Second, the eschatological character of the Eucharist was affirmed not merely in the sense of doing this till he comes, but in the sense of anticipatory evidence that Christ's vow of abstinence has now been overtaken by the reality of the Kingdom, a Kingdom which, though complete in heaven, is also established on earth in the believing community. The Sacrament was thus for Wilson a 'foretaste of that heavenly Supper of the Lamb'.[100] For Romaine it was so because 'here is *the bread which he brought down from heaven*'.[101] Bickersteth suggested that by his vow of abstinence, Christ 'seems to include a blessed promise of a peculiar communion with his people in their due observance of that Institution',[102] because it links the 'spiritual kingdom' on earth with the future 'heavenly kingdom'.[103] Finally, the Eucharist stimulates an unreserved level of self-oblation which, it would appear, was focused for the Evangelicals more on the moment of reception than on the post-communion Prayer of Oblation. Haweis commended his readers at the reception of the elements to 'Coolly, humbly, cheerfully and wholly, without partiality, and without hypocrisy, desire to give up your soul to God.'[104] The result, therefore, of the sacramental action is that the believer 'is strengthened...to be crucified to the world by the transforming lessons of the Cross'.[105]

CONCLUSION

The same person whose heart was warmed at Aldersgate received the Sacrament four to five times a week throughout his life. Wesley's eucharistic spirituality was not an isolated idiosyncrasy but, as John Bowmer has demonstrated, was widespread, at least in intention, throughout the beginnings of Methodism.[106] Ernst Rattenbury's verdict on the evidence is that the Wesleyan Revival was both Evangelical and sacramental.[107] This study of Wesley's thought has supported Rattenbury's claim, at least as far as the Lord's Supper is concerned, by revealing the intimacy of Gospel and Eucharist in his mind. It has also confirmed the argument of E. J. G. Rogers that the part of the Revival which remained in the Church of England was equally eucharistic.[108] It sought the same unity between Word and Sacrament which Whitefield enjoyed on 1 January 1739: '[I] Received the Holy Sacrament twice, preached twice, and found this to be the happiest New Year's Day that I ever saw.'[109]

There are elements in the sacramental theology of both branches of the Revival which will be reviewed more critically at a later stage, but at this point it is right to conclude with their achievements. First, their eucharistic thought was largely devoid of polemic – except that directed to lifeless formality or obvious hypocrisy. Secondly, it was marked by a freedom of expression which preferred to state the joy of experience and to encourage others to share its opportunities than negatively to define its limits. Thirdly, in so doing, it drew on the resources of the Reformers, and of the Puritan and the Anglican traditions – particularly High Church devotion, including, for Wesley, the Nonjurors. Fourthly and finally, the Revival's discovery of the Gospel led naturally to an enthusiasm for the Eucharist as an intended setting in which it could be proclaimed, celebrated and experienced in a unique way.

CHAPTER 6

Evangelicals, the tradition and the tension

The Evangelical party, which had emerged on the wave of Revival, had become, by the first third of the nineteenth century, a respected and powerful part of the Church of England. It was producing leaders destined to make a significant contribution to the Church of England and a decisive impact on the growth of the Anglican communion. But whilst it was poised on the edge of political power within the Church, there were two forces (later to be joined by a third) which were threatening to thwart its advance. The first grew out of its own internal life. Various disagreements and divisions developed amongst Evangelicals over peripheral theological concerns which, together with a gradual draining of talent as some of its best people went off to the mission field abroad, slowly but surely sapped their strength. The second came from the rise of Tractarianism. Tractarianism was to make a radical and lasting impression on the Church, leaving Evangelicals for many years at least one step (and sometimes many more) behind in theological creativity and ecclesiastical influence. Thirdly, the effects of both internal problems and external threat left Evangelicals ill-equipped to meet the challenge presented by Darwinism in particular and liberal intellectual pressure in general. It was the second of these forces which most affected the way Evangelicals viewed and valued the Eucharist, and so it is the effects of Tractarianism on Evangelical thought which will occupy us in the first part of this chapter. We shall then go on to look at the period when Evangelical defensiveness was at its height in the early years of this century, and conclude by considering some of the signs of recovery in Evangelical life from about 1930 to around 1960.

THE EVANGELICAL REACTION TO TRACTARIANISM 1833-1900

The initial sympathy which Evangelicals may have had for the ideals of the Tractarians soon turned to deep antipathy as the latter began to reinterpret the historical foundations and traditions of the Church of England in a way which appeared to give credibility to its increasing emphasis on the objectivity of sacramental grace and the mediation of a sacerdotal ministry. Both the shift of historical perspective and the underlying doctrinal motivation were seen as a direct threat to the Evangelical cause, and evoked a voluminous and impassioned reply. I shall trace the reaction to Tractarian teaching on the Eucharist by examining the thought of two theologians, William Goode and Nathaniel Dimock, who represent the main elements in the scholarly response, and the thought of one leader, John Charles Ryle, who represents features of the response on a more practical and popular level.

William Goode (1801–1868)

William Goode's massive study on the eucharistic presence, *The Nature of Christ's Presence in the Eucharist*, published in 1856,[1] formed a substantial Evangelical response to Tractarian teaching, which had by that stage reached a level of maturity. Goode was in no doubt as to the seriousness of the debate, which was on '*the very truths for which our martyred Reformers laid down their lives*'.[2] Although Goode acknowledged that the Tractarians did not formally maintain the doctrine of transubstantiation, he was nevertheless adamant that the motives and results of their teaching amounted to the essence of the Roman doctrine and, therefore, qualified for the same criticisms. The choice, he claimed, was not between transubstantiation, consubstantiation or any other theory which claims some form of real identity between the body and blood and the bread and wine, but between theologies which locate the activity of God either in the external material of the Sacrament or in the internal experience of the receiver. He claimed that doctrines which relate the presence to the elements in substantial categories are not supported by Scripture, reason or the tradition of the Fathers, the Reformers and the Anglican divines. They not only lead to the practical abuses of sacerdotalism and adoration of the elements but also result in a belief in the sacrifice of the Mass and, primarily for Goode's purposes, involve severe Christological and soteriological problems.

In Goode's eyes, the Christological error revolved around the definition of Christ's body. Doctrines of an objective presence imply its existence in two forms, one material and limited in location to one place, and the other immaterial, having the facility of multi-presence. Such constructions involve intolerable self-contradictions to the '*unity, locality*, and *quantity*'[3] of Christ's body. The soteriological error, for Goode, lay in the non-necessity of Christ's bodily presence and the ineffectuality of the *manducatio oralis*: 'The soul may feed upon Christ by faith, and spiritually receive the body and blood of Christ for its nourishment, as well when that body is in heaven as if it was in the stomach.'[4] The truth of this for Goode could be seen in the Tractarian Robert Wilberforce's acknowledgement that the *virtus sacramenti* can be received only by an act of faith – the bodily contact with the *res sacramenti* does not directly affect the soul. Indeed, Goode regarded Wilberforce's distinction between the *res sacramenti* and the *virtus sacramenti* as anomalous – not only because it is Christologically untenable, but because it misinterprets the eucharistic words of Christ. He argued that whereas the Tractarians were primarily interested in the substance of Christ's glorified body, the presence of which they attempted to define in immaterial terms, he was concerned for the salvation won by Christ which is made present by the contemplation of the material body of Christ once crucified on the Cross. Through such an act of faith the believer is united in communion with the glorified body of Christ in heaven: 'a difference of locality, therefore makes no difference in its presence to faith'.[5]

Goode went on to argue that just as the reception of Christ's body and blood is not contingent upon their substantial relationship with the elements, neither is the instrumentality of the Sacrament. A symbolic relation with the body and blood does not reduce the elements to a naked sign, for by means of the consecration they are set apart for a 'holy use and purpose' – even given a 'peculiar sanctity',[6] so that they become 'effective instruments...for bringing the communicant into a state of spiritual union and communion with Christ'.[7]

Nathaniel Dimock (1825–1909)

Nathaniel Dimock's prolific response to Tractarianism was published during the 1870s and 1880s. He began from the same starting point as Goode ('the question of preserving the purity of our Reformed faith is the question of the hour'[8]) and arrived at the same conclusions on the nature of the eucharistic presence (though by a less philosophical route), but he was more wide-ranging in the issues which he tackled.

Dimock's methodology was dominated by a concern to show that Tractarian theories of an objective presence and a real eucharistic sacrifice represented a new departure in the Church of England. He argued that the Tractarians' attempt to establish a precedent for their position in Anglican theological and liturgical tradition, and even in the motives of the English Reformers, could not be done. Cranmer's plan to 'uproot'[9] the doctrines of transubstantiation and the sacrifice of the Mass was complete: it was enshrined in the Prayer Book, expressed in the Articles and had been affirmed by Anglican divines, even of the highest sort. There is a doctrinal 'chasm'[10] first, between the 'Real Absence and the...Real Presence in or under the form of the consecrated elements considered in themselves',[11] and, secondly, between a '*nuda commemoratio*'[12] (that is, one devoid of any propitiatory efficacy, even of a derived sort) and a eucharistic sacrifice in which, in some way, the offering of Christ is continued. Anglican tradition has always remained on the side chosen by the Reformers (which according to Dimock was also the position of the Fathers) whereas the Tractarians placed themselves firmly on the Roman side of the divide.

Dimock argued that theories of an objective presence and an objective sacrifice destroyed the Gospel by positing a mode of presence which is independent of the apprehension of the meaning of Christ's death, and by implying that the efficacy of that sacrificial death is imperfect because it needs to be continued or perpetuated. Further, they not only undermine the character of the Gospel, but they are unnecessary to a full and satisfying appreciation of the sacramental event:

the change [to a Reformed understanding of the presence] would lose nothing of the *reality*, nothing of the blessedness, nothing of the fulness, nothing of the true joy of the Eucharistic Feast.[13]

And with this Sacrifice [the one oblation once offered] in full view of our faith, with this as the object of our remembrance, we want nothing more. Nay, we can see that there is room for nothing more.[14]

Tractarian claims that Christ's priesthood should be seen in terms of an ongoing sacrifice, which in turn should be linked with the activity of the ministerial priesthood in the Eucharist, were dismissed by Dimock. In the first place, Christ's priesthood, which was founded on his sacrifice on the Cross, makes all other priesthoods seen in terms of sacrificing for sin as 'not superfluous merely, but as anti-Christian impertinence'.[15] In the second place, Christ's priesthood is defined not by the action of sacrifice, for this was finished on the Cross, but by the image of the 'Great Shepherd'[16] who blesses his flock with the benefits of his past death.

Dimock's efforts were directed not only negatively against Tractarian doctrine but also positively towards establishing a necessary relationship between the Gospel and the sacraments. He described such a relation in terms of the 'subservience'[17] of the sacraments to the Gospel, and he defined the Gospel as 'the telling of a gift',[18] claiming that in God's 'appointment'

this gift should be made over to man not only by the general declaration of his Word, but by visible signs and seals of conveyance – seals which thus become effectual signs of the donation of the gift – sure witnesses and effectual signs of grace and God's goodness towards us.[19]

The response required by the 'telling' is one of faith in the meaning of Christ's death, but the activity of faith does not create the gift – it merely receives it by believing in its truth. Dimock thus placed the objectivity of sacramental grace not on the sacraments themselves but on the Gospel. However, the relationship between the two is such that the Eucharist, for example, is a means of grace because it actually *gives* the gift of the Gospel (the soteriological significance of Christ's body and blood) to all who participate. Hence, even the unworthy are confronted by the crisis of the Gospel. In order for the dynamics of faith to be maintained, there is no absolute identity between the *sacramentum* and the *res sacramenti*, and so the gift may be rejected – a decision which condemns the refuser as one 'guilty of profaning the body and blood of the Lord' (1 Cor. 11: 27). The 'effectual power'[20] of the Eucharist and its necessity lie not in its ontological exclusivity – for the same crisis of faith is possible in other contexts – but in its

ordained function to present and donate the reality of the Gospel in
sacramental form.

John Charles Ryle (1816–1900)

The mantle of the leadership of Evangelicals in the last quarter of the
nineteenth century was worn by Bishop Ryle. His writings reflect the
alarm felt by ordinary Evangelical clergy for the 'present distress'[21]
created by the Tractarian and Ritualist movements.

Ryle's doctrine of the Eucharist was essentially the same as
Goode's and Dimock's. He denied that the Sacrament has any
value *ex opere operato* and stressed instead that it must be rightly
received. He viewed the interpretative words in a representative way
and related them to faith in the meaning of Christ's death – a process
which leads to communion with the living Christ and his spiritual
presence in the heart of the believer. He regarded the real presence in
or under the elements as unscriptural and un-Anglican, involving the
most damaging Christological and soteriological errors. He maintained that the Eucharist is not a sacrifice, because it is not so called
in Scripture and because its purpose is for the 'continual remembrance'[22] of Christ's death – a sacrifice which, as 'once for all
finished',[23] removed the need for any Christian cultic activity.

He urged his readers to value the Sacrament and encouraged
participation whenever the opportunity was available not only on
the grounds that Christians are under command to do so, but because
it has

> a special and peculiar blessing attached to it. That blessing, I believe,
> consists in a special and peculiar presence of Christ, vouchsafed to the heart
> of every believing communicant…our Lord did mean to teach that every
> right-hearted believer, who ate that bread and drank that wine in
> remembrance of Christ, would in so doing find a special presence of Christ
> in his heart, and a special revelation of Christ's sacrifice of His own body and
> blood to his soul.[24]

Nevertheless, when we examine the position of the Sacrament in
Ryle's theological and practical priorities we meet a phenomenon
which, as we shall see, becomes a recurring theme in the history of
Evangelical attitudes to the Eucharist. It is the paradox of a relatively
high potential allowed to the Sacrament but a relatively low place
given to it, first in the theological scheme, and second, despite calls for

participation, in the practical system. This phenomenon, which was displayed amongst the Puritans, has its roots in the underlying theological and experiential tension between Evangelicalism and Sacramentalism – a tension which, as we have seen, is intensified by certain historical conditions and may result in the positive being subsumed by the polemic.

Ryle viewed the condition of the Church in the late nineteenth century in the most serious possible terms.[25] It was not just the Protestant character of the Church of England that was at stake but its very survival as the national Church. The cause of the 'present distress', he argued, was to be found in doctrinal error centred on the Lord's Supper. The policies of the extreme Ritualists were not neutral aesthetic practices but expressions of doctrinal positions which were Romanizing the Church from within. The Lincoln Judgement of 1890 (allowing the use of the Eastwood position amongst other practices which Evangelicals regarded as highly dubious) had signalled the sanction, even acceptance, of the drift towards Roman Catholicism. The 'younger men',[26] who were attracted by the ceremony of the Ritualists but not committed to their theology, had shown the extent to which the 'fog'[27] had permeated the Church. Although they were an unfashionable minority experiencing the turn of the tide. Evangelical clergy should 'stand firm in the old paths', 'shoulder to shoulder',[28] resist the temptation to secede, and fight in the battle they had not started: 'If we love the truth as it is in Jesus, if we love the Church of England, we must contend earnestly for the faith once delivered to the saints in the matter of the Lord's Supper.'[29]

The key strategy was to ensure that the Sacrament remain in its 'rightful position'[30] and assume the proportion in the scheme of Christian theology, spirituality and ministry which it finds in the Thirty-Nine Articles. The Articles deal first with the great Evangelical themes of Scripture, sin, justification and faith, and then only secondarily with the sacraments and other functions of the visible Church. This reflects the pattern of the New Testament itself which, apart from certain isolated passages, is largely silent over the Eucharist. Hence, Ryle argued, the contemporary priority given to the Eucharist, the increasing number of celebrations and the tendency to encourage all the baptized to attend, distracted people from the real concerns of religion (the inward and spiritual relation with Christ) and led to a concern with the non-essential (the outward

forms of the visible Church). The result was to reinforce the vague
notions of salvific, mechanical, sacramental grace in the ordinary
man who 'likes to go to heaven by formally using ordinances'.[31]

Ryle's attempt to meet this threat was twofold. First, he laid such
heavy qualifications on the efficacy of the Sacrament that the balance
Goode and Dimock had tried to retain between the objectivity of the
gift and the necessity of the subjective response to the gift was upset,
and the weight of emphasis placed heavily on the 'intelligent'[32]
activity of the participant:

'To discern the Lord's body' – that is, to understand what the elements of
bread and wine represent, and why they are appointed, and what is the
particular use of remembering Christ's death, – is an essential qualification
of a true communicant.[33]

Secondly, although Ryle defined the purpose of the Eucharist as for
the 'strengthening and refreshing'[34] of those who have already come
to Christ by faith, his writings encouraged a piety in which the
Sacrament plays little real part. For example, in *Holiness*, Ryle's
influential work on the process of sanctification, references to the
Sacrament are usually polemic calls that it should not be given 'the
honour due unto the Lord'[35] by usurping the role of inward spiritual
faith. The only commendation of its use is couched in a warning not
to expect too much on an experiential level; and where the marks of
a Christian's love for Christ are defined, a desire to be at his table is
not envisaged. Indeed, the life-blood of the faith rests in the
individual's own personal piety and not in the corporate activity of
the Church, whether it be Eucharist or evangelistic meeting, for
'private religion is the root of all vital Christianity'.[36]

I conclude by drawing up three points of comparison between the
character of Tractarian thought on the Eucharist and the Evangelical
reaction which it provoked. The Tractarian approach was marked,
first, by a degree of creativity: it was engaged in a dialectic between
an affirmation of certain catholic values – the essence of which it felt
had been preserved in the Anglican tradition – and a criticism of, at
least, the presenting face of Roman theology. Secondly, it was
marked by an element of imprecision: the dialectic, by nature, tried
to avoid the pitfalls of following one theological impulse to its logical
conclusion at the expense of the other, preferring instead to explore
new ways of holding them together. Thirdly, it was marked by a

thrust of sacramental spirituality: the pursuit of holiness found its source in the eucharistic celebration.

The Evangelical reaction, on the other hand, was traditional rather than creative: a restatement of Reformed doctrine in a largely uncritical way, and a conviction that Anglican tradition had been faithful to its foundation. Secondly, Evangelical thought was drawn to an increasing degree of precision: whereas pre-Tractarian Evangelicals had been, at times, unreserved in their comments on the Eucharist in an attempt to encourage expectant participation, the present generation found it necessary to set strict limits on the parameters of eucharistic experience. Thirdly, Evangelical thought tended to reinforce the incipient tendency in the Evangelical system towards a non-sacramental spirituality: the Gospel must be free and unfettered. The Reformers had sought to reform the Church by rediscovering the Word and by dismantling the mediatorial system – the Tractarians and Ritualists were reversing the process.

Nevertheless, there were positive areas in the eucharistic thought of Evangelicals. Goode and Dimock sought to retain and define the objectivity of the eucharistic gift. There was a belief, even in Ryle, in a specific role for the Sacrament and a conviction of a genuine communion with Christ through the informed reception of the elements. But in the climate of controversy these positive dimensions lost both their theological vitality and their opportunity for expression in the spirituality of Evangelicalism.

EVANGELICAL DEFENSIVENESS 1900–1930

The issues which were to dominate this period arose out of three developments. The first was the Royal Commission on Ecclesiastical Discipline which reported in 1906. Its 'Letters of Business' opened the door not only to a change in its rubrics on the vesture of ministers but to a revision of the Book of Common Prayer itself.[37] The second was the publication in 1901 of Charles Gore's *The Body of Christ* which expounded a moderate Catholic position and sought to dissociate itself more clearly from Roman theology than had later nineteenth-century Tractarian thought and extreme Ritualistic practice.[38] The third was Walter Frere's scholarly censure of the 1662 communion rite and his influential call for a period of experimentation in the use of alternative forms which adhered to a more primitive structure.[39]

In order to identify the main elements in the Evangelical response to these developments, I shall discuss the reaction of one of its most significant leaders, Edmund Knox, to the first issue, that of one of its emerging scholars, W. H. Griffith Thomas, to the second, and that of its most able liturgist, Thomas Drury, to the third. I shall then consider the underlying methodological question which faced Evangelicals by examining the emergence of an organized Liberal Evangelical element within the movement. I shall conclude by a brief comment on Evangelical objection to the communion rite of the Deposited Prayer Book.

Edmund Knox (1847–1937)

Edmund Knox believed the vestment controversy to be of crucial significance: 'vestments mean the Mass, and the Mass means the whole system of Roman theology'.[40] He argued that in the 1552 rite the Church had made a decisive break with sacrificial views of the Eucharist by replacing the sacrificial vestments with the sacramental surplice. It was symbolic of the theological conviction and an unambiguous signal to the worshippers that the Eucharist did not involve an exclusive sacrificial interaction. The significance of the change from vestments to surplice also spoke out against more modern attempts to revive the sacrificial dimension of the Eucharist by a doctrine of the pleading of Christ's sacrifice in union with his eternal act in heaven. Knox was prepared to accept that we do 'plead by the Sacrifice' but not that we 'plead the Sacrifice'.[41] He maintained that the liturgical difference was fundamental. The former is not restricted to the Eucharist; it is found, for example, in the Litany and the Absolution, but the latter inevitably leads to a direct relation with the elements, initially perhaps, in terms of a representation of the sacrifice but ultimately to an offering of Christ to the Father. The theological difference, he argued, is equally profound. In the former 'the absolute final completeness of the one Sacrifice in its relation to God'[42] is preserved. In the latter, both through its description of the heavenly life of Christ (in terms of representation or of offering his sacrifice) and through its concept of the eucharistic participation in this process, the completeness of Christ's sacrifice is compromised. The former meets the Evangelical criterion of direct personal access to God; the latter appeals to the Tractarian attempt to interpose the role of the Church. His plea therefore was that the Church must avoid a 'fatal counter-

Reformation', by altering 'not a word' of the 1662 rite and by not corrupting it 'with meretricious ornaments which belong to a distinct and alien tradition'.[43]

W. H. Griffith Thomas (1861–1924)

Griffith Thomas's basic criticism of Charles Gore's position was methodological.[44] Thomas argued that if Gore had begun with the Institution Narrative and had ensured that this remained the essential criterion for his eucharistic theology, he would have avoided the ambiguities, inconsistencies and imprecision which followed from his chosen method of approaching 'the Eucharist first from the outside'.[45]

In the first place, if Gore had followed his own exegesis of the interpretative words which concluded that 'the copula...is clearly indeterminate', he would not have tried to establish an objective presence 'attached'[46] to the elements independently of reception. And if Gore had accepted the implications of his view that the Last Supper was a 'true Communion',[47] involving the same kind of gift as subsequent Eucharists, he would not have posited a sacramental presence of the glorified body and blood. In the second place, if Gore had followed his instinct that 'at first sight' the 'New Testament does not suggest that the Eucharist is a sacrifice', he would not have been tempted to defend its traditional sacrificial status by claiming that 'the feast upon the sacrifice is the culmination of the sacrifice'.[48]

The real difference between Thomas and Gore lay in their definition of the sacrifice of Christ. For Gore, Christ's sacrifice must not be limited to his death. It should be identified with his priestly ministry, for which he was prepared by his death and which began with his entry into the holy place and continues in his life of intercession. Therefore, there is a soteriological continuity between his crucified and glorified body and blood. It is Christ who is 'our perpetual and all sufficient sacrifice',[49] and we participate in that sacrifice through contact with his glorified humanity – a process which is made possible in its 'completest degree'[50] in the Eucharist. For Thomas, on the other hand, Christ's sacrifice must be strictly identified with his death. There is therefore a soteriological discontinuity between the crucified and glorified body and blood because it is the latter which atones and not the former. Nevertheless, although the sacrifice is a past act, it remains permanently efficacious.

We participate in it by apprehending its meaning through faith. Such a grasp by faith that Christ is 'for us' leads to the presence of Christ 'in us'.[51] The role of the Eucharist is not to give an alleged eternal presence of the sacrifice in the form of the glorified body and blood; it is, rather, to provide a manward remembrance of the past sacrifice by revealing the 'force and efficacy' of the crucified body and blood. As such a remembrance can be made through other means as well as through the Eucharist, it should not be seen as the 'pivot and centre of our Christian life'.[52]

Thomas Drury (1847–1926)

From 1912 to 1920 Thomas Drury played a significant part in the revision of the 1662 communion rite – in particular, the restructuring of the Canon. The pilot of the project was Walter Frere, but Drury helped, sometimes unofficially, to navigate the chosen course through complex ecclesiastical seas. Frere believed that Drury held a 'mediating position' between those who desired change and the Evangelicals who would obstruct any attempt at it, and joined with him in an attempt to discover a form of revision which would be 'definitely accepted and welcomed by Evangelicals'.[53]

Frere's plan for the improvement of the 1662 rite involved the following restructuring of the Canon: moving the Prayer of Humble Access out, preferably to follow the Comfortable Words; moving the Prayer of Oblation into the Prayer of Consecration; moving the Lord's Prayer from a post-communion to a pre-communion position; and inserting an *epiclesis* into the Prayer of Consecration.

Drury agreed on the need to move Humble Access to follow the Comfortable Words, to return the Lord's Prayer to before the communion, and to revive an *anamnesis* which would include both thanksgiving and commemoration of the Passion together with the other 'mighty works'. He was personally strongly in favour of an *epiclesis* on both people and elements, and sympathetic, though still somewhat suspicious, of the Prayer of Oblation's return to the Canon.[54] His reservations on the 1549 position of the Prayer of Oblation centred on the pleading of Christ's passion in the *anamnesis*. He fully accepted that the Eucharist involves an individual and corporate 'pleading of Christ's merits' but he affirmed 1552's decision to dissociate this process from any hint of an oblation of the elements on the grounds that 'it is the whole service...by the whole congregation... that the merits of Christ's death is celebrated in the sight of God, and with earnest prayer that the merits of that sacrifice may be ours'.[55]

As well as being conscious of the limits imposed by the danger (proved in both past and present) that some liturgical forms are more open than others to theological misinterpretation, he was also conscious of the boundaries set by the Evangelical constituency which he represented. He was aware that a proportion of Evangelicals were prepared to accept '*some* modification of the Canon'[56] providing it did not involve a doctrinal departure from 1662. Although he did attempt to allay the fears of several 'prominent Evangelicals'[57] over the *epiclesis* and possibly the Prayer of Oblation, he felt that Frere's hopes for these were unrealistic and that it would be better for them both to concentrate on those areas (Humble Access, Lord's Prayer, *anamnesis*) which stood a greater chance of acceptance by Evangelicals.

Drury was thus in the curious and difficult position of, on the one hand, substantially agreeing with Frere's liturgical principles whilst holding different doctrinal views and being more cautious as to the appropriateness of certain liturgical forms in the given context, and, on the other hand, substantially agreeing with the doctrinal views of his fellow Evangelicals, whilst finding their liturgical principles somewhat inadequate and being much more adventurous as to the extent to which a liturgical departure from 1662 was desirable and justifiable.

Liberal Evangelicalism

The underlying issue facing Evangelicals during the period was the methodological question of whether the contemporary Evangelical position should be defined entirely by an appeal to the tradition of Evangelical Protestantism, or whether room should be made for a constructive interaction with other schools of thought at points which did not threaten the essence of the Evangelical tradition. There were signs that a significant body of Evangelical opinion was prepared to argue (in a manner similar to Drury) from a broader methodological base than were their more conservative brethren. In 1905 a number of younger Evangelical clergy formed themselves into the Group Brotherhood, which in 1923 led to the formation of the Anglican Evangelical Group Movement and the publication of *Liberal Evangelicalism*. In 1922 there was a split in the Church Missionary Society over its willingness to pay some heed to both the Higher Critical movement and the Ecumenical Movement, and its desire to allow some co-operation with Tractarians. An illustration of the application of the different methodologies to the theology of the Eucharist can be seen by a comparison of H. B. Gooding and A. E. Hughes, who were writing in a representative capacity for Liberal and Conservative positions respectively.[58]

Gooding's method involved maintaining the essence of the Evangelical 'heritage'[59] in such a way that it was integrated with other, perhaps new, dimensions of knowledge and experience. He justified his method on the hermeneutical grounds that as the New Testament does not give 'explicit guidance' in the area of sacramental theology, it is necessary to treat 'spiritual experience' and 'knowledge of reality'[60] as interpretative keys. He supported this method both by the theological principle that the Church, under the guidance of the Holy Spirit, is a developing organism rather than a fixed entity, and by the epistemological position of Liberal Evangelicalism, that neither the Evangelical tradition nor indeed the Church itself has the monopoly on all aspects of God's truth.

In contrast, Hughes set his theological parameters by the convictions, first, that 'what the Supper was when first instituted, that it is now, no more, no less' and, second, that Evangelical–Protestant tradition had accurately interpreted and faithfully passed down the meaning of that event, expressing it liturgically in 1662 in a way that 'cannot be exceeded'.[61] His own description of the interpretation, however, tended to heighten the negative aspects of the Evangelical tradition by so qualifying the working of the Sacrament that the fundamental question facing Evangelicals, of the value of the Eucharist over and against the preaching of the Word, remained starkly unanswered. His emphasis was on the way in which the communion service declares a 'Gospel Sermon'[62] and thereby facilitates the process of remembering which, providing it evokes belief in the meaning of Christ's death, will lead to one's faith in Christ, and therefore communion with him, being deepened.

Gooding's approach did not lead to a substantially different doctrinal position from that of Hughes but the nuances of his conclusions revealed real signs of a creative engagement with Catholic thought – particularly in his emphasis on the ecclesiological basis of the sacraments and his attempt to construct a positive role for the material in the life of faith. The result was twofold. First, the positive aspects of Evangelical thought figured much more prominently than they had in Hughes's thought. Secondly there were allusive suggestions for further theological developments rather than dogmatic definitions of an unalterable system. For example, he affirmed, albeit in a carefully qualified way, the instrumentality of the Sacrament on the grounds that 'matter is an expression of [God's] thought and an instrument of His Will'; he argued for the centrality of the Eucharist in the life of the Church as the 'fullest expression and chief means of growth' of our fellowship with God and with each other in Christ; and he attempted to identify a sacrificial movement within the Eucharist in terms of pleading Christ's one, past sacrifice 'at greater length, more impressively'[63] than we do in our prayers and by identifying with his attitude of self-surrender to the purposes of God through our closer association with his death.

The Deposited Prayer Book

When Frere and Drury's proposals passed into the hands of the National Assembly they lost their sensitivity and subtlety as they competed with the Bishops' own material and alternative proposals from all the main party groups apart from the Evangelicals. Some Liberal Evangelicals co-operated by concession rather than by conviction but were concerned that the limits imposed by the new book should be implemented in order to curb the extremes of Anglo-Catholic practice. The Conservatives consistently campaigned for the abandonment of any alternative to 1662's communion rite.

The Deposited Book presented to Parliament in 1927 therefore met with considerable Evangelical opposition. William Joynson-Hicks, who together with Thomas Inskip spearheaded the resistance to the book in Parliament, believed that the issue at stake was 'whether the work of the Reformation shall be undone'.[64] His specific criticisms centred on the alternative communion rite. His main objections were to the *epiclesis*, the Agnus Dei, the Benedictus, the Invitation to Communion and most particularly, the rubric allowing the reservation of the elements for the communion of the sick. His grounds were that they all imply – and when viewed cumulatively strongly suggest – a 'Presence of Christ in the consecrated Bread and Wine'.[65] He also objected to the restoration of vestments and the 1549 position of the Prayer of Oblation, on the grounds that the reversing of changes made in 1552 suggested a return to the doctrine which the

Reformers had rejected, namely on oblation of the body and blood of Christ. His more general criticisms were that the adoption of a party book would lead to further disunity, drive people out of the Church of England, make reunion with the Free Churches impossible and, given its lack of a clear statement of episcopal enforcement, would not lead to the control of Catholic excess. In short, the Evangelical position would gain nothing and stand to lose everything.

An example of the sort of alternative which may have been more acceptable to Evangelicals was provided by Albert Mitchell.[66] Mitchell had played a leading part in objecting to the machinations of the National Assembly, but although he did not want to compete with 1662 – which he described as 'the most perfect liturgical form yet devised or authorised' – he was prepared to respond to the 'present-day problems'[67] and to meet the practical need for a complete sacramental service of manageable length. His attempt to rationalize Holy Communion with the essentials of Morning Prayer, by the inclusion of an Old Testament lesson and canticles between the readings, was to anticipate future liturgical developments (as were his commendation of the westward position and his suggestions for supplementary consecration). As he was satisfied with the theology of 1662, he made no attempt to alter its sacramental order and language except to introduce a 'form of Epiklesis'. He regarded an invocation on the elements as teaching a 'change in the material of the Sacrament',[68] but was happy to pray for the sanctifying of the faithful in order that they might fulfil Christ's command. However, the prayer did ask for God's blessing on 'these gifts' and for his acceptance of 'our prayers and thanksgiving'.

SEEDS OF EVANGELICAL RECOVERY 1930–1960

It is generally accepted that Evangelicalism reached its lowest point in the 1920s. The tide of 'Catholicism' and 'Liberalism' which had steadily swelled since its beginnings in the nineteenth century had swept the majority of Evangelicals – apart from those who had risked the Liberal Evangelical lifeboat – into a private, protected and patrolled corner of the beach: antipathetic towards Catholics, antagonistic towards the accommodating ethos and authority of the Church of England and anxiously in retreat from serious theological engagement beyond that of repeating the principles and policies of the Reformation.

The distinctive feature of the period that followed was a gradual process of reorientation by which Evangelicals began to emerge from a defensive and reactionary position towards a more confident and positive attitude. It is possible to see at least three examples of this. First, there was a more healthy, though generally very cautious, interaction with Catholics, including an acceptance, in a qualified form, of the validity of their presence in the Church of England. Secondly, there was a willingness to step out of the ghetto and contribute to the life of the Church. Thirdly, there was a commitment to scholarly study which did not bypass the critical questions of the age but rose to their challenge by offering a convincing reply. The most significant aspect of the revival was that it was not led merely by an avant-garde Liberal element but involved, in some degree, the Conservative majority. It did so because it was based on an increase in confidence which in turn was being created by an internal renewal of strength and supported by a somewhat more sympathetic environment[69] in the Church. Of course, it was neither uniform nor complete. There was still a considerable spread of Liberal–Conservative opinion and many Evangelicals were untouched by the change. There was definitely, at least amongst Conservatives, a clear definition of party identity and, even by 1960, the process of theological dialogue and ecclesiastical involvement was still minimal. Nevertheless, it is clear that the Evangelicalism of the late 1950s was very different from that of the late 1920s and that the scene was being set for further developments in the 1960s and beyond.

The Evangelical relationship to the Eucharist was marked by the same dynamic. The concerns of the immediately preceding generation remained. Reservation and vestments were still rallying points for passion and polemic. Creative Catholic thought was often dismissed rather than discussed. The priority of the Word and the supportive function of the sacraments was stressed by some, with little real attempt to identify their integral unity. The Institution Narrative was claimed as the main criterion of eucharistic theology in such a way that it appeared in a vacuum divorced from the rest of the Bible, from theological reflection and from the later experience of even Evangelical Christians. The threat of Prayer Book revision provoked statements of support which implied that negotiations over its fallibility were, in principle, impossible. However, this was not the whole story. There was a serious challenge, led initially by Liberals but joined by Conservatives, to the negativism which had characterized Evangelical practice and thought in regard to the Eucharist since the rise of the Oxford Movement.

Practice

In 1933 the Liberal, Vernon Storr, noticed the beginnings of a 'new feeling for sacramentalism'[70] amongst Evangelicals, which he sought to maintain and develop. But by 1944 the Conservative J. Stafford Wright did not feel that it had permeated his constituency: 'Our present practice as Evangelicals is towards a minimizing of the Sacrament.[71] He described such an attitude as 'spiritually disastrous'[72] and called for a much more central place to be given to the Eucharist. His concern was echoed in the 1940s by Max Warren and Stephen Neill,[73] the latter calling for the adoption of a Parish Communion (that is, the Eucharist as the central act of Sunday worship) on at least a monthly basis. In 1953 Frank Colquhoun also castigated Evangelical tradition for treating the Sacrament as a 'liturgical luxury or pious extra' but he suggested that many Evangelicals, as shown by their use of the monthly Family Communion, were now showing a 'deepening desire' to restore the Eucharist to the 'centre of the Church's life'.[74] He commended others to do the same.

Thought

The apologetic was generated not by an attempt to imitate Catholic practice or to accept uncritically the persuasion of the Parish and People movement. It was, rather, fuelled by a recognition that contemporary Evangelical practice was not in line with, first, the life of the early Church, in which, it was admitted, the Eucharist was the main event of weekly worship; second, the intention of the Reformers, who wanted to unite the Word and Sacrament; third, the ideal of the Prayer Book; and fourth, as argued clearly and carefully by E. J. G. Rogers and Max Warren, the success and spirituality of the Evangelical revival.[75] Thus, the process of critically viewing the present position of Evangelicalism from the broader perspective of its long-term tradition, rather than of viewing the past through the problems of the present, helped to create a convincing case that an anti-sacramental attitude did not belong to the historic identity of Evangelicalism but was a recent intrusion arising from fears of Catholic excess. Hence, Evangelicals were able to claim that the

Parish Communion, though originating from the Catholic wing of the Church, had a perfectly respectable Evangelical pedigree. It was, in the words of Colquhoun, 'simply an attempt to celebrate the Communion in the manner laid down by the Prayer Book'.[76]

Similarly, Evangelicals began to admit that their recent theological approaches towards the Eucharist had been unnecessarily defensive and therefore had tended towards a false reductionalism. Evangelicals began to draw on the more positive aspects of their tradition, experiment with new ideas and enter into a tentative dialogue with Catholic emphases. The shift in style which resulted will be looked at in some detail.

Positive use of the Evangelical tradition

A significant number of Evangelicals sought to address the dichotomy which many Evangelicals perceived between the Word and the Sacrament. They argued that the Reformers' rediscovery of the Word was not made at the expense of the Sacrament; it was rather an attempt to unify the two into complementary expressions of the same Gospel. The position was stated succinctly in *The Fulness of Christ*, an Evangelical report commissioned by the Archbishops of Canterbury and York and published in 1950, which said that 'Jesus Christ gives himself to men by means of the word and the sacraments'.[77]

New categories of thought

As early as 1931, R. Birch-Hoyle called for a recovery of the Spirit's role in the Eucharist, not in terms of an *epiclesis* on the elements, but in terms of a dynamic action in the lives of the participants, so that the same grace available in the hearing and reading of the Word may be 'felt in a more intense degree'.[78] In 1944 Stafford Wright also posited a 'special blessing' to the Eucharist, by arguing for its ability to create, in a unique degree, a 'reception and apprehension' of the 'reality and inner meaning of the Cross'.[79] In 1946 Warren's evocative study of the Sacrament explicitly sought to interpret it from the *Christus Victor* model of the Atonement, which had been recently revived by Gustav Aulén:

the Atonement is conceived primarily as the victory of God over sin and death, and the forces of evil. On such a view the Sacrament of Holy Communion is in the first place a declaration by word and action of that victory in threefold form.[80]

He defined the threefold form in terms of memorial, communion and sacrifice. The Eucharist is a memorial because the 'victory completed' is celebrated in such a way that, by the Spirit's work on our faith, 'the sacrifice is here before our eyes'.[81] It is a communion because Christ shares his victory by uniting us with himself and thereby reconstituting his mystical body, the Church. It is a sacrifice because the Church is now in a position to respond in thanks, praise and in a style of service to humanity, in all its social and political complexity, marked by an obedience to the demands of the Cross.

Dialogue with catholic emphases

There was a concern to ensure that the contemporary Evangelical theology of the Eucharist included the best of Protestant and Catholic traditions. *The Evangelical Doctrine of Holy Communion* (a compendium of essays published in 1933 which was influential amongst Evangelicals and respected by others) surveyed the history of the Eucharist from the New Testament to eighteenth-century Anglicanism. The contributors argued that authentic Evangelical sacramental theory (dubbed 'dynamic symbolism'[82] by the editor A. J. Macdonald), was the dominant position until the eleventh century and, in the form of Berengar's presentation, only narrowly missed official approval. They argued that it was still present in the underlying motifs of Aquinas, was revived by Wycliffe and the Reformers, and was accepted Anglican doctrine until the Oxford Movement. Storr and Smith were prepared to acknowledge that the Reformers did not fully utilize the potential of the tradition, and Macdonald claimed that Berengar's symbolic but effective categories were constructive sources for a reinterpretation of Anglican teaching in ways which combined the Reformed emphasis on the faith of the recipient and the Catholic stress on the instrumentality of the sacramental action.[83]

Similarly, in *Evangelicals Affirm* (a compendium of essays by Evangelical writers, published before the 1948 Lambeth Conference), W. F. P. Chadwick tried to maintain the balance between the objective and subjective dimensions by the concepts of the 'giftedness' of grace (the '"stooping mercies" of a God who condescends to draw near to us in this way'[84]) and the 'meeting' required by the grace of a God who treats us as persons rather than as 'things': 'for us the Bread and Wine "are" the body and Blood of Christ. But they are so in relationship.'[85]

In its vision for the ecumenical possibilities of the Church, *The*

Fulness of Christ identified the 'objective character of the sacraments'[86] as one of the Catholic emphases which must be embodied in a future united Church. Indeed, the way it related the objective to the subjective state represented a departure from the cerebral under-standing, which had been such a dominant feature of traditional Evangelical thought:

The sacraments are something to be done. They carry the assurance that, provided the Christian does his part to the best of his ability, God does indeed give his grace, however dim the understanding and however feeble may be his faith.[87]

However, in the more specific area of eucharistic sacrifice the Report made no attempt to domesticate the Catholic emphasis:

The Eucharist is the divinely instituted remembrance of Christ's sacri-fice... the Church is enabled to make that offering of praise, thanksgiving, and self-oblation which (apart from alms) is the only sacrifice actually offered in the Eucharist. Only as united to Christ in his death and resurrection through receiving the Body and Blood of Christ is the Church able to offer itself acceptably to the Father.[88]

Writing as an observer of Evangelicalism rather than as a member of the movement, Alan Richardson identified this as the only distinc-tively Evangelical element in the Report and regarded it as a debilitating limitation, which ignored Christ's offering of the Church to the Father in union with the Church's own eucharistic offering.[89]

The underlying issue revolved around the questions of how the Church's sacrifice is related to Christ's and of how this relationship should be expressed liturgically. The overwhelming Evangelical answer was that, as we contribute nothing to our salvation, the Church's offering is solely one of response. Therefore, the 1662 order of commemoration, communion, followed by oblation is the correct liturgical expression of the soteriological order of relationship: 'we make our self-oblation not "in union with" but *in response to* the perfect offering of Himself for us and for our salvation'.[90] Never-theless, despite Stephen Neill's claim that the Evangelical and Catholic concepts of the eucharistic sacrifice were not 'ultimately reconcilable', attempts were made to form a partnership during this period.

For Charles Moule, the biblical concepts of *koinonia* and *en Christo* were the 'keys to the meaning of the Eucharistic Sacrifice'.[91] God has expiated or 'neutralized' man's sin by the perfect obedience of Christ the 'perfect man'[92] even to death. Although this was a once-for-all event, its work, in some sense, is continued in us through our lives of obedience. Our status *en Christo* means that our obedience is joined to his obedience. The Eucharist is a 'focal point' of this process: the result of the *koinonia* which it realizes is that 'our offering becomes a part of his'.[93] However, Moule affirmed the 1662 position of the self-oblation, because it preserved the uniqueness of Christ's sacrifice, and he preferred to talk of the Church offering itself in Christ, rather than Christ offering himself in the Church. He was still, therefore, firmly within the traditional Evangelical framework of commemoration–communion–oblation.

Very Lutheran

Leslie Brown, who as a CMS missionary and contributor to *The Churchman* must be counted as at least within the Evangelical orbit, was prepared to break with the framework. He related the Church's offering directly to both the *anamnesis* of Christ's sacrifice and the action of Christ in the Church, arguing that 'We are taken into Christ's sacrifice and he offers himself in us and we in him do the Father's will.'[94]

It may well be said that through his influence on the Lambeth Conference in 1958, Brown set the immediate theological agenda for Evangelical eucharistic thought for the early 1960s. Indeed, it may also be suggested that the whole issue of whether we join our offering to Christ's sacrifice, or whether we just respond to it, became the vital and dominant eucharistic question for Evangelicals throughout the 1960s and the 1970s, and probably beyond.

A useful summary.

PART II

The recent period

The nature of Anglican Evangelicalism in the recent period

The Evangelical reawakening, which was conceived in the 1930s and developed embryonically in the 1950s, was finally born in the 1960s (and baptized at the Keele Congress in 1967[1]). It grew in the exciting way that healthy children do, in the 1970s, only to face the inevitable adolescent crisis of identity (confirmed at the Nottingham Congress in 1977[2]) and then to meet the choice (defined at the Caister Celebration in 1988[3]) which adulthood always brings between fragmented existence (in which the various aspects of personality do not cohere or even relate) and the maturity of integrated life-style (in which the dimensions not only cohere but provide the resources for a critical engagement with the life of others).

Liberal Evangelicalism may have been paternally related to the process by fathering the ethos of modern Evangelicalism, maternally related by nourishing its values, and even fraternally related by forging ahead to model a new kind of Evangelicalism with all its potential and pitfalls. Nevertheless, the remarkable feature of the recent period is that by the early 1960s Liberal Evangelicalism had ceased to exist as a distinct and recognizable entity within the Church, and had thus left Conservative Evangelicalism free to take the Evangelical label as its own. Hence, in the following survey, the word 'Evangelical', unless otherwise indicated, refers to the Conservative Evangelical grouping within the Church of England – though, of course, always in its many-faceted form.

For reasons which were made clear in chapter 1, our study of the recent period of Evangelicalism's history will concentrate on the period from just before 1960 to soon after 1980, though reference will be made where appropriate to developments during the rest of the 1980s. These decades saw a renaissance in Evangelicalism which was not merely an increase in numbers (though the growth in numerical strength did have an immense effect on its psychology) but essentially a change in character.[4] Previously, Evangelicalism had seen itself as the Reformed, and therefore the only authentic element within the Church of England, and had sought to extend its ideals mainly in pragmatic ways through its own parochial, interdenominational and missionary networks, and (occasionally) in ideological ways through Protestant polemics cast at the contemporary Anglican scene. Now, however, it began to move from a self-sufficient to a self-critical understanding of itself. It repented of the negativity of much of its immediate history; it pledged itself to a radical commitment to the logic of the Gospel (from whichever tradition should bring it to light); and it desired to reform the Church not by distanced attack but by loving involvement.

There were various ecclesiastical cross-currents which helped to mould the redefinition of Evangelicalism. The increasing numerical strength gave Evangelicals a new feeling of political confidence. The ecumenical context of modern Church life and theology (including the realigned dynamics within the Church of England) encouraged a cross-fertilization of ideas. The Charismatic Movement proved irresistible to the pietistic strain of the Evangelical consciousness and thereby intensified the tension with its Reformed side.

There were also theological cross-currents at work in the reshaping of modern Evangelicalism. I can do little more than mention them. First, Evangelicals rediscovered the social dimension of the Gospel. Secondly, they realized the complexity of the hermeneutical process by which the Word spoken yesterday becomes God's Word for today. Thirdly (though first in chronological terms), they re-emphasized the doctrine of the Church in a way which led them from Troeltsch's 'cult-mentality' (with its exclusive terms of membership and its esoteric terms of reference) to his 'church-mentality' (with its inclusive terms of membership and wider terms of reference)[5] and paved a way to greater interest in the sacraments as the signs which mark out the presence of the visible Church. Included within these winds of change was the rise of a liturgical movement amongst Evangelicals in which the whole package of their worship – and particularly the role of the Eucharist – was placed under critical review.

However, whether in liturgy or theology, ethos or ethics, policies or principles, not all Evangelicals moved at the same pace and some did not move at all. In a valuable piece of research (from which I shall draw on several occasions), William Hopkinson has analysed the changing self-identity of Evangelicals in the period 1960–80. He claimed his findings had

suggested in a number of instances that evangelicals have divided into two rough groups. Some have followed the church in the transition [that is, the Church of England's own movement of change during the period], and been subject to a loss of traditional evangelical identity symbols as a result. A second group have taken a more reactionary stance and resisted change, continuing the tendency to adhere to reformation formularies, largely maintaining their identity, although at the cost of increasing marginalization.[6]

We could add that the more reactionary group had its own spread of approaches ranging from those who would relive the sixteenth century to those who were concerned merely to add a careful but controlling Reformation critique to the life of Evangelicalism. Similarly, a spectrum of opinion could be identified amongst the more progressive majority. On the right were those with Reformed theological ideals still high on their agenda but who were prepared to engage in a dialogue with others in the Church of England. In the centre were those who were determined to make their principled contribution to the Church of England by a credible political profile. On the left were those with more avant-garde experiments in liturgical or activist directions. Amidst them all, by the 1970s, were the Charismatics with their new and potentially threatening set of priorities.

However, Hopkinson's delineation of 'two rough groups' provides a helpful categorization of the complex life of Evangelicalism in the 1960s, 1970s and even the 1980s. We shall see that it broadly corresponds with the story of the Evangelical response to the process of liturgical revision, the production of ecumenical statements and the development of issues concerning spirituality as each in its own way touched on eucharistic theology and spirituality. It is to the first of these that we must now turn.

CHAPTER 7

Fearing liturgical revision: Evangelicals and Lambeth 1958

The Report of the Prayer Book sub-Committee, which formed part of the 1958 Lambeth Conference Statement,[1] is a natural starting point for our study of Evangelical reaction to and involvement in liturgical revision. First, the Report offered a justification for the revision of the Prayer Book in a way that cohered with the Liturgical Commission's memorandum *Prayer Book Revision in the Church of England* (1957); both argued that the Prayer Book should no longer be regarded as the doctrinal norm governing future revision. Secondly, it provided various liturgical guidelines to direct the process of revision. Thirdly, it suggested that the controversy over eucharistic sacrifice had been transcended by the convergence of opinion created by modern scholarship, and that accordingly, it should be possible to give a form of liturgical expression to the doctrine that would be generally acceptable.[2]

As the issue of eucharistic sacrifice will be found to be a dominant one throughout the period of liturgical revision, the Evangelical reaction to Lambeth's claim that a consensus had been reached will be given detailed attention.[3] This will enable us to gauge the Evangelical position on the subject in the early 1960s and also to set the scene for the later discussions and disputes by identifying the central theological questions around which the issue revolved, or was seen to revolve, by Anglican Evangelicals. The survey will be concluded by a comment on the attitude of Evangelicals to the whole question of liturgical revision in the light of the Lambeth Statement.

EVANGELICAL REACTION TO LAMBETH'S UNDERSTANDING
OF EUCHARISTIC SACRIFICE

The Statement failed to convince Evangelicals that the controversies over eucharistic sacrifice had now been overcome. Indeed, although Lambeth's theology did not in fact prove to be entirely acceptable to Catholic opinion,[4] Evangelicals perceived it as a distillation (albeit in an ambiguous frame) of modern Anglo-Catholic theories of eucharistic sacrifice. For example, in its widened definition of Christ's sacrifice ('This sacrifice is an act of willing obedience'), Evangelicals detected the thesis of Nugent Hicks,[5] that the efficacy of sacrifice lies in the life offered, not the death endured. In its concept of the eternal dimension of Christ's sacrifice ('This sacrifice...is not only an event in history but the revelation of eternal truth'), they identified S. C. Gayford's understanding of Christ's heavenly sacrifice.[6] In its delineation of a Godward movement to the Eucharist ('we offer our praise and thanksgiving for Christ's sacrifice for us and so present it again'), they sensed Gregory Dix's[7] assumption that the *anamnesis* is directed towards God rather than the people. In the relationship it claimed between the Church and Christ ('Christ with us offers us in himself to God'), they discovered the 'ontological and realistic' association which was the basis of E. L. Mascall's theology of eucharistic sacrifice.[8]

The Statement was thus seen as a capitulation to Anglo-Catholicism and therefore as a betrayal of Reformation principles. James Packer described it as 'the product of theological intentions completely opposite to those of historic reformed Anglican teaching on the Holy Communion'.[9] Hence, it acted as a catalyst, setting off a series of vehement Evangelical attacks on Anglo-Catholic theories of eucharistic sacrifice. They were fuelled by the underlying fear that all such theories – including modern Anglican ones – undermine the very essence of the New Testament Gospel:

We must beware of teaching which seems to imply that the church, in union with Christ, saves itself by offering...[10]
Any piety or doctrine and any liturgy or action which obscures the centrality and reality of God's grace, putting in its place, even partially, man's moral sensitivity and power, does not arise from the cross of Christ and his offering.[11]

The facts that Leslie Brown was the Chairman of the Prayer Book sub-committee (and was known to have heavily influenced the Report) and that the Report drew on the theology of Charles Moule, did nothing to allay Evangelical concern. Their part in the process simply reinforced the view that Liberal Evangelicals had been so willing to accommodate catholic concerns that they could no longer be trusted to defend evangelical ones – at least in the area of eucharistic theology.

The attack on Lambeth aimed to establish the following. First, it sought to prove an identification between Christ's sacrifice and his death:

> We cannot escape the uniform and insistent New Testament teaching that 'Christ *died* for our sins'. He 'bare our sins *in his own body on the tree*': 'he died unto sin *once*'. Behind this teaching lies the New Testament assumption that there is a connection between sins and death.[12]

Secondly, it sought to show that the Church's relationship to Christ's sacrifice is one of reception of its benefits and not involvement in either its making or its offering, for 'Man the sinner cannot take part in this offering of Christ. All he provides is the sin and guilt which the saviour bare.'[13] Thirdly, it sought to make clear that the Eucharist is the sacramental expression of this relationship:

> What the Saviour offers us is His body crucified and his blood outpoured for the sins of the world, that we may take to ourselves and make our own the whole virtue and meaning of this 'one perfect and sufficient sacrifice, oblation and satisfaction made once for all upon the Cross' – that is 'the remission of our sins and all other benefits of His passion'.[14]

The eucharistic elements represent Christ's crucified, sacrificed form, so that his death might be proclaimed for the benefit of the believers present, and that in receiving them, they might appropriate anew the redemption Christ's death achieved. Accordingly, the liturgical structure of the Sacrament should reflect the inner movement of the Gospel message itself – the offering the Church makes can only be in response to the one, final offering made by Christ. The 1662 structure was given whole-hearted support, for when, in the 1552 order, Cranmer relocated the people's oblation to the end of the service, he was giving (in the one remark of Gregory Dix which Evangelicals loved to quote) 'the only effective attempt ever made to give liturgical expression to the doctrine of justification by faith alone'.[15] Hence, there was strong resistance to the liturgical implications of Lambeth's doctrine which would return the Prayer of Oblation to its 1549 position.

Evangelicals were even more anxious to resist any offering of the consecrated elements to God. The fact that an offering of the elements was either directly attacked or at least felt to be the inevitable outcome of Lambeth's assumptions, even though it was not mentioned in the Report itself, shows again that the Evangelical response sparked off by Lambeth was directed not just at the sub-committee's Statement but at Anglo-Catholic eucharistic theology, as this was seen to have provided the conceptual framework for the Report.

The real theological issue behind the liturgical debate was whether the Eucharist should involve, as Lambeth believed, a presentation to God of Christ's one sacrifice. Evangelicals interpreted the dominical command to 'do this in *anamnesis* of me' in terms of proclaiming before people the meaning of Christ's sacrifice, not as a means of calling on God to remember the sacrifice of his Son. According to J. R. S. Taylor, 'the plain meaning of these words is that the sacrament was ordained for the continual remembrance by us of the sacrifice of the death of Christ and the benefits that we receive thereby'.[16]

Whilst detailed analysis was made of biblical, patristic and Reformation evidence in order to show that 'reminding us' rather than 'presenting to God' is the most natural interpretation of Jesus' command, the following overriding principles dominated the Evangelical apologetic. First, Christ's priesthood is unique and exclusive – only he can offer his sacrifice to the Father. Secondly, Christ's sacrificial work is finished and complete – any presentation or offering is at best unnecessary and at worst destructive because it threatens a proper recognition of the finished nature of Christ's work. Thirdly, and most significantly, any theology or practice that implies, however obliquely, offering the Son to the Father involves a blurring of the distinction between Christ's sacrifice and ours, and therefore undermines the very nature of the Gospel. Any attempt to assimilate the life and worship of the Church with the sacrifice and eternal priesthood of Christ implies that we can contribute to our own salvation and thereby erodes the very foundation stone of New Testament theology which was rediscovered by the Reformers and expressed in Anglican doctrine and liturgy.[17]

The differences between Lambeth's theology and that of the Evangelicals derived largely from the different definitions of Christ's sacrifice. In the approach adopted by Lambeth, Christ's sacrifice had a wide term of reference and could include both his earthly and his heavenly ministry. However, in the Evangelical framework Christ's sacrifice was much more narrowly defined to mean his death on the Cross. These two contrasting terms of reference for the notion of sacrifice produced two conflicting understandings of eucharistic sacrifice. Lambeth was quite able to affirm that Christ's sacrifice was complete on the Cross and yet at the same time talk of it being an eternal event. For, if sacrifice is defined in terms of 'willing obedience' it is an appropriate description of both his life before the Cross and his life after the Cross, because it is the mode of relationship between Father and Son. Similarly, Lambeth was quite able to affirm that Christ's sacrifice was 'for us' and talk at the same time of Christ offering 'us in himself' as we present his one sacrifice to God. For, if his sacrifice is defined in terms of 'willing obedience' rather than in terms defined by Evangelicals, as 'our Lord's substitutionary suffering as the representative sinner',[18] it has a much more inclusive capacity. In the theological approach represented by Lambeth, the Eucharist could be described as the sacramental reflection, enactment and realization of the Church's life of sacrifice to the Father which has, at its heart, the ritual and liturgical presentation of the one sacrifice of Christ to the Father. To Evangelical theology, with its different terms of reference and different understanding of Christ's sacrifice, this made very little sense at all.

ATTITUDES TO LITURGICAL REVISION IN THE LIGHT OF LAMBETH

There is no doubt that Evangelicals had a great love for the 1662 communion service. They saw it as essentially Cranmer's rite. They had profound respect for his skill in devising a liturgy of great beauty which was profoundly devotional and an apt expression of Reformed doctrine. However, despite this admiration there was, on the one hand, an increasing recognition of the inevitability of liturgical revision and, on the other, an acceptance that at many points it could be improved and that a more modern form was necessary.[19]

The weight of opinion in the early 1960s was still that the revision should be as minimal as possible – a modernization preserving its basic structure and flavour. However, there were also calls for a more radical structural revision.[20] Indeed, at the request of a joint meeting of four Evangelical theological colleges in 1962, their lecturers in worship (under the leadership of Leo Stephens-Hodge), devised a revision of 1662 entitled *An Evangelical Eucharist* (1963).[21] The rite was more than a modernization of the 1662 rite. Westward position was adopted. The Prayer of Humble Access and the Lord's Prayer were moved to before communion. The manual acts in the Narrative of Institution were abandoned. A Fraction was introduced after the Eucharistic Prayer. And, most significantly, in the light of the ensuing debate over Series Two, the rite injected a greater emphasis on thanksgiving. The Sursum Corda, Preface and Sanctus were reunited in one prayer of thanks to the Father, which included a commemoration of the mighty works of God in both creation and redemption, led into the Narrative of Institution and concluded with a petition for the Spirit's work in the life of the faithful receiver.

Nevertheless, although there were shades of opinion over the extent and style of the future revision, there was full agreement that it should not deviate doctrinally from the 1662 order. Evangelicals were from the outset adamant that either the Thirty-nine Articles or the Book of Common Prayer should be used as its doctrinal norm. Lambeth's departure from the 1662 rite as a norm for the communion service and its perceived movement away from the Reformed Anglican position was viewed with the most serious concern by Evangelicals: 'Prayer Book revision is a matter of the gravest importance. Should it take a wrong turning, our worship will become "vain" and fail in its purpose.'[22]

CONCLUSION

The Evangelical reaction to Lambeth displayed some of the classic tensions which (as was established in chapter 1) have undermined the expression of an Evangelical form of sacramental spirituality in the past.

The antipathy directed towards Lambeth arose not so much out of anti-sacramentalism as out of a concern that the Sacrament should be put to the use for which it was designed:

The Evangelical view of the Sacrament is the highest. We believe more about its efficacy and spiritual work than any other section of the Church. Because of this, we ought to be most careful about its administration.[23]

As we shall see in chapter 11, there was a feeling in some quarters that to place such a high value on the Sacrament should mean that it ought to be more fully integrated into the life of the whole Church rather than being an optional service at 8 a.m. on a Sunday morning.

Unfortunately, however, such positive approaches were swamped by the need to defend the Evangelical cause which was seen to be seriously under attack. Evangelicals were overpowered by the weight of creative Catholic thinking, fearful that future liturgical reunion would be in a Catholic direction,[24] and impoverished by the lack of creative Evangelical thinking on eucharistic theology and its liturgical expression. Hence, the Evangelical response to Lambeth reads to a large extent like a sixteenth- or nineteenth-century polemic. It is interesting that a commentary on the Prayer Book published at about the same time and written on a more popular, devotional level displayed a rich and moving sacramentalism without denying any of the Evangelical insights which those reacting to Lambeth were themselves trying to defend.[25] We shall see that when Evangelicals were able to rise from their defensive positions, the positive sacramentalism which is implicit in Evangelical Christianity began to find an outlet on a more widespread level.

A side glance at the work of Vincent Taylor on Sacrifice would at come amiss.

CHAPTER 8

Facing liturgical revision: Evangelicals and Series Two

The Liturgical Commission had been asked (at its own request) to provide a 'radical revision'[1] of the 1662 communion service. It did so in the form of the 'Draft Order for Holy Communion' (published in December 1965).[2] After a warm reception at the Liturgical Conference in February 1966,[3] it was worked on by the Commission in March and then, on 1 April 1966, presented as a definitive report to the Archbishops.[4] However, the Report did not represent the unanimous views of the Commission. The Commission's newest member, Colin Buchanan, had been forced into dissent by the wording of the *anamnesis* and primarily by the oblation of the bread and the cup. He also dissented over the optional petition for the departed in the intercessions.[5]

Buchanan's dissent was significant not only because he was an Evangelical but also because he was seen and saw himself in a representative capacity for the Conservative Evangelical wing of the Church of England.[6] He had been invited on to the Commission as a result of some Evangelical pressure on the Archbishops to include a presence on the Commission to which they could clearly relate. The existing Evangelical representation was thus seen as of too liberal a variety to gain their confidence.[7] Buchanan accepted this mantle and assumed its dual responsibility. His self-determined brief was to commend the Commission's work to the Evangelical constituency, providing it did not rule itself out of acceptance by breaching fundamental doctrinal criteria.[8]

The oblation of the bread and the cup and the petitions for the departed clearly failed the doctrinal test. For Buchanan these did not fall into the category of unsatisfactory but, in the last resort, permissible liturgical changes. They carried with them innovations to the Church of England's doctrine. He knew that fellow Evangelicals in the Church of England would feel exactly the same.

EVANGELICAL REACTION

Before examining the precise theological issues involved in the dissent and the Evangelical contribution to its solution, let us briefly assess the Evangelical reaction to the service as a whole.

The service

The whole concept of a 'radical revision' was viewed with suspicion by James Packer. Against such a policy he suggested that 'we should embrace the principle that revision should be as conservative as is consistent with linguistic clarity and force on the one hand, and pastoral utility on the other'.[9] Whilst he undoubtedly spoke for a substantial section of Evangelicalism[10] there were also, as we have seen, movements within the party which favoured a more thorough-going reform of the 1662 rite.[11]

Some of the structural changes in Second Series – such as the movement of the Prayer of Humble Access to the preparation – were received with approval. Its flexibility was welcomed, though with some reservations. And its greater potential for congregational involvement was commended. However, its understanding of consecration in terms of thanksgiving was not wholly accepted. Its attempt to reduce the penitential element of the Prayer Book service was seriously questioned. And its principle of so devising potentially controversial items that they allowed for a latitude of interpretation was rejected.[12] In fact, not only were Evangelicals highly critical of the principle of ambiguity, but they felt that the Commission had failed in its attempt to provide for a variety of interpretations and had actually swung heavily towards the new-Catholic side.[13] Indeed, it was seen by some as the realization of all their fears in the wake of the Lambeth Statement.[14]

The thanksgiving

The heart of the Evangelical dissatisfaction with Second Series centred on the thanksgiving. It revolved around the following points, all of which were, in some way, liturgical departures from 1662 and which were seen as expressing, or at least implying, unacceptable movements away from the doctrine of the Prayer Book.[15]

First, the 'sacrifice of praise' which Cranmer in 1552 transposed to the post-communion, was brought, by the Commission, into the Canon. Evangelicals did not feel this was wise. Not only did it place the offering of human praise before the gift of God's grace but it also had a dangerous potential for ambiguity. Evangelicals noted with concern how Ronald Jasper, the chairman of the Commission, had extolled its virtues on the grounds that it could be interpreted by some quite literally as our offering of praise and thanksgiving whilst for others it could only 'refer to the sacrifice of Christ himself – a praiseworthy and eucharistic sacrifice'.[16]

Secondly, in a further return to 1549-type terminology, Second Series asked that the bread and wine may 'be unto us his body and blood'. Evangelicals felt that the petition, seen together with the optional Agnus Dei, the shorter words of the administration and the omission of the Black Rubric, pointed to a presence in the bread rather than the believer's heart.[17]

Thirdly, the Pauline edict that we do this 'until he comes' received only very muted expression in Series Two. Although the eschatological dimension did not receive much attention in the 1662 order, it did, at least refer to Christ's personal return, not just (as in Series Two) to the 'coming of his Kingdom'. Evangelicals objected to the demythologization.[18]

Fourthly, Cranmer's absolute statement on the completed nature of Christ's sacrificial work and the clear connection he made between the Cross and the Sacrament were not given the same unmistakable reference in Second Series.[19] Evangelicals regarded this as a serious deviation from the spirit of the Prayer Book: it raised the following fears in them. First, on a general level, Evangelicals sensed that when it was seen together with certain other elements in the service Christ's redemptive work was being left open rather than closed: 'the whole idea of the finality of the Atonement has disappeared'.[20] Secondly, Evangelicals stressed that one of the central purposes of the Sacrament was to 'show forth' Christ's death. It had a didactic function: to proclaim Christ's death as the only basis of man's salvation. Second Series failed to do so adequately. Thirdly, Evangelicals felt that recent Anglo-Catholic theology, which they viewed as defective at key soteriological points, was finding a clear and unmistakable liturgical voice in the Commission's work.[21]

Still a formulat
Negative stance.

The oblation

Thus Evangelical objection to the oblation was not an obstinate reaction to a single, isolated phrase which, though loved by many Churchmen, did not meet certain, perhaps narrow, Evangelical criteria. It was both the tip of the iceberg and the straw that broke the camel's back. It was not just an uncomfortable nuance in an otherwise acceptable rite, it was the unbearable amidst the just bearable. It was seen as the flowering of a theology which the 'sacrifice of praise' and the lack of emphasis on Christ's once-for-all sacrifice implied. The dissentient, Buchanan, was prepared to accept the other four departures from 1662 and to take the responsibility of commending the service to Evangelicals but he could not, with integrity, tolerate an offering of the bread and the cup, and moreover, he knew that it would be futile to try to campaign for its acceptance amongst other Evangelicals.

The starting point for the Evangelical objection to offering the bread and the cup was its absence from the narratives of the Last Supper: 'offering is not one of the instituted acts of Christ, and is therefore an intrusion'.[22] However, they did not consider it to be a neutral intrusion which, although lacking direct biblical precedent, did not actually offend significant biblical principles. Neither did they see it as a harmless archaism which returned the English liturgy to its origins before the Reformation dispute in a purer heritage in the second and third centuries. It was, according to the Evangelical dissent, a misinterpretation of Christ's command to 'Do this...' Buchanan argued that, whereas for Cranmer the fulfilment of the *anamnesis* was in the reception of the elements, in Series Two it was in the offering of the elements. It therefore took a very definite position in the Reformation debate. In so doing, it distorted the nature and purpose of the Sacrament: it obscured both its historical setting as a meal and its theological basis in the initiative of God. It also inevitably involved an attempt to express, however loosely, a doctrine of eucharistic sacrifice. Hippolytus' phrase therefore, like pre-Nicene Trinitarian and Christological language, could not be seen in its third-century innocence, for it 'merely provides a convenient peg on which to hang the modern doctrine, and would never have been copied otherwise'.[23]

Buchanan argued that every theology of eucharistic sacrifice fails precisely because, by attempting to make an offering which is peculiar to the Eucharist, it necessarily links such an offering with the bread and the cup. Evangelicals were quite prepared to apply sacrificial language to the Church's life and even, though somewhat reluctantly, to relate it to the Eucharist. But when such sacrifice was made distinctive to the Eucharist by theological and liturgical attempts to tie it to the bread and wine at the climax of the thanksgiving for the work of God in Christ, it raised, for them, serious theological question marks over the nature and uniqueness, sufficiency and completion of that work. Therefore, Evangelicals argued, the correct understanding of the death of Christ (by which they meant their own) and the need to preserve that meaning from possible misinterpretation must provide the liturgical criteria for deciding what is appropriate and what is not appropriate to say in the Eucharistic Prayer and particularly in the *anamnesis*.

CONTRASTING MODELS OF EUCHARISTIC THEOLOGY

In a significant contribution to the debate Leslie Houlden presented a telling critique of the Evangelical reaction, when he described the Evangelical view of the Eucharist as a 'recapitulation of one's conversion experience'.[24] His point was that the liturgical structure preferred by Evangelicals – that is, one which reflects the movement of God's redemptive activity – is not necessarily the appropriate one for the central celebration of those who are already redeemed. In short, a purely manward view of the Eucharist fails to take seriously our status as baptized members of Christ. In reply, Evangelicals admitted that absolute categories of manward and Godward direction could not adequately describe the eucharistic event, as the very act of giving thanks involves a movement towards God. Despite this, Evangelicals argued that such categories are still relevant when discussing priority and order. The purpose of the Eucharist is primarily to receive God's undeserved and unwarranted grace, not in terms of reliving one's 'conversion', but in terms of those already 'in Christ' receiving him anew in the ongoing life of sanctification.[25]

The exchange highlighted the two different models of eucharistic theology and practice being used by the two sides of the debate. The Liturgical Commission owed much to the ideas of two of its members: E. C. Ratcliff and – in many ways the popularizer of his thought – Arthur Couratin. Drawing on the sacrificial imagery of the Old Testament and the eucharistic life of the early Church (as seen through the eyes of Justin and Hippolytus), they defined the Eucharist as the means by which we give, with bread and wine, our thanks and praise to God for his work of creation and redemption. Thanksgiving is not only given over bread and wine but is offered with bread and wine. It is in this way that we make the memorial of Christ's death. Hence, thanksgiving, memorial and offering are interdependent moments in the Church's central act of worship to the Father. And all three aspects converge liturgically in the oblation of the bread and the cup.[26]

Conversely, the Evangelical dissent defined the Eucharist as the means by which we receive, through bread and wine, the fruits of the redemption which are ours but to which we did not and do not contribute. Whereas Ratcliff argued that as we cannot, according to the Deuteronomic principle, 'appear before the Lord [our] God empty', we have to represent 'the Lord's passion with the bread and the cup... (as it were) bearing it in [our] hands as [our] offering',[27] Evangelicals argued that we must enter his presence with empty hands because it is only then that we are in a position to have them filled with the benefits of his sacrifice (that is, it is only then that faith is able to operate). Hence, dictating the course of the debate was the underlying difference between, on the one hand, a view of the Eucharist as primarily a context for an act of worship which is made on the basis of Christ's sacrifice and, on the other, a view of the Eucharist as primarily a context for a renewed appropriation of Christ's sacrifice through the exercise of evangelical faith. However, it should be made clear that Evangelicals were showing a readiness to accept that the bread was not just to be received with thanksgiving but was to be 'given thanks over' and that this eucharistic (and, therefore, Godward) dimension to the Lord's Supper had not been given sufficient expression in 1662.[28]

THE PRACTICAL SOLUTION

As a way out of the impasse Buchanan proposed: 'we give thanks...' as an alternative to 'we offer...'[29] Although this had been discussed and rejected by the Liturgical Commission, he claimed that it still held real possibilities for agreement because it expressed the essentials on which all sides were agreed (giving thanks) without going on to give a party interpretation (giving thanks and offering or giving thanks and receiving) which, though preferred by the different groups, would not be considered by them as absolutely necessary.[30] It therefore transcended the party problem. In later correspondence Buchanan was at pains to show that 'we give thanks' should not be seen as the pure and perfect Evangelical text jousting with the pure and perfect Catholic text 'we offer' for supremacy. He pointed out that although the text had first been made public by an Evangelical, it had been originally proposed by a Commission member who was far from the Evangelical constituency. He also noted that 'we give thanks' did not say all that an Evangelical would want to say and that 'we offer' had been criticized by many prominent Catholics who did not feel that it accurately expressed the Catholic position.

Indeed, the Evangelical dissent was shown a good measure of sympathy at the May Convocation which debated the Liturgical Commission's Report. At the end of a protracted debate, the Liturgical Commission Steering Committee was ordered to set up a representative team of theologians with the brief of arriving at a unitive text.[31] Peter Johnston and Leo Stephens-Hodge were its Evangelical representatives. Buchanan was in informal dialogue with the group via Eric Kemp, one of its Catholic members, and so had the opportunity of commenting on various possible alternatives. At a preliminary stage the possibility of a reworking of the post-Sanctus petition as well as the *anamnesis* was suggested. The text ran as follows:

Sanctus...
Hear us, O Father, through the same Christ thy Son our Lord, who made upon the Cross, by his one oblation of himself once offered, a full, perfect and sufficient sacrifice, oblation and satisfaction for the sins of the whole world; through him accept our sacrifice of praise; and grant that these gifts of bread and wine may be to us his body and blood.
Narrative of Institution...
Wherefore, O Lord and heavenly Father, having in remembrance the saving passion of thy dear Son, his resurrection from the dead and his glorious ascension into heaven, and looking for the coming of his Kingdom, we do this in obedience to his command, and as we eat this bread of eternal life and drink this cup of everlasting salvation we show forth the Lord's death till he come. We pray thee to accept this our duty and service and we give thanks to thee through the same Christ, our Lord...
Doxology...

Buchanan described this as a 'most generous attempt to meet evangelical hesitations about the Commission's text' and that it would '*as it stands* be all that evangelicals could properly ask for in the present situation'.[32] However, the suggestion did not gain much further ground in the Group. In fact the Group's final recommendation bore little resemblance to it and was a disappointment to Evangelicals[33] but, out of loyalty to the representative nature of the Group, Buchanan was prepared to accept its text and to attempt to encourage other Evangelicals to do the same.

Evangelicals may have been dissatisfied with the result but, for very different reasons, significant and powerful members of the Liturgical Commission, a sizeable proportion of Bishops and the Archbishop of Canterbury were mortified. The proposed text was ousted in October 1966 by the House of Bishops and replaced by the Commission's original text. But on 12 October 1966 Convocations voted for 'we give thanks' to be included in the *anamnesis* as an alternative to 'we offer...' This was not seen as a great victory by Evangelicals. They still objected to the very existence of 'we offer...' in what would become an authorized liturgy, and were also genuinely concerned to find 'a single text which would unite men of different schools of thought'.[34] For Colin Buchanan and Roger Beckwith 'we give thanks' was still the most hopeful prospect for a unitive text.

In February 1967 the House of Laity, which included a larger proportion of Evangelicals following recent elections, showed itself to be against the idea of alternatives and asked that the Liturgical Conference planned for April 1967 might discuss the Eucharist. In the meantime the Steering Committee produced a text which avoided the impasse simply by omitting both alternatives.[35] It was proposed to the Conference on 25 April 1967 but was overtaken by a proposal from Ronald Jasper which, with no mention of offering, was neutral enough to pacify Evangelicals but, by attempting to give a more positive content to the *anamnesis*, as compared with the Steering Committee's somewhat vacuous suggestion, was more likely to receive Catholic support: 'Wherefore, O Lord, with this bread and this cup we make the memorial of his saving passion...'[36] It met with an agreeable reception at the Liturgical Conference, was approved by Convocation the following day, the House of Laity in July and was finally authorized in the September Convocations in 1967.

EVANGELICAL LITURGIES

Although it was acceptable to Evangelicals, the authorized form of the *anamnesis* in particular and the thanksgiving as a whole, were by no means ideal in Evangelical eyes. Preferred ways of handling the revision of the eucharistic liturgy were provided by three different Evangelical alternatives to the Liturgical Commission's work. They all have their origin in the Latimer House Liturgical Group and represent the Group's ongoing response to Series Two. However, they clearly show two different policies towards liturgical revision. Indicative of the tension was the fact that all three texts were published under the names of individuals rather than of the Group as a whole.[37] Two of them (*1662 Revised* and *Series 2–3 Revised* by Roger Beckwith and John Tiller) were attempts to present a definitive Evangelical text expressing the Reformed position as received. The third (*A Eucharist for the Seventies* by Christopher Byworth and Trevor Lloyd), as its introductory note made clear, was a radical experiment designed to stimulate debate amongst fellow Evangelicals and in the Church at large:

we must help forward the debate which we pray will result in a living, modern, Anglican liturgical tradition, however much we may wish to keep 1662 as a doctrinal standard. We must face up to the [liturgical] drawbacks of 1662 ... Even doctrinally, 1662 is in need of help, with its omission, apart from one phrase of the doctrine of the second coming, with its inadequate view of consecration, and with its failure to emphasize sufficiently the corporate nature of communion and so involve the laity in the action of the service.[38]

Here the traditional methodology which sought to correct on the basis of the norm provided by the 1662 rite had given way to a willingness to contribute on the basis of a shared learning experience to the quest for a modern, unitive eucharistic liturgy.

The two approaches expressed, on the one hand, in *1662 Revised* and *Series 2–3 Revised*, and on the other, in *A Eucharist for the Seventies* reflect the conservative–progressive spectrum which we saw to be evident at the beginning of the debate but which, by now, had become more marked. Indeed, as we will see, it eventually led to the Liturgical Group splitting away from Latimer House to form *The Group for the Renewal of Worship*. Before the debate and in its earlier stages, the conservative approach was representative of the majority of Evangelicals. Probably by its end, and certainly after some use of Series Two, the second approach predominated.[39]

CONCLUSION

Series Two became an authorized alternative to the Prayer Book rite on 7 July 1967, for a period of four years. The debate which had been set off by a determined Evangelical dissent and which had delayed the process of liturgical reform in England for eighteen months was finally over. It had two important effects. First, it left the machinery of revision – the Liturgical Commission and the Church Assembly (soon to be replaced by the General Synod) – in no doubt that Evangelicals were interested in the revision of the Church's liturgy and were determined to ensure that they were given a fair opportunity to make their contribution. Secondly, the reworking of the *anamnesis* (and of the prayers for the departed) helped to convince Evangelicals that, as it had been possible to bring Evangelical pressure to bear on the revision, Series Two, though not ideal, still deserved to be tried and tested. This also helped to prove to them that they were now in a position to influence the future course of liturgical revision. They were becoming part of the very process which they had traditionally viewed with so much suspicion.

The historical factors which have militated against the expression of an Evangelical form of sacramental spirituality were beginning, by the end of the debate, to take on a different form. A Catholic majority was no longer seen to be riding roughshod over an Evangelical minority. Rather, the Church of England had seen the necessity of listening to Evangelical opinion. We have shown that some Evangelicals were prepared to respond realistically to the new opportunity and that the ensuing dialogue was already showing signs of movement in areas of their understanding of the Eucharist. As long as the ongoing process of liturgical revision maintained the essential theological concerns of Evangelicals and so released them from defensive mentalities, this creative spirit could continue and increase.

However, by no means all Evangelicals were persuaded that these concerns were safeguarded in Series Two. For example, speaking on behalf of the right wing of the conservative end of the Evangelical spectrum, David Scales regarded Series Two as a reversal of the Reformation: 'we can only regard it as a studied and deliberate attempt to re-introduce those doctrines which were so carefully rejected by the Reformers'.[40] His detailed commentary on the authorized text of Series Two detected transubstantiation and the sacrifice of the Mass at almost every point of difference between the new service and the 1662 service. He urged Evangelicals in the strongest terms never to use Series Two and to work for its eviction in 1971.

As suggested earlier, Evangelicalism was undergoing an internal realignment. Indeed, the debate over Series Two helped to identify the shifting sands of loyalty and identity. In the reply to Lambeth and the early response to Second Series (symbolized by the partnership between Roger Beckwith and Colin Buchanan), Evangelicals generally spoke with one voice. At the end of the debate, the conservative/progressive tension was not only unmistakable, it was also becoming clear that the weight of opinion (or, at least, political control) was shifting from the former to the latter. A factor in this process was the increasing marginalization of the reactionary ideology represented by Scales. For certain, the experiment of Series Two (and the forthcoming *Eucharist for the Seventies*), rather than unflinching commitment to the Prayer Book, reflected the mood of Evangelicalism expressed in the first National Evangelical Anglican Congress held at Keele in 1967.

The availability of a doctrinally serviceable modern liturgy – and the real hope that it could be improved in the near future – was significant. It ensured that Evangelicals would not be forced into using a seventeenth-century eucharistic liturgy when the rest of the Church was using a modern one, and when they themselves were using revised forms of other services and experimenting with various forms of family services. Such a course of events would have made Keele's call for Evangelicals 'to work towards the practice of a weekly celebration of the sacrament as the central corporate service of the Church'[41] an even more difficult task to put into practice than it proved to be. Hopkinson has shown that as Evangelical parishes moved towards the implementation of the Keele intention, they turned to the new services on the grounds that they were structurally and linguistically more suitable for a regular main service communion than was the 1662 rite. Hence, if Evangelicals had found it necessary to close the door on the whole process of liturgical revision of the Eucharist, there would have been even more pressure on them to confine the Eucharist within the strictures of 8 a.m.' and 'staying-behind' communions, rather than setting the possibilities for its

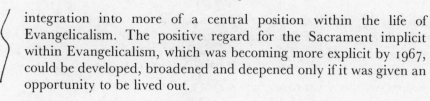

integration into more of a central position within the life of Evangelicalism. The positive regard for the Sacrament implicit within Evangelicalism, which was becoming more explicit by 1967, could be developed, broadened and deepened only if it was given an opportunity to be lived out.

CHAPTER 9

Welcoming liturgical revision: Evangelicals and Series Three to the ASB and beyond

Even whilst Series Two was being debated in Convocations, the Liturgical Commission was working on its revision.[1] But the ongoing débâcle was affecting the dynamics of the Commission. The Evangelical position was clearly a stronger force than the numerical make-up of the Commission had suggested. Colin Buchanan may have been the only definable Conservative Evangelical member but he represented a considerable and growing power group. The Commission's dynamics were also disturbed and rearranged in the years immediately following Series Two by its own internal movements. Another Evangelical (Leo Stephens-Hodge) was invited to serve and, through death or resignation, five distinguished Catholic members were lost to the Commission. The most significant of these departures were those of E. C. Ratcliff and Arthur Couratin, whose theological and ideological concerns had been such a major influence on Series Two. A third factor which helped to create a more promising prospect for Evangelical concerns was the result of the Liturgical Commission's questionnaire on Series Two, which was distributed to the dioceses in 1969. The returns called for a stronger reference to the completeness of the Atonement, as well as for more congregational involvement in the thanksgiving.

These various influences led to the chairman of the Commission (Ronald Jasper) instituting a dialogue on the Eucharistic Prayer in 1970 between Kenneth Ross (a Catholic), Colin Buchanan and himself. The discussions used the recent agreement on aspects of the theology of eucharistic sacrifice between Eric Mascall and Michael Green (which will be discussed in detail in chapter 10) as a theological guideline for the construction of the prayer.[2] Buchanan was pleased with the result. He was later able to say that they 'were able to reach agreement which made the whole text look more clearly biblical than had Series 2'.[3] The *anamnesis* was completely rewritten. The key, as far as Evangelicals were concerned, was the identity established between Christ's sacrifice and his death which in turn allowed the clear statement that his sacrifice was 'made once for all'. In addition to the changes in the thanksgiving, Series Two's words of distribution were lengthened from 'the Body of Christ' to 'the Body of Christ keep you in eternal life', which also helped to endear the text to Evangelical ears.

, The Commission published its proposed revision in September 1971 and was proudly and appropriately able to boast of its unanimity.[4] After revision in the November (1971), February and July (1972) sessions of the newly formed General Synod, a referral to the House of Bishops and a subsequent report from them, Series Three was given final approval by Synod in November and authorized for use from 1 February 1973.[5] The *anamnesis* had been reworded in the process and although somewhat more reminiscent of Series Two than the original version, it retained the emphasis on Christ's once-for-all sacrifice and so was still a great improvement at the critical point on Series Two as far as Evangelicals were concerned. However, Synod also introduced an optional use of text from 1 Chronicles 29 at the taking which, as we shall see, led to suspicion and criticism from Evangelicals.

EVANGELICAL REACTION TO SERIES THREE

Whilst Series Three was in Synodical revision the Latimer House Liturgy Group began an ambitious project designed to respond in critical creativity to the changing scene of Anglican worship. The choice between 'the definitive Evangelical statement' and 'the experimental Evangelical contribution' had been made by the majority of the Group as they planned a series of booklets (Grove Ministry and Worship Series, later to become Grove Worship Series) on the pastoral implications, problems and opportunities provided by the changing liturgical context in the Church of England. In 1971 Colin Buchanan replaced Roger Beckwith as Chairman of the Group. This was a significant and symbolic change in leadership. These two prominent Evangelicals symbolized the two different reactions to liturgical revision identified in chapters 7 and 8. Buchanan was clearly committed to the process of revision and was prepared, on the one hand to broaden his horizon of eucharistic theology – or at least to widen his liturgical sources – and, on the other hand, to accept liturgical forms that did not perfectly meet his criteria in the interests of wider ecclesiological concerns.[6] Beckwith, however, whilst fully admitting the need for liturgical revision, remained convinced that the ideal form this should take would be a modernization of the 1662 rite. He was willing to allow for alternative services provided that they were seen to maintain doctrinal purity and that the Prayer Book service was given a realistic opportunity to compete as a viable alternative.[7]

In terms of Series Three these two approaches consisted of positive affirmation (though retaining a judicious instinct), and critical suspicion (though eventually coming to a measure of acceptance). Of course these were not just the attitudes of two men, or two policies in Latimer House; they represented the spectrum of Evangelical opinion in regard to Series Three. On several occasions Beckwith went as far as to claim that Series Three had split the Evangelical party.[8] Certainly there were those who felt happy to use the service as it stood and those who would not use it at all, but the alleged split should not be blamed entirely on Series Three – it should be seen in the context of the dynamics of Evangelicalism at this stage in its history. However, the ideological difference did lead to the eventual separation of the Group from Latimer House in 1976. As we have seen it renamed itself the Group for the Renewal of Worship (GROW).

A crucial question that had to be faced was the extent to which late-twentieth-century Evangelicalism should remain faithful to the Reformers in the sixteenth century and their interpretative sons in the seventeenth, eighteenth and nineteenth centuries. Inevitably this issue was focused sharply in the differing attitudes towards liturgical revision. The answer to the question in many ways determined the approach to Series Three. The Grove Ministry and Worship Series, though recognizably Evangelical in its underlying sacramental concerns, was prepared to sit reasonably lightly to its inherited tradition. Colin Buchanan was proprietor of Grove Books (which published the Booklets), as well as chairman of Latimer House Liturgy Group. In 1972 he claimed that the series had become 'an overall programme for reform'.[9] But it was a reform that cut two ways: both into the wider Church and her liturgical life and into Evangelicalism itself. In 1973 (and in 1976) he defined its aim as the 'quest for a scriptural "high" churchmanship' and its method as an exploration of 'those areas in which the "Catholic" end of the spectrum may have something to teach us'.[10] Although Series Three was never put beyond criticism, the Grove Ministry and Worship Series could be seen as an attempt to commend and improve its use amongst Evangelicals and non-Evangelicals alike.[11]

Roger Beckwith, on the other hand, representing a considerable though arguably diminishing group within Evangelicalism, attempted to hold a tighter and more visible link with Evangelicalism's past. He campaigned for an official 'modernization of 1662' and maintained a concerted and rigorous critique of Series Three. Although he admitted that the reference to Christ's finished work at Calvary in the *anamnesis* and the longer words of distribution had 'persuaded many Evangelicals that Series Three is doctrinally tolerable', he argued that the three original doctrinal failings of Series Two (namely, prayers for the departed, eucharistic sacrifice and reservation) had been 'disguised rather than solved' in the new service.[12] He was also far from sympathetic to Series Three's doctrine of consecration. The following analysis of the debate begins with the discussion over consecration and then moves on to consider the issues of eucharistic sacrifice and reservation. The matter of prayers for the departed is not pursued as it did not – at least as far as it was discussed in relation to Series Three – raise matters specifically related to the Eucharist.

Consecration

It had long been the policy of the Liturgical Commission to move away from the Western understanding of consecration as effected by the recital of the interpretative words of Christ, towards the more primitive notion of consecration through a Prayer of Thanksgiving set in the context of the other three sacramental actions. Beckwith and Tiller, however, were critical of the contemporary emphasis on both thanksgiving and the four-action shape. They claimed that Jesus' original nine actions were rightly conflated in the second and third centuries into seven and not the four of modern liturgical orthodoxy. Such, they argued, was the structure of Cranmer's rite, which had been taken over in 1662, and maintained in both their modernization of the 1662 rite and also in their revision of Series Two and Three. In turn, whilst thanking has a part in the consecration, it is only a part of the seven- rather than four-action shape which has its high point not in the thanking, but in the recital of Christ's interpretative words over the bread and wine which are to be received in faith: 'the thing that differentiates this meal from any other meal on the Jewish pattern, and so turns a common meal into a sacrament, is the recital of our Lord's interpretive words'.[13] Needless to say, Buchanan, as one of the compilers of Series Three, was fully in support of the four-action shape and indeed was critical of anything that might disrupt that structure. He was also highly critical of the Western formula of consecration, arguing instead that 'the whole eucharistic prayer – from the initial greeting to the final doxology – must be viewed as consecratory'.[14]

Eucharistic sacrifice

Although Beckwith acknowledged that the reference to Christ's sacrifice being 'once for all' in Series Three's *anamnesis* had been a safeguard against overt doctrines of eucharistic sacrifice, he maintained that the petition to 'accept... this our sacrifice of thanks and praise' could, for the following two reasons, still be interpreted as an offering of Christ himself. First, the context of the petition related it to the bread and the cup rather than to the act of thanksgiving. Secondly, it was originally introduced into Series Two's thanksgiving because it allowed for a spectrum of interpretation. Its retention in Series Three showed that 'every effort has been made to ensure that the Roman interpretation fits as naturally as a Reformed one'.[15] In order to excise the possibility of the former, Beckwith recommended that Cranmer's precedent should be followed and the phrase transferred to the post-communion Prayer of Oblation. In contrast, it did not raise any doctrinal problems for Buchanan. He later argued that it had acceptable biblical roots in Hebrews 3:15 and that the *anamnesis* in Series Three kept a clear distinction between Christ's atoning sacrifice 'made once for all' and our responsive sacrifice of thanks and praise, which is made through him.

The differing assessment of the petition is an example of the different methodologies which were being employed. There clearly was a link of some kind in the *anamnesis* between the bread and the cup and the sacrifice of thanks and praise. By being the material focus for the act of remembrance, the elements were in turn the material focus for the sacrifice of 'thanks and praise'. For Beckwith this was an unacceptable connection because it left room for the 'dangerous deceit and blasphemous fable' which Cranmer (and, therefore, the

1662 rite) had gone to such great lengths to avoid. Although Buchanan did not specifically admit the link, the fact that he regarded the petition in this position as perfectly innocent does show that he was prepared to break with the Prayer Book's order which placed 'the sacrifice of praise' (or at least the phrase) after the communion. It also shows that he was prepared to follow through the principle for which he argued in the debate over Series Two, that we should express 'the thanksgiving *totally* in terms of thanksgiving'.[16]

Clearly some Evangelicals were moving away from their historical succession and were broadening their eucharistic theology and practice in a dialogue with the early liturgies and with the contemporary debate over eucharistic theology and liturgy.[17] David Scales, speaking on behalf of the right wing of Evangelicalism was in no doubt about this:

To those who love the Scripture's doctrine of the Lord's Supper, to those who share the Reformers' earnest desire that full and free forgiveness through the atoning sacrificial death of Christ should be proclaimed, to those who wish to be the twentieth century custodians of the evangelical heritage, the Series 3 order must be unacceptable.[18]

But clearly the progressive response to liturgical revision within the party felt that love for Scripture's doctrine of the Lord's Supper and a desire for an expression of God's full and free forgiveness in Christ could be combined with, and enhanced by, a discovery of a wider eucharistic heritage than that provided by the received Evangelical tradition.

Reservation

Roger Beckwith was convinced that Series Three permitted unlimited and uncontrolled reservation of the Sacrament. The origins of his concern lay in a decision of Chancellor Moore in 1967 which judged that rubric 40 of Series Two had legalized reservation. Beckwith believed that the corresponding rubric in the Report form of Series Three was substantially the same and, therefore, the permission which the Church Assembly had unwittingly given in its authorization of Series Two had been continued in the new service. He called for General Synod to correct the mistake in the revision process, warning that 'only thus can the hope of united action over Prayer-Book revision with evangelical participation be kept genuinely alive'.[19]

Beckwith had not been able to count on the support of Buchanan, who did not believe that the wording legalized reservation.[20] Buchanan maintained that the fault was not in the rubric's wording but in the misjudgement of Garth Moore. The Chancellor had failed to recognize that since the Church of England had no authorized form (at that time) of administering communion, except within the actual context of an authorized communion service, the rubric could not have legalized reservation for the purposes of an eventual communion.

THE REVISION OF SERIES THREE

With the revision of Series Three, which began in 1976, the Church of England was moving into a new phase of liturgical development. The new rite would not only be a part of the forthcoming Alternative Service Book, it would also be the standard by which common features in other rites would be adapted. Aware of the significance of the revision, Roger Beckwith seized the opportunity to influence its course. Again he singled out the three issues of petitions for the departed, eucharistic sacrifice and reservation of the elements as those areas in vital need of reform. He called for a concerted effort by Evangelicals to campaign for their removal and suggested small changes to the text which would unambiguously exclude them and therefore 'would be sufficient to correct the service at the three traditional points of controversy, and could be regarded as a minimum necessary to make the service permanently acceptable to Evangelical consciences'.[21] His concern was supported in 1977 by an initiative of five London clergymen ('The East-End Five'). They sought to expose the extent of Evangelical dissatisfaction with Series Three. The results of their survey showed that almost half of the Evangelicals who used the new service did so in an amended form.[22]

However, in 1977, the second National Evangelical Anglican Congress did not respond to Beckwith's call that it should register Evangelical dissatisfaction with Series Three by using an amended text at its own main celebration of Holy Communion. In fact, it showed a sympathy for the ethos of Series Three both in its actual celebration and in its statement on worship:

we enjoy our written liturgy and welcome in the Series 3 services the emphasis on joy, freedom, flexibility and congregational involvement. We should like to see these features extended.[23]

Nevertheless, in commenting on the future revision the Statement registered the following fear:

> we are concerned lest any revision should give greater weight to the concepts of petition for the departed, eucharistic sacrifice or permanent reservation of the elements. We are also concerned because a number of our brethren believe that these concepts are already emphasised too greatly, so much so that they feel conscientiously unable to use the service without grave misgivings.[24]

Hence the Congress admitted the divide which Series Three had created in Evangelical opinion but did not go as far as Beckwith (and others further to the right of the party) would have wanted, for it did not recommend the removal of the contentious elements from the service. Accordingly, David Samuel, speaking for the right wing of the conservative end of the Evangelical spectrum, accused the Congress of a 'high tolerance of unreformed teaching in the Communion Service'.[25]

Buchanan refused to be drawn into a detailed defence of Series Three over these specific points. Instead, he argued that any theological criticism of the service should be on much broader grounds. He believed that only those with theological or political axes to grind would find that it failed to meet acceptable doctrinal criteria.[26]

However, he did direct substantial criticism to one element in Series Three. In the Synodical procedures of the original service, verses from 1 Chronicles 29 had been introduced into the taking, thereby encouraging the questionable – as far as Evangelicals were concerned – offertory theology with all its attendant practices. During the revision of Series Three, Buchanan argued for the extraction of the offertory concept from the sacramental action. On theological grounds, he maintained that a presentation to God of the bread and wine distorts the initiative of grace which is the basis of the Sacrament. On liturgical grounds, he argued for a distinction between the preparation of the elements and the act of taking, claiming that in identifying the two, Dix's theory has been like a 'beacon which has consciously or unconsciously led a whole fleet astray'.[27]

The Liturgical Commission published its revision on 16 May 1978 (*Series Three Revised*).[28] Colin Buchanan had played an important part in working on the revised *anamnesis* with Hugh Craig (who had joined the Commission as another Evangelical representative after the retirement of Leo Stephens-Hodge) and two Catholic members of the Commission. As chairman of the Steering Committee responsible for the revision's passage through Synod, it fell to him to commend the text to the Synod at its July session. According to procedure, the text was passed on to the Revision Committee, which was chaired by Cyril Bowles and included an equal number of Evangelical and Catholic representatives.

Series Three Revised did not allay Roger Beckwith's fears. Indeed, he saw it as 'somewhat less acceptable'[29] than the original service. Nor, it would appear, did the Evangelical representation on the Revision Committee inspire him with confidence, for he pursued an independent line of attack. In an unlikely alliance, he joined with the Anglo-Catholic campaigner Brian Brindley to forge a deal which would provide Evangelicals and Catholics with their own preferred sacramental emphases whilst, at the same time, providing safeguards to ensure that each emphasis remained within acceptable doctrinal boundaries. The result was twofold: first, a Hippolytan-inspired prayer which included an identification between Christ's death on the Cross and his 'one perfect sacrifice made once for the sins of all'; secondly, a modernized form of the 1662 rite.[30] The Revision Committee agreed to consider the proposal. The Evangelical members had misgivings over the wording of the Hippolytan prayer, particularly 'we bring before you these gifts, this bread and this cup' and 'send the Holy Spirit on all that your Church sets before you'. However, they were satisfied by the agreed omission of 'these gifts' and by the change in the *epiclesis* which made it into an unambiguous invocation on the people.

Although the modernized form of the 1662 rite was duly fitted into the revision in full text form, Buchanan claimed that as far as the Evangelical cause was concerned, the Brindley–Beckwith deal was an unnecessary collusion. He divulged that the Revision Committee had already agreed to the inclusion of a modernized form of the Prayer Book service in the projected ASB.[31] However, the initiative was significant in terms of its impact on the right wing of the party. First, it showed that 'uncompromising representatives'[32] could work together to produce a eucharistic prayer which, whilst not meeting Evangelical preferences, did contain sufficient safety valves to make its presence (if not their use of it) broadly acceptable to them. Secondly, it did at least create the impression that the conservative position had been able to win a battle by securing the future of the Prayer Book service in the Church's alternative liturgy.

In addition to the Brindley–Beckwith submission, the Committee had to consider hundreds of other textual amendments to *Series Three Revised*. Michael Saward, one of its Evangelical members, later described how 'to the amazement of almost everyone not only one, but four Eucharistic prayers were prepared which all fourteen [members] were prepared to commend and use'.[33] By the end of the process Roger Beckwith offered his 'warm thanks' to the Committee for its work on the Liturgical Commission's text. Its revision of *Series Three Revised*[34] and its inclusion of the modernized form of the Prayer Book service enabled him to commend the Committee's report in the following way:

the new text of Series Three which the revision committee has produced 'deserves the Synod's support. It is not the final goal of revision, but it is a real step towards that goal. It is not a substitute for the Prayer Book service, but it is a text which can be discriminatingly used alongside the Prayer Book service, with fewer misgivings, and with greater confidence of God's blessing, than any of its predecessors in England since the beginning of the century.[35]

The far right may not have been convinced to accept the revision but the public support given to it by this erudite Evangelical spokesman of the conservative approach – who had previously opposed Series Three on theological as well as liturgical grounds – was a clear sign that the process of the liturgical revision of the Eucharist had won its way even amongst many of those Evangelicals who objected to the very principles on which it was based. Some Evangelicals may have continued to reject the service but, deprived of Beckwith's theological and political back-up, they were in danger of becoming isolated.

On 7 November 1979, after a series of minimal changes in Synodical debates in February and July, the Revision Committee's text was authorized for use from 1 May, and on 9 November it became a part of the ASB. The present round of liturgical revision was over. The preceding two decades had seen a remarkable change in both the liturgical life of the Church of England and in the liturgical ethos of its Evangelical wing. In 1960 Dix's charge that '"Evangelicals" would offer the most determined and conscientious opposition'[36] to liturgical change, was still largely true. But by 1980, indeed well before, the accusation had become quite inaccurate. In short, Evangelicals were experiencing their own Liturgical Movement. The reform had been propelled by the sustained vision, incisive mind and organizational skill of Colin Buchanan. As we have seen, he acquired a considerable level of political power which he used to great effect. It would be wrong to say that he created the Evangelical Liturgical Movement – for it evolved from the dynamics of Anglican Evangelicalism in the 1960s and 1970s – but it would be true to say that he gave it voice in Commission, Synod, conference, press, article and booklet, and that he trained it to think and speak for itself.

BEYOND THE ASB

Whilst the text of the ASB was being prepared by the publishers, the Liturgical Commission was working on forms of service for the sick. Its proposals included the use of communion by extension which necessarily involved some form of limited reservation of the elements. Although tension was being caused on the Commission through its work on the blessing of oils and the ministry of reconciliation, over which Buchanan and Craig were forced into dissension, its plans for services for the sick found ready Evangelical acceptance. Indeed, as we shall see in chapter 11, Buchanan had been a supporter of communion by extension for many years. Although Evangelicals fought hard against the report on *The Blessing of the Oils and the Reconciliation of the Penitent* (eventually defeating it), the report on *Services for the Sick* was generally well received and duly authorized.[37]

When the new Liturgical Commission was appointed in 1981, its Evangelical representation was strengthened by the inclusion of Trevor Lloyd. Trevor Lloyd, who was committed to the centrality of the Eucharist, had already played a quiet and self-effacing but highly significant and strategic role in Evangelical liturgical life. He had provided support, friendship and advice to Colin Buchanan; he had been an important member of GROW; he had provided guidance, advice and inspiration to the Evangelical world as it experimented with new forms of worship both through his writing and speaking, and through his own creative practice in his ministry as vicar of a parish. Now his influence and creativity were being given official recognition and an official channel. The Commission in which he first served dealt with little that was directly to do with the Eucharist. But its successor worked on new Eucharistic Prayers and alternative structures for the Eucharist. Under the chairmanship of Colin James (the Bishop of Winchester), this Commission had welcomed to its

ranks a younger generation of liturgists who showed a remarkable
capacity to work together with great energy and unanimity. Because
of length of service Colin Buchanan was not reappointed, but Trevor
Lloyd remained and was joined by a higher proportion of Evangelicals than had previously served on the Liturgical Commission.

Trevor Lloyd and Kenneth Stevenson worked on suggestions for
Eucharistic Prayers to be included in the Commission's planned
response to the request for suitable material for family services and
worship in urban priority areas. Lloyd and Stevenson were both
committed but open members of their respective Evangelical and
Catholic traditions, and were able to work effectively together. As the
Commission worked on the texts, hesitation was voiced by Evangelicals over the reference to pleading Christ's sacrifice in the *anamnesis*
and in the invocation on the elements as well as the people in the
epiclesis in one of the proposed Eucharistic Prayers. In deference to
Evangelical desire to state clearly our assurance that Christ's sacrifice
has been accepted, the Commission inserted the words 'with
confidence' into the *anamnesis* so that it ran: 'we plead with
confidence his sacrifice made once for all'.

Patterns for Worship was published in 1989.[38] With its Directory
approach to worship, the Report appealed to the wider liturgical
instincts of Evangelicals – particularly those influenced by the
Charismatic Movement – and was generally well received by them.
Meanwhile the Evangelical members of the Commission turned their
attention, with the Commission as a whole, to the issue that would
dominate liturgical discussion in the Evangelical world and in the
Church as a whole over the last decade of the twentieth century – the
revision of the ASB.

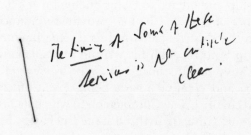

The timing of some of these revisions is not entirely clear.

CHAPTER 10

Evangelicals and ecumenical statements on the Eucharist

[handwritten marginalia: Then hlaved a significant... informed fait but were the originators?]

The Ecumenical Movement may have originated from the initiatives *[handwritten: what t. gone or...]* of Evangelicals at the turn of the century but it soon lost the confidence of their successors. With their ecclesiology of an invisible Church united in common testimony to the truth of Christ, Evangelicals found it difficult to relate to the modern Ecumenical Movement's ideals for institutional unity and its perceived method of defining the truth in as broad a way as possible.

Various attempts were made in England during the period under review to translate the goodwill of the Ecumenical Movement into concrete forms – either in the form of schemes for reunion (as with the Methodists) or in statements of agreed doctrine. Evangelicals were thus forced to reflect on and then articulate their relationship with institutional ecumenism. Their decision was to commit themselves to the quest for 'the unity of the visible church'.[1] The pledge was grounded in a shift of ecclesiological categories. The Keswick cry of 'All One in Christ Jesus' began to be seen as an inadequate expression of the New Testament principle of 'All in Each Place'[2] – that is, the biblical precedent and demand for there to be only 'one church in one place'.[3]

The Charismatic Movement added a further dynamic to the changing ecumenical psychology of Evangelicals. Although it had a tendency to reinforce the notions of unity on the basis of common spiritual experience, the discovery that the experience was not restricted to Evangelicals and the Movement's inherent affirmation of both community and visible form, helped to foster a seed-bed of ecumenical energy.[4]

Nevertheless, despite the new-found stress on the visible unity of Christians in a given area, with its corresponding preference for local organic growth rather than imposed structural unity, and the widening of the definition of spiritual experience engendered by the

Charismatic Movement, Evangelicals remained adamant that the process towards institutional unity should be based on genuine agreement on the essentials of the Gospel.[5] This chapter will examine their contribution to and criticism of the bilateral and multilateral attempts to arrive at such an agreement in regard to the doctrine of the Eucharist.[6]

ANGLICAN–METHODIST DIALOGUE

The Report: 1963

The section on the Eucharist in the 1963 Report[7] of the Conversations between the Church of England and the Methodist Church consisted largely of a statement of Methodist doctrine. The hope that this would prove acceptable to Anglicans was dashed by the critical reception it received from Evangelicals.[8] Indeed, the belief that the statement was representative of Methodist opinion was challenged even earlier. Four Methodist members dissented over various aspects of the Report's theology including its expression of the doctrine of eucharistic sacrifice.

One of the main voices in the Evangelical response was that of Roger Beckwith. By a detailed source criticism of the statement he established a line of connection between various Methodist scholars and the theology of Hicks, Dix and Mascall. Therefore, although he acknowledged that the statement could be understood in a Reformed way, the background to its ideas and its own 'studied ambiguity'[9] led him to the conclusion that it was designed to accommodate, and at points actually to express, the main concerns of contemporary Anglo-Catholic eucharistic theology.

The force of his attack was directed at the statement's interpretation of the remembrance as 'the renewal of the corporate memory of the Church by the Holy Spirit', the consequence of which is that 'the great "salvation" events culminating in the Cross are re-enacted'.[10] Here, for Beckwith, was pure 'Dixian' theology: Christ's sacrifice is 're-presented', that is, literally made present again, 'by the mysterious power of *anamnesis*'.[11] He argued that Dix's theory was inconsistent with the New Testament for the following reasons. First, the meaning of *anamnesis* in Dix's proof-texts does not sufficiently support the theory which he builds upon them. Secondly, the object of the New Testament's symbolism of the rite is to point to Christ's 'state of death', not his 'act of dying'.[12] Thirdly, the identity which the theory posits between Calvary and the Eucharist necessarily implies a repetition of Christ's death.

In the light of its emphasis on *anamnesis*, Beckwith regarded the statement's use of the phrase 'real presence' with great suspicion. He noted that Dix's theory of the ontological effect of the *anamnesis* involved, as a consequence, a belief in the real presence of Christ's flesh and blood (for the sacrifice cannot be present without the victim). He listed the classic pneumatological, Christological and soteriological objections to the doctrine of the real presence and concluded that the signatories should give a 'public assurance' that they intend 'only to affirm the spiritual presence of the risen Christ, promised to His people not just at the eucharist but wherever they meet'.[13]

In a similar way to the Lambeth Statement, the Methodists talked of Christ's sacrifice being an act of obedience which in some sense is both eternal and united with the Church's offering. Hence, in a similar way to those who replied to Lambeth, Beckwith argued that the New Testament regards Christ's sacrifice more in terms of 'vicarious sin-bearing'[14] (understood in a penal substitutionary way) than in terms of the offering of perfect human obedience. Further, it sees this atoning act as completed on the Cross and as presented to God, not eternally, but once for all, at his ascension. The Church's action at the Eucharist is sacrificial in the sense that we offer our praise, our thanks and ourselves, but these are qualitatively distinguished from Christ's sacrifice which 'unlike ours, belongs to the past not the present, was unblemished by sin, necessarily involved death, and atoned for mankind'.[15] Thus, the role of the Eucharist is not to unite our offering with Christ's sacrifice at Calvary, but to commemorate that event and to participate in it by means of a symbolic 'post-sacrificial feast'.[16] It is in his description of the feast on the sacrifice that we find Beckwith's most positive comments on the sacrificial associations of the Eucharist. Drawing on the function of such meals in Old Testament life and worship, he claimed that the Eucharist maintains and renews the believer's part in the New Covenant by 'cementing *koinonia*' between himself and God.[17]

Invalidates point in Gylett's R. (handwritten)

Interim Statement: 1967

The Evangelical presence on the original Commission clearly did not gain the confidence of Conservative Evangelicals.[18] Hence, in view of the dissatisfaction voiced by them, not just over the sacramental section of the Report, but also regarding its doctrines of episcopacy and priesthood as embodied in the Service or Reconciliation, James Packer and Gordon Savage were invited to join the second Commission.

1967. (handwritten)

The new Commission produced an Interim Statement (*Towards Reconciliation*[19]) of its attempt to meet the disputed areas of the 1963 Report. The method it chose was to state the common ground between the Churches and then to identify, but not harmonize, the areas of disagreement which existed both within each Church and also between the Churches. Beckwith regarded the Statement's description of the common eucharistic doctrine as entirely acceptable and approved of its relegation of the more contentious issues to a description of the belief held by some, rather than an expression of the official belief of either Church.[20]

This Statement was incorporated in the Commission's final Report.[21] However, many Evangelicals objected to the two-stage scheme of reunion which it envisaged and the Service of Reconciliation which it proposed (with its implication of defective Methodist orders), and thus refused to give the Report their support.[22]

Growing into the union: 1969–1970

One result of the Report's proposals was the formation of an unlikely alliance between Conservative Evangelicals and those Conservative Catholics who were also dissatisfied with the scheme and the Service of Reconciliation. In response to demands that those who rejected the scheme should offer a positive alternative, Colin Buchanan and James Packer joined with Eric Mascall and Graham Leonard (two leading Catholics) to present a detailed plan for a gradual (but one-stage), locally based, piecemeal integration of the two Churches.[23] Their proposal for the process of 'growing into union' was built on an attempt (which they considered successful) to reach a theological agreement over the areas that had traditionally divided Evangelical from Catholic. Their section on the Eucharist addressed the vexed

There was a total misunderstanding of likelihood. The book was appallingly insensitive. (handwritten)

question, raised in the 1963 Report, of the relationship between the Church's activity in the Eucharist and the sacrifice of Christ on the Cross. Their agreement was a significant and influential one which deserves to be quoted at length:

what can we offer at the Eucharist? Not mere bread and wine...not merely 'the fruit of our lips'; not merely undefined 'spiritual sacrifices'; not ourselves considered apart from Christ; not even ourselves in Christ, if that is seen in separation from our feeding on Christ; but ourselves as reappropriated by Christ. If the sacrament is to communicate to us afresh the benefits of Christ's passion, then it must reaffirm quickly that it also communicates to us the demands of it. It may be good liturgically to express our self-offering as responsive to God's grace...but there is no real time sequence to be represented.[24]

The intimacy of the relationship between grace and response, gift and sacrifice, offer and demand, was reaffirmed in an appendix by Michael Green and Eric Mascall: 'In the act of communicating, the Church, reintegrated and reappropriated by the one means of grace, is made a living sacrifice to God.'[25] Green and Mascall were able to agree that as we 'partake in the benefits' of Christ's sacrifice our 'imperfect' offering and our 'non-propitiatory' sufferings are 'joined with' his perfect offering and redemptive sufferings.[26]

The essay also picked up a further theme of the Methodist Statement – that of the eternal dimension of Christ's sacrifice and ministry. It attempted to clear up some of the 'semantic confusions'[27] surrounding talk of pleading Christ's sacrifice and of him presenting his sacrifice in heaven. It concluded that Catholic use of such terms is passive rather than active and, therefore, acceptable to Evangelicals. It is not a case of persuading a reluctant Father or of Christ being in a permanent state of atoning offering, but of expressing the belief that Christ's presence in heaven, as 'the Lamb who was slain', is both the 'silent plea for our acceptance' and the 'pledge of our acceptance'.[28]

ANGLICAN–ROMAN CATHOLIC INTERNATIONAL COMMISSION

Surveying the Evangelical response to ARCIC's statement on the Eucharist is a complex task. First, in a similar way to the Methodist Conversations, ARCIC's publications spanned a whole decade and elicited Evangelical reaction at each stage.[29] Secondly, the character of the response needs to be seen in the context of the deep antipathy

with which Evangelicalism had historically regarded Roman Catholicism. Major areas of Roman dogma were seen as thoroughly
erroneous and the Roman Catholic Church was believed to be
committed to a position of irreformability. However, their positive
response to Cardinal Heenan's call for Evangelicals to be involved in
any future process of Anglican–Roman dialogue, their willingness at
Keele to 'rejoice...at signs of biblical reformation'[30] in Rome and
their acceptance at Nottingham of 'Roman Catholics as fellow
Christians',[31] reveal that Evangelicals were involved in a costly
reappraisal of their inherited attitudes.

The third reason for the complexity of the task of surveying the
Evangelical response to ARCIC is that the Commission's work was
received – as we would expect – in different ways across the Evangelical spectrum. At the risk of over-simplification, I would suggest
that the reactions fell into three groups. On the right wing,
represented by David Samuel, the Statement, along with the whole
process of dialogue, was rejected in an absolute fashion. In the centre,
represented by the Anglican Evangelical–Roman Catholic Dialogue
Team and by the Church of England Evangelical Council (voiced
respectively by Roger Beckwith and John Stott), much of the
Statement was welcomed as entirely biblical. However, over the
main issues of the relation of Christ's presence to the elements and the
relation of the Eucharist to Calvary, the old differences were detected
only slightly below the surface. On the left wing, represented by
Julian Charley (a member of the Commission),[32] Colin Buchanan
(involved in some way in the background),[33] and George Carey (a
firm supporter of the ARCIC process and future Archbishop of
Canterbury),[34] the Statement was viewed as acceptable to Anglican
Evangelicals.

The Statement, which was first published in 1971, tackled head-on
the traditional areas of controversy and so elicited a response which
concentrated mainly on the issues of sacrifice and presence. In order
to clarify various points within the Statement, ARCIC published
Elucidations in 1979.

Sacrifice

ARCIC treated the concept of *anamnesis* as the key to unlocking the
traditional controversy over the relationship between the Eucharist
and Christ's sacrifice. However, behind its use of the term Samuel
and Beckwith detected the theology of Casel and Dix in which the

anamnesis involves the making present of Christ's past sacrifice.[35] As we have seen, Beckwith did not accept the etymological or theological basis of this theory. However, he did feel that *Elucidations* had made enough concessions to safeguard the uniqueness of Calvary.[36] Samuel, though was not appeased. He argued that ARCIC's concept of *anamnesis* led to the identification of the Cross and the Eucharist and thus 'cancelled out' all that the Statement says elsewhere about the 'finality and sufficiency of Christ's sacrifice'.[37] Alternatively, Buchanan, himself no lover of the 'Dixian' approach, noted that despite the Statement's emphasis on the *anamnesis*, it did not actually talk of the sacrifice being made present. He found its definition of the *anamnesis* as 'the making effective in the present' entirely acceptable.[38]

Behind the Evangelicals' suspicion of the concept lay the fear that ARCIC was positing some form of cultic exchange to the *anamnesis* which either dissociated it from the communion or inappropriately associated the Church with the atoning action of Christ. For example, Beckwith believed that the Statement implied that the worshippers participate in the benefits of Christ's sacrifice by the effect of the Eucharistic Prayer rather than through the reception of the elements.[39] And John Stott claimed that ARCIC's understanding of the Church entering into 'the movement of [Christ's] self-offering' unacceptably confused the roles of Calvary and the Church in the eucharistic event. Understood in the sense of the present efficacy of the sacrifice in the Eucharist, the Statement's use of *anamnesis* was quite proper. But if it meant to extend the reference to an inclusion of the Church's action in the Eucharist with the action of Christ's self-offering on the Cross, then it is quite improper.[40] The same view was expressed in three 'Open letters' by Evangelicals in 1972 (on the ARCIC Statement on the Eucharist), 1977 (on the whole subject of Anglican relations with Catholic and Orthodox Churches) and 1988 (on the work of the ARCIC I and II and signed by Anglican Evangelicals throughout the Communion).[41]

Buchanan met both Beckwith's and Stott's fears by the following parenthetic gloss on the text:

In the eucharistic prayer the church continues to make a perpetual memorial of Christ's death, and his members, united with God and one another, give thanks for all his mercies, entreat the benefits of his passion on behalf of the whole church, [in communion] *participate in these benefits and* [*in response*] *enter into the movement of his self-offering* (my emphasis).[42]

Charley quoted this interpretation and described it as the 'intention of the drafters'.[43]

Presence

All three spheres of Evangelical response agreed that the Statement used strong sacramental language when describing the relation of Christ's presence to the elements. The divide came over what the Statement meant by such language. Did it teach a presence of Christ in the elements, or merely a presence of Christ offered through the elements?

Although the term 'transubstantiation' occurred only in a footnote to the Statement, the Right and Centre were convinced that the essence of the doctrine remained. Samuel identified a 'spatial conjunction between the sign and the thing signified';[44] Beckwith believed that the Statement deliberately excluded the doctrine of receptionism;[45] the 'Open letter' of 1977 was 'dissatisfied with the declaration of an objective change in the elements';[46] and the 'Open letter' of 1988 claimed that 'what the word [transubstantiation] stood for is still retained, namely "a change in the inner reality of the elements"'. John Stott argued that despite the assurances of *Elucidations* that it does not mean to imply a material change of limitation of Christ's presence to the elements, the presence 'certainly appears to be localized there'.[47]

However, the Left argued that the use of realistic language was validated first, by the precedent set by Christ and followed in liturgical history (including Protestant history) and, secondly, by the objective basis of the eucharistic gift. It maintained that the correct approach to ARCIC is not to dismiss its sacramental language but to judge it by the Statement's overall understanding. Charley argued that ARCIC aimed to keep the two 'moments'[48] of consecration and communion in the closest possible relationship – the former affirming that a real gift is really to be offered, and the latter underlining the personal categories in which the gift is to be understood: 'So long as the eucharistic action is seen as a whole, this logical order of Christ's "offering to the believer awaiting his welcome" presents no difficulties.'[49]

Hence, ARCIC's concept of consecration amounts to no more than the classical Anglican and Puritan notion of 'the setting apart for a holy use'. Seen in these terms, Buchanan urged Evangelicals not to fear language of *being* and *becoming* when applied to the elements after the process of consecration – it merely comments on their new 'use' or 'valuation'.[50]

THE LIMA TEXT

The World Council of Churches' Statement on the Eucharist in the Lima Text of 1982[51] did not produce the same passion amongst Evangelicals as its ARCIC contemporary. The heat generated by the historical tensions was obviously not present in the same way – a fact reflected in the character of the Statement itself. Rather than concentrating on the predictable, controversial themes, Lima attempted a more wide-ranging theological treatment. This helped to realign the Evangelical response. The ARCIC pattern of rejection, criticism or acceptance was replaced by a twofold reaction of either dissatisfaction or satisfaction, with the further significant factor that the Church of England Evangelical Council sided firmly with the latter.[52] On their behalf, Tony Price, having noted both Lima's enthusiasm for the Eucharist and the breadth of its theological approach, concluded that 'a study and application of it could enrich our own [that is, Evangelical] devotion and church life'. He detected a 'degree of ecumenical convergence' which not only expressed a 'growing towards concensus' but, alongside the Statements on Baptism and Ministry, created a whole new phase in practical ecumenical possibilities.[53] However, the Evangelical replies naturally singled out the traditional areas of disagreement, and it is to those we must turn.

Presence

Roger Beckwith described the Lima Statement on the Eucharist as 'a very confused and confusing text'.[54] It would seem that he was thinking particularly of the Statement's concept of the eucharistic presence. He claimed that it understands the interpretative words in a literal way and that the Statement throughout seems to hint at the presence *in* the elements although it does not actually assert the doctrine. By contrast, Tony Price felt that Lima did no more than state the fact of Christ's presence – it 'wishes to recognize Christ's presence, without trying to define the exact mode of it'.[55] Similarly, Colin Buchanan defended the Statement's use of strong sacramental language as consistent with a functional view of their status. He was

quite happy with its emphasis on the work of the Spirit in relation to
the role of the elements: for this 'is our assurance that they *are* (or,
indeed, *become*...) the body and blood of Christ'.[56]

Sacrifice

Lima laid great stress on the dynamic and objective character of the
anamnesis in the Eucharist. Beckwith was critical of this approach on
three scores. First, he considered 'commemoration' to be a preferable
translation of *anamnesis* to Lima's 'memorial'. Secondly, in its
interpretation of the *anamnesis* as the 'present efficacy of God's work
when it is celebrated by God's people in liturgy', he detected the
whole theory (which he considered to be unacceptable) of the
making present of a past event. Thirdly, he argued that Lima's broad
reference to the living Christ in the various aspects of his person and
work, from Incarnation to Pentecost, went beyond the New
Testament's specification of his death as the content of the *anamnesis*.[57]

Beckwith's unease with the emphasis on *anamnesis* was present in
both Buchanan's and Price's responses to Lima. However, they felt
that although erroneous constructions are often built on the objective
interpretation of *anamnesis*, Lima itself had stayed safely within
acceptable limits:

While [Evangelicals] might prefer to avoid this language altogether, we
would not want to disagree with [the] explanation of the memorial of Christ
as 'the living and effective sign of his sacrifice'; that is, a means by which
God's work accomplished in the past becomes fully effective today.[58]

Nevertheless, in line with Beckwith, Price noted that Evangelicals
would have preferred a much clearer emphasis on the death of Christ
as the primary content of the *anamnesis*.

ANGLICAN–LUTHERAN, ORTHODOX AND REFORMED STATEMENTS

Although the Statements issuing from Anglican dialogue with the
Lutheran, Orthodox and Reformed traditions produced little Evangelical response, it is still appropriate to make a brief comment on
them, as each Commission included at least one Evangelical
representative.

The Anglican–Lutheran Conversations of 1970–2 resulted in the
Pullach Report in 1972.[59] The dialogue was followed up in 1980–2 by

the Anglican–Lutheran European Commission, which reported at
Helsinki in 1982.[60] James Atkinson was the Evangelical representative on both. Pullach's section concerning the Eucharist affirmed
'the real presence of Christ in this sacrament' but, by declining to
define 'how this happens' and by placing great weight on the whole
eucharistic action, it left little that would be objectionable to
Evangelicals. However, it described the Sacrament as 'in some sense'
involving sacrifice. It defended this description not only on the
grounds that in the Eucharist we offer our praise and ourselves, but
also because 'we make before God the memorial of Christ's sacrifice
– Christ's redemptive act becomes present for our participation'.
Nevertheless, this strong use of *anamnesis* was softened by the way in
which the Report set the Word on the same essential footing as the
Sacrament. Both were seen as 'occasions of [Christ's] coming in
anamnesis of his first advent'.[61]

The European Commission was asked to seek further clarification
in the area of eucharistic theology. The result, on the one hand, was
to 'raise' Pullach's doctrine of the presence by identifying 'a
particular sacramental presence of Christ', and by referring to Christ
being both 'truly present' (in his body and blood) and 'coming to us'
'under the elements of bread and wine'. On the other hand, it
'lowered' Pullach's theory of *anamnesis*: rather than speaking of the
presence of the past, it kept to the ARCIC-type language of 'the
Church's effectual proclamation of God's saving acts in Christ' – the
purpose of which is 'the contemporary application of Christ's
salvation'.[62]

Roger Beckwith was a member of the Anglican–Orthodox
Commission which produced the Moscow Agreed Statement in
1977.[63] He was joined by Oliver O'Donovan in the preparation for
the 1984 Dublin Agreed Statement.[64] Moscow laid great stress on the
role of the Holy Spirit in the Eucharist. The Spirit was seen as active
in the consecration to the extent of coming 'upon the elements'. But
its corresponding emphasis on the coming of the Spirit on the
community – not only in the Eucharist but continually – and its
reference to consecration occurring as a result of the 'whole
sacramental liturgy' left room for an understanding of the Spirit's
work as the enabling of a reception of the body and blood, in the
hearts of the faithful, by the use of the elements.[65]

However, the Orthodox members of the Commission were clearly
not satisfied. We are told that many, if not all of them, would have

preferred a clear reaffirmation of the 1935 Bucharest Statement, rather than the mere noting of it, as actually appeared.[66] The Bucharest Statement between Orthodox Christians and Anglicans was quite specific in the assertion of the presence *in* the elements and of the perpetual presentation of Calvary in a 'bloodless fashion' at each Eucharist.[67] Roger Beckwith played a leading part amongst the 'several Anglicans'[68] who resisted the move. For example, on the question of the presence, as with his response to ARCIC, he insisted that the 'essential thing to safeguard is not the *how*, but the truth *that*, in the Eucharist Christians...feed on Christ's Body and drink his Blood'.[69] Hence, the Orthodox call (which was heeded) for the Bucharest Statement to be published with the Moscow Statement, was regarded by him and some of his Anglican colleagues as purely for the 'purposes of information',[70] and not as an expression of the Commission's mind.

The Dublin Statement underlined the fact that the Commission as a whole had not discussed in detail the 'change'[71] resulting from the consecratory prayer or the extent to which the Eucharist may be described as a sacrifice. It merely noted that the Commission was agreed in describing the Eucharist as 'an anamnesis and participation in the death and resurrection of Christ',[72] and in reaffirming Moscow's expression of the effect of consecration:

the bread and wine become the Body and Blood of the glorified Christ by the action of the Holy Spirit in such a way that the faithful people of God receiving Christ may feed upon him in the sacrament.[73]

When comparing ARCIC, Lima and Moscow, Beckwith cited this comment as evidence that out of the three, Moscow 'came nearest to a Reformed understanding of [the] question'.[74]

Andrew Kirk represented Evangelicals in the Anglican–Reformed International Commission which first met in 1981 and reported in 1984.[75] Ironically, out of all the Statements, it was this one which used the most unguarded language when discussing the Eucharist. This is particularly evident in its use of *anamnesis* and its understanding of the relationship between Calvary and the Church's offering:

The Eucharist is a making present of the once-for-all sacrifice of Christ. Joined to Christ, in that sacrifice, the Church makes an acceptable offering of itself in thanksgiving to the Father.[76]

And, when discussing the presence of Christ it argued that statements associating his presence with the elements were equally as true as those relating it to the reception in the heart through faith.

However, such comments, when read as a whole, were quite capable of an interpretation acceptable to Evangelicals. For example, the Statement quoted Lima's definition of the *anamnesis* as the 'living and effective sign of Christ's sacrifice' and applied it to the Word as well as to the Sacrament. It made it clear that the Eucharist is a 'participation in the benefits of [Christ's] death and resurrection' and that his sacrifice was offered by him alone once for all to the Father. Thus its language of offering meant no more than as the Church is united as beneficiary to Christ's 'unique'[77] sacrifice, so it is in a position to offer itself in thanks and praise to the Father. Likewise, its acceptance of statements which relate the presence to the elements as well as to the faithful recipients, was merely to underline the agreement reflected in ARCIC, that the Eucharist involves both real gift and real reception.

CONCLUDING ANALYSIS

Having considered the general features of the Evangelical response to the ecumenical statements we are now in a position to dig a little deeper into three issues which the Reports (particularly ARCIC and Lima) exposed. The first was the question of whether the central focus of the Eucharist is the death of Christ, or the other 'mighty works' of God before and after that death, or the living reality of his presence. In a Reformed critique of ARCIC and Lima, Gerald Bray accused the Statements of shifting the Sacrament's centre of interest away from the Atonement and towards the Incarnation.[78] Defining the Atonement in terms of Christ's death, he argued that the Cross should be seen as the thing signified (*res significata*) in the Eucharist. In contrast, although Julian Charley similarly located the atoning activity of Christ in his death and described the elements as the 'sacrament of his death', he also pointed out that Jesus actually said: '"Do this in remembrance of *me*", that is of the incarnate, crucified, raised, and ascended Lord'.[79] Hence, whereas Bray related the *res significata* in the Sacrament to the work of Christ, Charley directed it to his person. Colin Buchanan warned against creating a false dichotomy between Christ's person and work: 'The person cannot be proclaimed without his work ... and his work cannot be known unless it belongs to the living Lord.'[80] Nevertheless, his suggestion that our starting point should be the 'affirmation that the living present Lord "has the virtue of his death in him"',[81] still identified the primary reference point as the ascended Christ rather than the death of Christ.

The second issue raised by the Reports was the question of the role of the *anamnesis*. Bray considered that the purpose of the Sacrament 'is not to re-present the sacrifice of Christ, but to proclaim it'.[82] Its objectivity is rooted, therefore, not in the liturgical act but in the event of Calvary. The role of the *anamnesis* is to remind us of the Cross in order that we may grasp the 'full meaning'[83] of Christ's work and, in so doing, be brought into and sustained in the personal relationship God offers us with him, in the person of his Son. Whilst Buchanan would clearly have wanted to underline Bray's emphasis on the Cross as the objective basis of the Sacrament, he was prepared to allow certain objective features to the *anamnesis*. First, the commemoration has a given content because the calling to mind of Christ's death cannot be abstracted from the reality of his presence – '"remembrance" involves a union with the living Christ'.[84] Secondly, the value of the commemoration is not to be sought solely in its impact on the devotion of each participant but also in the fact that it is being celebrated in a communal setting. Therefore, the liturgical act itself may be said to have a given objectivity because the remembrance is taking place in the presence of the living Christ and in the community of his people.

David Gregg attempted to address his own detailed research into the etymology of *anamnesis* to the ecumenical scene. His conclusions formed a highly original Evangelical contribution to the debate. He was critical of theories which claim an 'actualization'[85] of Christ's sacrifice in the present – believing that ARCIC and Lima's approach fell into this category. However, concerned that we should appreciate the dynamic quality of the biblical notion of an historical event, he commended the following interpretation of the dominical command:

Take, give thanks, break the bread and say the interpretative words, at each weekly festal communal meal, as the commemorative act in which you initiate a genuine encounter in the present by means of a moment of redemptive time from the past.[86]

He defined the Cross as the sole content of the 'commemorative act'. Clearly this resonated with the sort of traditional Evangelical understanding of the Sacrament that was being presented by Bray. However, Gregg did make significant departures from other Evangelical axioms. He maintained that the *anamnesis* is an objective cultic act. Its purpose is to create the possibility of an encounter with Christ through the liturgical function of a series of designated actions. At this point he did not necessarily go beyond the objectivity posited by Buchanan (in terms of the communal aspect) or of Beckwith (in terms of the post-sacrificial meal). However, his advice that we should not see the *anamnesis* in exclusively manward terms but should allow for its mutual effect on both sides of the covenant relationship showed a marked difference: 'there will be, in every commemorative act, dynamic consequences, as both God and man grasp the whole and act accordingly'.[87]

The third question raised by the Statements was over the role of the elements in the eucharistic experience. In an attempt to refute ARCIC's (alleged) doctrine of the real presence in the elements, James Packer argued that the New Testament gives

basis enough for asserting a 'real' (in the sense of 'genuine') presence of the Lord Jesus by his Spirit *at* the Supper, *among* the communicants, *mediated by* the elements, and thus *in* each believer's heart – but not for asserting a bodily presence in or under the consecrated bread and wine.[88]

The various strands within the Evangelical debate would have agreed with Packer's definition of the presence including his affirmation of the instrumental function of the elements. However, there were contrasting nuances in the way the instrumental activity was understood.

For example, Bray saw the role of the elements as pointing to the grace of God shown in Christ's death and thus provoking the appropriate response in the individual: 'When we take the bread and the cup we make a conscious decision which is at the same time a test of our ability to discern what Christ has done for us.'[89] The elements are thus the foci of the whole sacramental action of reminding the participants of the objective act of God in Christ's death. The result, one hopes, is that the elements will elicit the appropriate soteriological understanding and thereby enable the personal meeting in Christ with the same God of grace. Therefore, their role is essentially affective.

Julian Charley described the role of the elements more in effective terms: 'By the gracious initiative of God something profound occurs

by which the life of Christ is transmitted to the members of his
body.'[90] He made it clear that his understanding of that 'trans-
mission' was in fully personal categories and thus that the offer
requires a reception in faith before the 'life-giving encounter'[91] can
take place. However, it is still true to say that the elements themselves,
on the basis of their consecration, '"become" the appointed means'[92]
of such an encounter. Whereas with Bray they are instrumental in the
sense that they encourage the individual to meditate on the life-
giving significance of the Cross, with Charley they are instrumental
in the sense that they mediate that reality to the receiving faith of the
individual. The distinctions may be subtle but they are still
significant. The one answers our fundamental dilemma of identifying
the real value of the Eucharist over and against hearing and believing
the Word, by saying that here is a dominically appointed, and
therefore particularly potent, visual aid. The other answers it by
saying that here the same grace of the Gospel is itself linked to a
material form in such a way that, in this moment of God's activity,
the reception of his grace cannot be isolated from the reception of the
elements. In short, in one approach we are left with food for thought,
in the other we have the bread of life.

CHAPTER II

Evangelicals, the Eucharist and spirituality

TOWARDS A MORE CENTRAL PLACE FOR THE EUCHARIST IN EVANGELICAL PRACTICE

In 1958 John Stott wrote that the 'chief expression of fellowship between Christians is the Holy Communion service. It is the central service of the Church.' He argued against multiple communions and regarded the Family Communion or the Parish Communion as 'a step in the right direction'.[1] His comments may be seen as a summary of the theological and practical agenda that Evangelicals in the 1960s set themselves in relation to the place of the Eucharist in the local Church's life of worship.

The emphasis on fellowship not only appealed to a significant theme in Evangelical spirituality; it also avoided the more complex issues surrounding the areas of 'sacrament', 'presence' and 'sacrifice', and thus provided a relatively non-controversial rationale for the centrality of the Eucharist. In line with the Parish and People movement (though institutionally quite separate), Evangelicals described the Eucharist as the biblical means of both expressing and fostering the unity of the Church. They were critical of the individualistic understanding of the Sacrament in traditional Evangelical thought and of its outworking in the contemporary Evangelical practice of 8 a.m. and 'staying-behind' communions. As a result, they continued the moves made in the 1950s to translate the principle of 'corporate centrality' into parish practice, by establishing the Holy Communion as the main Sunday service on at least a monthly basis.

The calls for the adoption of a weekly Parish Communion model were heeded in some quarters but the norm in Evangelical parishes became the monthly rather than the weekly service. This was not acceptable to certain leading (or rising) Evangelical strategists who

153

did not miss the political opportunity provided by the Keele Congress in 1967 to turn the campaign into policy. Despite a large minority against a clear recommendation for a weekly pattern, the Congress committed itself to 'work towards the practice of a weekly celebration of the sacrament as the central corporate Service of the church'.[2]

In 1972 Charles Hutchings noted that the 'pledge itself has been hotly disputed in evangelical circles'[3] and in 1973 Colin Buchanan claimed that the monthly main-service pattern had developed to 'possibly the "mainstream" Evangelical practice'.[4] As with the process of liturgical revision, the conservative end of the Evangelical spectrum found it difficult to relate on a theological level to Keele's reorientation of Evangelical practice. However, it seems that most of the objections were in terms of the practical difficulties that a weekly celebration would involve. There were worries that insufficient time would be available for preaching; that the uncommitted would be either excluded from worship or forced into premature participation; that the Sacrament would be devalued by familiarity and by lack of preparation; that, if the morning Parish Communion were adopted, the evening service would be crowded out; and finally that the presence of children in the service would make it unworkable.

In reply, a rigorous refutation of the reservations and a vigorous demand for the implementation of Keele was made by Hutchings and Buchanan during the early 1970s. Hutchings built his case on the corporate dimension of the Eucharist: 'the sacrament must clearly be at the centre of our worship as an effective sign in our community'.[5] Buchanan combined an appeal to the corporate function of the Sacrament with a heavy stress on the dominical command: 'There can only be one top priority for all Christians. And it is communion. Any other service must fall into the category of helpful but not mandatory.'[6]

There were several other factors in the 1970s which added to the movement for centrality. First, liturgical revision – particularly the authorization of Series Three communion. In his analysis of the changing character of Evangelical worship during the 1960–80 period, Hopkinson claimed that 'Evangelical churches tried the service [Series Three], and found it congenial ... it made it possible to catch up with the liturgical movement and use a communion service regularly'.[7] Secondly, further encouragement was provided from 1971 by the Latimer House Liturgy Group. As we have seen, the

Group became independent of Latimer House in 1976 and renamed itself the Group for the Renewal of Worship. The Group brought together younger Evangelicals with an interest in worship. GROW's membership was continually open to change as some, having made their contribution, left and as other emerging Evangelical thinkers and writers on matters of worship were invited to join. Members of the Group wrote, commissioned, edited and generally oversaw the publication of the Grove Ministry and Worship Series which later became the Grove Worship Series. We have already seen how the backcloth to the series was the 'recovery of a healthy sacra-mentalism'.[8] The size, style and price of the booklets made them easily accessible and highly influential. The booklets assumed that the Eucharist would be playing a prominent part in the mainstream worship, and several offered ideas for its integration into other areas of the Church's life and ministry. A significant number dealt directly with Series Three, either commending its use or providing a variety of suggestions for its performance. The third factor which encouraged Evangelicals to give the Eucharist a more central place in their worship was the Charismatic Movement, with its potential for a robust eucharistic spirituality.

However, by 1977 the ideal of a weekly main service communion still had not received overwhelming support from Evangelicals and certainly had not been implemented in the majority of Evangelical parishes. Despite Trevor Lloyd's stance in favour of a weekly model in the preparatory material for the Nottingham Congress in 1977,[9] the Congress Statement wavered over the principle: 'we are equally divided over whether we should reaffirm (Keele Para 76) that the main church meeting on a Sunday should be Eucharistic in its worship'.[10] Its vision for Sunday worship, which emphasized the need for teaching, family worship and flexibility 'in pattern', suggested that the pastoral issue, rather than the theological case, was still the real blockage. At the end of the decade, Buchanan claimed that the situation was substantially the same: Evangelical reluctance to adopt the weekly model was caused by practical reservations, not by lack of theological conviction.[11]

By the late 1980s and early 1990s it had become clear that the case for a weekly main service pattern had not been thoroughly won in Evangelical circles and, indeed, that some of the ground gained was in danger of being lost. The reaction against the weekly model on the basis of pastoral and evangelistic expediency had become firmer and, in some cases, the theological misgivings were being stated more clearly. The conservative and more protestant end of the Evangelical world had by now regrouped and was reasserting its emphasis on the centrality of the Word rather than the frequency of the Sacrament, through the Church Society and the Proclamation Trust. Other Evangelicals, whilst affirming the importance of the Eucharist, were focusing their attention and energy on the urgent missionary needs of the country and commending appropriate steps to meet these which were not immediately compatible with a weekly pattern. In 1992, on the advice of GROW, Colin Buchanan attempted to halt the regression. He appealed to the corporate character of Christian existence and claimed that the Holy Communion was the Christ-given way by which the early Christians expressed, sustained and developed their common life. Once again he sought to convince Evangelicals that the Eucharist should be the central event of the local church's week, giving advice on how to manage the service in order that it may function effectively as 'the *place of meeting*' in which the people meet with God 'as they meet with each other'.[12]

Although pastoral and evangelistic concerns may help to explain the reluctance of some Evangelicals to adopt a weekly pattern, it seems entirely possible that the theological argument was not *sufficiently* convincing to make the necessary inroads into the pastoral hesitancy. It is at least worth considering that the theological case may have been too narrowly based on an appeal to community and that, in order to win over the 'Gospel and Bible people', a more wide-ranging attempt was needed – one which defined the necessity and centrality of the Eucharist on wider and deeper theological grounds.

THE INFLUENCE OF THE CHARISMATIC MOVEMENT ON EVANGELICAL EUCHARISTIC SPIRITUALITY

There is a somewhat ambivalent relationship between the Eucharist and the Charismatic Renewal. On the one hand, the historical precedent set by the fourth-century Messalians, the medieval Cathari and the Reformation Quakers suggests that the experience of renewal in the modern Charismatic Movement 'may be so firmly situated at the level of the *res* that the *sacramentum* may be underestimated'.[13] Displaying all the characteristics of Troeltsch's sect-type Christianity – immediacy of experience, lay initiative, small esoteric groups and spontaneous spirituality – the movement has been prone to the mentality which 'frequently ... replaces the ecclesiastical doctrine of the sacraments by the Primitive doctrine of the Spirit and by "enthusiasm"'.[14] According to the Roman Catholic Report, '*The Charismatic Renewal and Ecumenism* (1978),[15] some Catholic Charismatics, having received their experience in a non-sacramental context, have concluded that 'the church does not know where to locate the transforming power of God', and have become convinced that the focus should be transferred from the 'sacramental–liturgical life of the church' to 'individual religious experience'[16] – a tendency which various Roman Catholic (and Lutheran) guidelines on the Renewal have been concerned to correct.[17] Again, J. B. Hillyer's study of three Anglican Churches in Cambridge, reveals that, for some time, the Eucharist played only a very incidental part in the life of a Charismatic Church.[18] And during Josephine Bax's research into the Charismatic Renewal in the Church of England (1986), 'only one person actually alluded to the total experience of the Eucharist as an ongoing form of spiritual renewal'.[19]

On the other hand, it is often alleged by both observers and participants in the movement that a discovery or rediscovery of eucharistic experience is a common result of Charismatic experience.[20] Lutherans, Presbyterians and Anglicans admit to a new love for the Eucharist.[21] Roman Catholics describe a renewed sense of Christ's presence and desire to praise.[22] And the Report '*The Charismatic Movement in the Church of England*' (1981) identified a 'positive sacramentalism even amongst those who had previously been non-sacramentalist, or even anti-sacramentalist'.[23]

I would suggest that the cause of both the negative and the positive interaction is to be found in the structural relationship that may be identified between the Eucharist and Charismatic Renewal, in terms of the coincidence of certain dominant themes. The result is that the Renewal both creates the appropriate theological and experiential setting for the development of eucharistic piety and provides a non-sacramental alternative to the fulfilment of the same thematic concerns. In order to discern whether it has been a help or a hindrance to the development of Evangelical eucharistic piety I shall first discuss the central themes of the general movement of Renewal. I shall then identify their place in Evangelical Charismatic Renewal, at times comparing the effect of their presence on the traditional Evangelical terms of reference.

The Renewal

Epiclesis

Central to the Renewal is the experience of the power and presence
of God in a new way, often described as the baptism in, with, or of the
Holy Spirit. It is an experience which intensifies the individual's
awareness of the presence of Christ.

Sacrament

The encounter is always (in classic Assemblies of God Pentecostalism)
or often (in other Pentecostal and Charismatic circles) evidenced by
the sign of speaking in tongues, accompanied in time and in the
community of the Church, by several other manifestations of the
Spirit's work. The Roman Catholic Charismatic Simon Tugwell talks
of the 'sacramentality of speaking in tongues'. He claims that the
activity corresponds with the 'fullest catholic' understanding of a
sacrament: 'it is a human act given to men to do, in which however,
according to their belief, we may unequivocally and without reserve
identify an act of God himself'.[24] Charismatics display a 'gut level
understanding of created order'[25] and a holistic view of man.
Ignoring the Western dichotomy between matter and spirit, they
treat created material, bodily activity and suprarational mental
processes as means of worship and media of ministry.

Eucharist

From the experience of the *epiclesis* and sacrament, indeed often using
the 'sacrament of tongues', there emerges an invigorated desire and
ability to worship. Worship is seen as the priority of the Church and
is described in explicitly sacrificial terms.[26]

Anamnesis

The Charismatic Movement affirms the continuity of the forms of the
Spirit's work in the first century with his activity in the twentieth.
The saving work of God in Christ is not trapped in the historical past
or bound up in Scripture. However, neither is it transhistorical nor at
the discretion of the tradition. In this way, according to Peter Hocken
(another Roman Catholic Charismatic), the Movement 'manifests a
distinctive understanding of the relationship between the work of the

Spirit in the once-for-all event of Jesus Christ and the work of the Spirit in making that salvation present and effective in the course of history'.[27]

Ecclesia

The Baptism is often mediated by hands, the gifts are for the community, the worship is that of the Church, the Spirit's ministerial activity is for the body and the world: thus Charismatics discover that Christian existence is communal and are often surprised by the breadth of that community. In the immediate term at least, institutional and doctrinal differences are overcome by a deeper unity of the Spirit.

Charismatic Evangelicals and the Eucharist

Epiclesis and anamnesis

When comparing the most influential figures in contemporary Anglican Evangelicalism, Hopkinson makes use of the sociological method of identifying the 'evil' which the individual believes needs to be exposed.[28] Whereas for John Stott (who does not claim to be a Charismatic), the 'evil' is man's guilt before God, which may be met by the Gospel of the substitutionary death of Christ, for David Watson (who played a leading part in the Charismatic Movement), it is man's hopelessness in the face of the absence of reality – a condition which may be met by 'the concrete of the experience of God'.[29] These are instructive results which bear development.

The urgent priority of the Church for Watson was not, as it was for Stott, the informed preaching of the truth of Christ to the rational receptivity of the hearer; it was rather the recovery of the power of the presence of God (*epiclesis*), shown by the signs of the presence of his power (sacraments), leading to the praise of his people (eucharist) in their life together (*ecclesia*), thereby creating the experiential involvement of the individual with the person and work of Jesus Christ (*anamnesis*). It is this event of 'God revealing himself to Man'[30] which constitutes the Word of God, and as such, it cannot be strictly identified with the Bible or with preaching but may be mediated by the Spirit's use of a multiplicity of media.

Michael Harper passionately argued that the personal *epiclesis* is not an apostolic experience replaced now by apostolic teaching, but a fundamental datum of Christian existence. It is not an option. It is a necessity: 'The Pentecostal experience of the Spirit is not *a* way, it is *the* way for all God's people.'[31] However, in contrast to classic Pentecostalism, it is not, for most Evangelical Charismatics, a once-for-all event, but a repeatable experience, even a continuous state as one lives in openness to the Spirit.[32]

Evangelical Charismatics discovered that the activity of the Spirit in the present moment often occurred in a eucharistic setting. Watson detailed conversions, rededications, convictions of sin, healing and filling of the Spirit in the context of the Sacrament.[33] Green considered the Communion service to be the appropriate place for the exercise of spiritual gifts.[34] Similarly, David Pytches advised those who permitted the use of spiritual gifts to expect to see them manifested within the Eucharist.[35]

Nevertheless, although the Spirit has been seen as continually creating an *anamnesis* of Christ's historic work in the present life of the individual, and although it has been recognized that this encounter may occur in a eucharistic context, little attempt has been made systematically to relate the two in either theology or practice. For example, on the one hand, Watson allowed that in the Sacrament the believer 'not only remembers the once-for-all sacrifice ... in one sense he relives the events of the Upper Room and Calvary',[36] but on the other hand, he did not apply his widened definition of the Word of God to the eucharistic event and, further, in his various outlines for the development of personal spiritual growth, he did not even refer to the Eucharist.[37]

Sacrament

Following the Orthodox theologian Alexander Schmemann, Watson defined the Church as 'the sacrament of Christ's presence'.[38] It is through the quality of the Church's love and worship that the unbeliever may perceive a tangible manifestation of Christ's presence. David Gregg described how involvement with Charismatic Renewal led him to a sacramental world-view and then to a deeper appreciation of the centrality (and reality) of the Eucharist.[39] Harper made explicit the sacramental character of *glossolalia*: 'speaking in tongues is a sacrament, an outward and visible sign of an inward and spiritual grace'. It is a process which operates by 'transcending the intellectual process'.[40] Indeed, the sacramental principle has a more sinister side. Green described how evil influences may be transmitted by material objects.[41]

In comparison, non-Charismatic Evangelicals were either critical of the emphasis on the visible and tangible, or, in the end, regarded it as unnecessary. Stibbs and Stott stressed that the real evidence of the Spirit's work is not in miraculous manifestations but in moral change.[42] Packer's sympathetic appraisal of the Charismatic Movement still worked within an essentially dispensationalist philosophy, and thus he concluded by commending the inward and spiritual dimensions of the Movement whilst demythologizing its external phenomena.[43] This may help to explain the vast difference between Stott's understanding of the Sacrament as a rational reminder, a visual aid, appealing to the mind of the individual and therefore to be accompanied by the Word,[44] and Green's suggestions for the use of the Sacrament in the ministry of deliverance. The Eucharist, Green argued, will diagnose the demonized (who will literally not be able to receive the cup); it will cleanse a person and a place, and it will consolidate the ministry of deliverance by giving a 'tangible demonstration of the love of God'.[45]

Eucharist

Harper recounted how, as a direct result of his Charismatic experience, worship took on 'a priority it never had before'.[46] Watson was adamant that the offering of sacrificial worship is the primary task of the Church. It must precede its witness. Indeed, it should be seen as the correct setting for evangelism.[47] Again we see a significant reorientation of Evangelical tradition. The stress for Charismatics is on worship as ministry to God (eucharist) rather than as ministry to man (edification). Stott defined worship as the 'intelligent response to God's self-revelation'[48] (viewed in terms of history and Scripture). It is therefore impossible without preaching and involves as much announcement to each other as gift to God. But for Charismatics it is seen primarily as a 'spiritual sacrifice' and involves a much more intimate relationship between worship and proclamation: 'we not only talk about the magnificent banquet of the Gospel but let people experience it through the joyful and festive context in which the Gospel is proclaimed'.[49]

Despite the emphasis Charismatic Evangelicals have placed on worship, and the 'quasi-sacramental'[50] character of the worship they commend, there has been a reluctance to relate the Eucharist itself to the business of worship. At one point Watson even contrasted the worship occurring during a communion service with the Sacrament itself, instead of seeing both worship and Sacrament as one total eucharistic event.[51] It seems reasonable to suggest that at this point Charismatic Evangelicals remained thoroughly Evangelical in defining the Eucharist in manward terms: 'the Eucharist should be a declaration of God's agape not primarily a celebration of our love for God'.[52] Thus, the potential that their emphasis on worship offered to integrate the Godward and manward dimensions in the Eucharist was not fully realized.

Ecclesia

Although an ecclesiological emphasis was not new to the theology of modern Evangelicalism, it would be true to say that the experience of Renewal, and the ensuing contact which Charismatics have had with Roman Catholics, injected a fresh dynamic into their understanding of the Church.[53] They saw it as the setting for the real activity of the Spirit of the present Christ, in the life of worship, ministry and witness: 'it is through his Body, the church, that Christ today expresses himself to the world'.[54] It is significant that Watson's strongest words for the Eucharist were reserved for its corporate dimension. In his book on discipleship he did not refer to the Sacrament until he discussed the fellowship of the Church[55] and in his book on the Church, he affirmed that it is when the body of Christ comes together in love – as it does most clearly in the eucharistic context – that 'the life of the risen Christ will be manifested amongst us'.[56] Accordingly, the Peace became, as it did in the Renewal generally, a high point in Charismatic Evangelical Eucharists.

It is possible to discern a deepened eucharistic spirituality amongst Evangelicals as a result of their involvement in Charismatic Renewal. I would suggest that this is partly accounted for by the coincidence of structural themes in the Sacrament and the Renewal. However, the non-institutionalized alternative provided by Charismatic spirituality may have at points restricted the development of eucharistic piety. It also seems that the Evangelical tradition which Evangelical Charismatics have generally not discarded, may have added to the restrictive function by not providing the categories for the integration of the Renewal's subliminal sacramentalism into a full eucharistic spirituality. Both of these tendencies were offset, to some extent, by the authorization of the Series Three communion rite at a time when the Renewal was making great headway in the Evangelical world.

The service suited the 'modern' orientation of many Charismatics and gave them permission to be flexible and even spontaneous. It also lent them a liturgy in which many of their experiential priorities found an explicit form. It thereby offered the integrating facility that their theology was not always able to provide. In short, therefore, despite an element of negative feedback, the balance still remains firmly on the side of a positive interaction between the Renewal and the Eucharist in Evangelical circles.

This increased appreciation of the Eucharist was in part the result of the methodological shift which can be discerned amongst Evangelicals who became involved in the Charismatic Movement. First, Charismatic Evangelicals came to place a higher value on the role of experience. This is not to say that experience has been seen as a rival to Scripture but rather that it has been regarded as important theological data because it has provided helpful interpretative keys to unlock some of Scripture's hidden treasure. Secondly, they have come to see the Evangelical presentation of Christian life, and even the Evangelical heritage itself, as deficient in some areas and in need of addition. Consequently, a more eschatological, rather than definitive, concept of truth has emerged in which an ongoing dialogue between practice and theology is expected. This has been combined with an exposure to other dimensions of the Church – often in the context of worship – and a willingness to receive from them in the sure trust that the Spirit will lead them together into all truth.

THE CHARACTER OF EVANGELICAL EUCHARISTS

A study of the character of a worship event can be properly undertaken only by an analysis of the participants' perception of the event. A detailed attempt to do so is not possible in this context for the following reasons. First, it is beyond the parameters of the study. Restrictions on time and space have necessitated concentration on the theological issues involved, and where necessary, allusion to the effect of the historical context on their expression. Secondly, Pastoral Liturgical Studies, that is the attempt to identify the worshippers' experience of a liturgical event, is still an infant discipline. Its methodologies have not been sufficiently formalized to provide us with tested theological (rather than anthropological or sociological) techniques of analysis.

Nevertheless, one of its pioneers, Mark Searle, warns that we should not be so eager to uncover the psychological impact of a liturgical event that we miss its outward and visible aspects.[57] It is on this level of surface ritual that we do have evidence of the changing character of Evangelical Eucharists and thus the following analysis will concentrate on this level. Indeed, we would expect that by noting the external features, we may also glean a hint on the relationship between those outward forms and the inward reality which is, or is not, experienced through them. Such a relationship may be either on the level of expression – where the outward witnesses to a different perception – or on the level of education – where the outward creates a different perception. As a conclusion to this section and to the chapter as a whole, I shall comment on the deeper question of the relation between the practical changes in the Evangelical Eucharist (in terms of both 'centrality' and 'character') and the Evangelical theology of the Sacrament.

Liturgical ethos

In the early 1960s Evangelical celebrations of Holy Communion were marked by the same distinct set of 'liturgical identity symbols'[58] which had distinguished their Fathers from the ethos of most of the rest of the Church of England, as it succumbed, in one form or another, to Tractarian influence. For the majority of Evangelicals, by 1980 these recognition symbols had lost their power as a source of identity and précis of theology.

The North Side position was vigorously defended in 1963 by publications from the Church Society and the CPAS.[59] Both were aware that Evangelicals could well be attracted to the westward position (which was beginning to be popularized in other sections of the Church), and thus, as well as condemning the eastward position, they sought to discourage any flirtation with the western alternative. However, by the mid-1960s the tide had begun to turn. In 1966 the CPAS ceased to regard North Side as a necessary condition for the award of a grant for curates.[60] In 1967 the Keele Congress commended 'consideration of the westward position'.[61] A positive reply clearly followed, for by 1977, it was regarded as quite proper that the westward position should be used at the Nottingham Congress's own communion service.[62]

Traditionally, the question of the use of vestments had served to rally Evangelicals into an emotive defence of their fundamental theological and liturgical position. But the 1960s and 1970s saw it being pushed to the periphery. In an age of Evangelical commitment to the contemporary Church of England, rather than to its pre-Tractarian past, the battle was no longer considered worth fighting. Besides, as Evangelicals began to serve in non-Evangelical parishes they found themselves exchanging the scarf for the stole and even wearing full eucharistic vestments. Indeed, there is some evidence that Evangelicals, particularly Charismatics, were prepared actually to introduce the stole into definable Evangelical parishes.[63]

Similarly, a faithful use of the Prayer Book service, which had been a hallmark of Evangelical communions, gave way to an increasing use of the new services. Hopkinson has shown that the use of the new services has exposed Evangelicals to a much wider theological agenda than that set by the 1662 rite,[64] inevitably influencing – albeit implicitly – both the theology of the clergy and the experience of the laity.

Illustrative of the changing mood of the external features was the shift in title from 'Lord's Supper' to 'Eucharist'. Although the propriety of 'Eucharist' as a title had long been accepted by Evangelicals, their preferred description was the 'Lord's Supper' or 'Holy Communion'. But in Evangelical writing during the 1960s and 1970s (though not in Evangelical parishes) 'Eucharist' gained currency as the natural title.[65] No doubt this was due in part to its grammatical and ecumenical advantages over the other names for the Sacrament, but its adoption as the natural name may indicate that rather than thanksgiving being seen as one element occurring within the event, it came to be seen as an overarching category within which other elements take place. Whereas the primary emphasis had been on the Sacrament as an instructional event which, through its dramatic symbolism, communicates the meaning of Christ's body and blood, there was a developing understanding of it as a celebrational event, which provides the media for rejoicing in as well as learning about the present reality of the salvation won by the broken body and poured-out blood.

The character of the Evangelical Eucharist was affected – and would continue to be so – by four areas of influence. The first was political. As has been shown, a significant proportion of Evangelicals moved from a sect-type to a church-type mentality. Instead of seeking to recreate others in their own image, they committed themselves to the Church of England, and the Church at large, in its multifaceted form. Inevitably the process involved conceding the clarity of their distinct liturgical identity and compromising their immediate liturgical ideals for the sake of broader theological objectives. The second was sociological. Contemporary society was changing rapidly, and Evangelicals took the lead in adapting the face of worship accordingly. The third was theological. Worship ceased to be the Cinderella of Evangelical theology: the three decades of Evangelical life since 1960 have seen an unprecedented investment of Evangelical energy and time into reflecting theologically on the significance of worship and in responding to the fulfilment of its potential in the life of the Church. The essence of the Evangelical Liturgical Movement has been a reorientation of reference away from the received Evangelical tradition, and towards the renewal of the tradition according to the needs of the present. However, it would be wrong to give the impression of uncritical acceptance of current liturgical fashion. For example, the concept of the offertory and particularly the Offertory Procession received very little support from Evangelicals.[66] Although some writers were prepared to tolerate its use, they generally put up warning signs and, as we have seen, Colin Buchanan issued a substantial critique of its theological value and its historical pedigree.[67] Likewise, the practice of concelebration was viewed with considerable suspicion.[68]

The fourth influence was experiential. This operated on two levels. First, the Charismatic Movement reinforced the theological emphasis on the significance of worship. In broad terms, its major contribution was to translate the agenda of a minority of liturgically enlightened clerics into the desire of the laity. In specific terms, by creating a distinct liturgical ethos of its own, it shifted the centre of loyalty from a defence of an Evangelical form of worship, with one set of identity symbols, to the development of an Evangelical–Charismatic form of worship, which had its own set of characteristics. Secondly, as we shall see in the following section, the higher profile that the Eucharist gained in Evangelical circles affected Evangelical thought and practice in a significant way.

Liturgical theology

The Roman Catholic theologian Aidan Kavanagh has argued that the liturgical event itself is the true locus of theology. It is as the Church worships that it thinks:

> Theology on this primordial level is thus dialectic. Its *thesis* is the assembly as it enters into the liturgical act; its *antithesis* is the assembly's changed condition as it comes away from the encounter with the living God in Word and sacrament; its *synthesis* is the assembly's adjustment in faith and works to that encounter.[69]

The way some Evangelicals rethought their practice over the communion of the sick and the age of admission to communion, provides two areas of support for Kavanagh's claim.

In regard to the former, reservation of the elements was unacceptable to Evangelicals for a variety of reasons. It was assumed thereafter that the only acceptable way of providing for the needs of the sick was through a separate celebration. In regard to the latter, Evangelicals had been quite happy with the Anglican practice of regarding confirmation as the qualification for communion. Indeed, they were unhappy about the tendency to lower the age of confirmation below an age at which an independent profession of faith could be expected. However, partly through the experimentation occurring in other quarters of the Church but mainly through their renewed emphasis on the importance of communion and the frequency of 'main-service Eucharists', Evangelicals began to consider the use of extended communion and child communion.[70]

The Sacrament had always been seen as a sign of the unity of the body of Christ. But, as the Eucharist took on a more central place in Evangelical life, the belief moved from the notional level to the empirical (that is, it was found in experience to realize that unity) and therefore it began to be felt that the central, unifying event should be extended both to those who were absent through illness and to the young.

Evangelical theology had also always defined the Sacrament as a means of grace. But, again, as the Eucharist took on a more central place (and was thus experienced as a means of grace by the majority), demand grew for its provision for the sick and the young. Thus, rather than appealing to the theological principle enshrined in the Prayer Book's rubric for the Communion of the Sick (that is, that a sacramental context is not intrinsically necessary for the feeding on Christ's body and blood), some Evangelicals began to press for all to be regularly involved in the eucharistic means of grace. Both practices not only brought about a departure from the Evangelical tradition; they also involved a reorientation of the inherited theology. By lessening the emphasis on the didactic function of the Sacrament they implied a heightening of its objective capacity.

The approach may be contrasted with Roger Beckwith's attempt to correct Evangelical experimentation with both practices.[71] The essence of his argument was that sacramental participation is not a sufficiently important facet of Christian life to be made into a determinative influence on Christian theology. He argued that it is 'devout observance not weekly observance' which is really necessary to fulfilling the biblical ideal. And on this score, he considered both extended communion and child communion to be deficient. Indeed, he suggested that as God's grace is available through other means, admission to communion should await maturity, that is adulthood. Hence, whereas others were arriving at theological convictions through their experience of the role of the Sacrament in the life of their churches – or at least having their convictions reinforced by their experience – Beckwith was ensuring that his prior theological principle remained the sole influence on his practical policy. And the result tended towards the marginalization of the Eucharist.

Liturgical dilemma

A further area in which some Evangelicals had been reassessing their own practice of the Eucharist was the question of eucharistic presidency. Despite commitment to the priesthood of all believers, Evangelical tradition had remained, for reasons which were as much sociological and practical as theological, quite satisfied with the restriction of a eucharistic ministry to those ordained as priests. However, as the sociological and practical ground shifted, the theological issues began to be discussed.

The whole matter was raised in Evangelical circles during the response to the 1963 Report of the *Conversations between the Church of England and the Methodist Church*. Evangelicals supported the dissentients to the Report who defended the integrity and validity of the Methodist practice of lay presidency in certain controlled circumstances. However, it was not until the mid-1970s that there were significant signs of Evangelicals actively supporting and, in some cases, even campaigning for a limited form of lay presidency at the Eucharist. Peter Johnston in his presidential address to the Islington Conference in 1975 urged Evangelicals to 'give serious consideration to the question' and then elaborated on the theme in the following year.[72] In the preparation material for the Nottingham Congress, Trevor Lloyd floated the idea of home-group communions being led by lay people.[73] At the same time, he brought the debate to the pages of Grove Booklets, by editing and introducing a Liturgical Study which presented theological arguments for and against the issue (by Robin Nixon and Douglas Davies respectively), framed by a historical survey of Anglican practice by Colin Buchanan.[74] In 1983 and 1987 the question was debated by the Anglican Evangelical Assembly and both occasions resulted in an overwhelming majority in support of a motion for a controlled form of lay presidency.

Some of the impetus on the matter had come from Evangelicals serving in other parts of the Anglican Communion. Roger Bowen reported from Tanzania how thousands of Christians there were becoming increasingly impatient with a system which denied so many of them a regular experience of the Eucharist through a paucity of eucharistic presidents.[75] But it was through the experience of Evangelicals in Chile that the debate on lay presidency received an airing throughout the Communion and almost found its way into the text of the 1988 Lambeth Statement, as an issue at least worth discussing. As Brian Skinner, Bishop of the Valparaíso region, developed and implemented (in the late 1970s and early 1980s) the Church-planting policies of his former diocesan Bishop, David Pytches, he found that lay presidency had become an urgent need. New congregations were sprouting but were not sufficiently mature to produce ordinands. Hence, Skinner argued, without the authorization of appropriate lay people the new Christians would be starved of a frequent and regular eucharistic life. His active support for the idea of lay presidency took the issue to diocesan level for discussion and then, through the backing of the Bishop of Chile, Colin Bazley, to provincial level – where, at a Synod of the Southern Cone, a motion calling for an experimental period of diaconal or lay authorization was narrowly defeated.[76] However, since returning from Chile, Brian Skinner has again joined forces with David Pytches and together they have pursued the possibility of lay presidency in England through their ministry at St Andrew's Chorleywood. They have claimed that there is 'little justification on biblical or theological grounds'[77] for restricting eucharistic presidency to ordained priests, and have suggested that Bishops should respond to the needs of the time and modify traditional practices accordingly.

In summary, we may say that the pressure for the authorization of lay people in certain circumstances to preside at the Eucharist which has come from some Evangelicals has been driven by three factors. The first has been ecclesiological. Evangelicals have argued that as the Church is constituted by the people rather than the priest, and as the Eucharist is celebrated by the whole people of God rather than by individual priests, there can be no fundamental theological objection to allowing a suitably authorized member of the congregation to preside in the absence of a priest. The second factor has been one of spirituality. As Evangelicals have become more sacramentally conscious and have sought to integrate the Eucharist more fully into their life, the demand for the Sacrament has outstripped the supply of those able to provide the appropriate ministry. The third, consequently, has been one of practicality. In an age when the sacramental expectations of existing congregations are high, the number of clergy is falling and the missionary character of contemporary Britain is being taken with increasing seriousness (with even the call to plant new churches being heeded in many circles), some Evangelicals have found themselves unable to ignore the issue of eucharistic presidency.

This is very much the Methodist position though we see as a Connexional decision not just a local one.

CONCLUSION

As we conclude our study of Evangelicals and the Eucharist from the early 1960s, it is worth underlining the considerable changes that have taken place in their attitude to the Eucharist. The minister standing at the North End at the beginning of the 1960s, canonically dressed and reciting the Prayer Book's Prayer of Consecration to the faithful worshippers who had stayed behind after the main service, could still be found at the end of the 1980s, but by and large, he and they had been replaced by congregations who expected the Eucharist to play a central role in their worship, and who enjoyed the form and flexibility of ASB Rite A, even experimenting with alternative patterns (both those suggested by the Liturgical Commission and those devised by themselves). Many Evangelical congregations had also created a whole new setting for their worship in terms of the use of buildings and music and the development of symbols and style, which made their sacramental life look, sound and feel very different from that of thirty years earlier. And many individuals and some congregations were calling for communion to be extended to the young and absent and for the Eucharist to be celebrated in contexts where the ministry of an ordained priest was unavailable. The sixteenth century had seen a momentous change in eucharistic life in a similarly brief period, effected by the Reformation. The eighteenth century had also witnessed a massive change over a short time-span through the Revival. And now in the twentieth century, Evangelical eucharistic life has experienced another profound change during the renewal of its life and fortunes.

An important summary.

PART III

Theological analysis

CHAPTER 12

The Eucharist as sacrament

As was established in chapter 1, the challenge to Evangelical sacramental theology is to identify the real value of the Eucharist over and against that of hearing and believing the Word. By this we mean: what is the real value of the Sacrament if, in Calvin's words, 'Christ was given to us by God's generosity to be grasped and possessed by us in faith',[1] or indeed in Paul's words, 'faith comes from what is heard, and what is heard comes by the preaching of Christ' (Rom. 10: 17)?

The problem is encapsulated in Augustine's exegesis of John 6: 29): 'Believe and thou hast eaten.'[2] We have seen it running throughout the stages of Evangelicalism's history. In the sixteenth century Luther admitted that he could 'hold Mass every day, indeed, every hour' by feeding on the words of Christ.[3] Zwingli was quite sure that 'when Christ referred to eating his flesh and drinking his blood he simply meant believing in him as the one who has given his flesh and blood for our redemption and the cleansing of our sins'.[4] Calvin, like Zwingli and Cranmer, saw the Words of Institution recited in the Eucharist as 'living preaching which edifies its hearers, penetrates into their very minds, impresses itself upon their hearts and settles there'.[5] In the seventeenth century, despite the deep regard for the Sacrament amongst the Puritans, the real heart of their encounter with the Gospel lay in their experience of the effect of preaching. In the eighteenth century some of the Moravians pushed the dilemma to a crisis, by insisting that if Christ is to be received by faith, then even the preaching of the Word is an unnecessary attempt to mediate God's free salvation. They were preceded by the seventeenth-century Quakers and succeeded by the twentieth-century Charismatics in their tendency to bypass the usual means of grace. Finally, much nineteenth-century and twentieth-century Evangelical theology emphasized the priority of the Word to such an extent that the Sacrament was forced into practical redundancy. In Evangelical polemic, the Prayer Book's caveat for anyone for whom reception of the Sacrament was impossible was often quoted as the first principle of sacramental theology:

if he do truly repent him of his sins, and steadfastly believe that Jesus Christ hath suffered death upon the Cross...he doth eat and drink the Body and Blood of the Saviour Christ profitably to his Soul's health, although he do not receive the Sacrament with his mouth.[6]

Of course, Evangelical theology was not content merely to live with the problem. It sought to solve the problem by establishing an integrated relationship between Word and Sacrament. However, we have also seen that the historical context in which the attempt was made, often militated against the practical expression of the theoretical interdependency between the two. Hence, Evangelical sacramental history has often been marked by the anomaly of allowing a relatively high potential to the Eucharist in Evangelical theology, whilst restricting it to a relatively low place in practice. For example, the Puritan rediscovery of preaching, and its desire for the authenticity of the local congregation, displaced the Sacrament from the importance ascribed to it in its theology. Similarly, J. C. Ryle's reaction to Tractarianism led him to omit almost all but the most negative reference to the Eucharist in his seminal work on *Holiness*. This was despite his belief that in the Sacrament we meet a special presence of Christ. Finally, Roger Beckwith's crusade against both the new services and the drift of contemporary Evangelical theology and practice did not give the impression that he was committed to the principle of a weekly main-service Eucharist and even led him to recommend that reception of the Sacrament await adulthood. This was despite his rich theology of the Eucharist as a post-sacrificial feast in which we maintain and renew our part in God's covenant.

However, as this study has shown, in those times when Evangelicals have felt less pressure to defend their cause and constituency, the theological tension between evangelical theology and sacramental spirituality has had a less restrictive effect. For example, the freedom in thought and expression created by the confidence of Evangelicalism before the rise of Tractarianism and Liberalism allowed the

Eucharist to be described as 'the nearest approaches to the Divine Presence, our state in this world admits'.[7] And the open mentality of contemporary Evangelicalism produced by the Ecumenical Movement, the Charismatic Movement and by its own political confidence has enabled Evangelicals to rediscover their sacramental heritage and thus to release the Eucharist from its practical marginalization and polemical qualifications.

Nevertheless, even at those times when the historical context has been at its most hostile and Evangelical theology at its most precise, the Eucharist has retained a unique hold on devotional life. In the middle of his Reformed interpretation of the presence of Christ in the Eucharist, Calvin admitted that his mind was 'overcome by the greatness of the thing' and that ultimately, all he could do was 'to break forth in wonder at the mystery, which plainly neither the mind is able to conceive nor the tongue confess'.[8] The magnificence of John Owen's preaching and the power he experienced in prayer did not detract from his belief that in the Sacrament 'there is an eating and drinking of the body and blood of Christ, with a spiritual incorporation ensuing, which are peculiar unto this ordinance'.[9] Finally, as has been noted, Ryle's antipathy towards the priority given to the Sacrament in Tractarian theology and Ritualistic practice did not stop him claiming that every 'believing communicant' would 'find a special presence of Christ in his heart, and a special revelation of Christ's sacrifice of his body and blood to his soul'.[10] The task of this chapter is to account for this experience of the Eucharist amongst some Evangelicals as a unique (even the highest) means of grace, in terms which coheres with the Evangelical experience of justification by faith. However, before doing so, some preliminary comments should be made on the doctrine of justification by faith.

First, as we saw in chapter 1, faith is simply the acknowledgement that it is God who saves and the acceptance of the salvation he freely gives. The doctrine's apparent emphasis on faith is merely a deflected emphasis on grace. The doctrine claims that without an acknowledgement of helplessness (faith) there cannot be the knowledge and experience of God's helpfulness (grace). A fuller précis of the doctrine is the reminder to the Ephesians that it is 'by grace you have been saved through faith' (Eph. 2: 8). And, as the Epistle makes abundantly clear, both are a 'gift of God' – that is the faith to receive is as much a work of God as the giving of the grace.

Secondly, Evangelical theology has always framed the doctrine of justification by faith within certain qualifications. The first is that it cannot be divorced from works. Faith may not be the result of works but it must result in works – for 'faith apart from works is dead' (Jas. 2: 26). The second is that it cannot be dislocated from the Church. As Calvin made clear (echoing Cyprian), the Church is Mother to those for whom God is Father – 'for there is no other way to enter into life unless this mother conceive us in her womb, give us birth, nourish us at her breast'.[11] The third is that it cannot be distanced from the sacraments. Even during the heated debates of the nineteenth century, Dimock was able to say that 'there is a teaching of Sacramental Grace, which may be regarded as the true comp- lement of the doctrine of Justification by Faith, in so much that there is danger, at least, of that doctrine being made to be, in a sense, maimed and incomplete without it'.[12]

LEX ORANDI AND *LEX CREDENDI*

The attempt to account for the unique experience of the Eucharist turns on the crucial question of the relationship between experience and doctrine. As we saw in chapter 11, Aidan Kavanagh has argued that the event of worship is the raw material out of which Christian theology is formed. Indeed, for Kavanagh it *is* theology in its most primary sense. It gives birth to theology in the secondary sense of reflection on and adjustment to the encounter with God in worship.[13] In a related way, Geoffrey Wainwright describes worship as 'a source of doctrine in so far as it is the place in which God makes himself known to humanity in a saving encounter'.[14] However, he insists that the raw material must be smelted by the three tests of 'origin' (dominical, apostolic and scriptural), 'spread' (historical and ecclesiastical) and 'ethical correspondence' (ability to create a holy Church and just society). He envisages a dialectical relationship between worship and doctrine in which the teaching function of the Church both learns from the experience of worship and corrects any developments which 'distort the true faith'.[15] He is critical of Kavanagh for not providing the necessary criteria for deciding whether a religious experience is a genuinely Christian experience.[16]

However, the relationship between experience and doctrine in Evangelicalism, which was outlined in chapter 1, is actually more intrinsic than Wainwright allows. Rather than an external dialogue between two separate orders of knowledge, it is an internal conversation within the dynamics of the one evangelical event. A glance at the Orthodox perspective on the relationship between worship and doctrine provided by Alexander Schmemann[17] will help to clarify what is meant by this 'internal conversation'. Like Kavanagh, Schmemann believes that the law of prayer establishes and constitutes the law of belief. However, like Wainwright, he is concerned to set up the critical criteria by which contemporary – and traditional – elements in the life of prayer may be judged. In contrast to Wainwright, his tests are not external theological principles, but rather develop out of the essence of the law of prayer itself. In short, he seeks first to uncover the original *lex orandi* and then to use it to criticize later Orthodox liturgical practice.

Schmemann's academic method corresponds with what happened existentially in the Reformation and in the Revival. The genuine freeness of the apostolic experience of God's grace was realized afresh in the subjective depths of individual lives. It then became the hermeneutical key which unlocked the treasures of Scripture and the liturgical impulse which sought, in Wainwright's term, doxological expression. Therefore, the authentic evangelical criterion by which we may judge whether a religious experience is a genuinely Christian one may be defined as the extent to which it coheres with the fundamental apostolic experience of the Gospel – which itself is grounded in the recognition that it is 'by grace you have been saved through faith'.

It follows that the relationship between the apostolic experience of the free grace of God in Christ and the apostolic experience of the Eucharist is of key interest. If we can indicate a correspondence between the experience of the Eucharist as unique in Evangelical tradition and the apostolic experience of the Eucharist, then we have gone a considerable way towards justifying the claim that it should be dogmatically and practically treated as, in Wesley's words, 'the grand channel of God's grace'.

THE APOSTOLIC EXPERIENCE OF THE EUCHARIST

Clearly we cannot here attempt a detailed study of the place of the Eucharist in the New Testament. However, by focusing on the Lucan narrative of the resurrection appearance on the way to Emmaus and the Johannine discourse of the bread of life, we will be able to point to some significant connections between the apostolic experience of the Gospel and the apostolic experience of the Eucharist.

Luke 24: 13-35: the road to Emmaus

We must first face the disputed question of whether Luke is actually referring to the Eucharist when he talks here, and in Acts, of the breaking of bread. Much recent study and commentary (for example, Cullmann, Leaney, Jeremias, Tinsley, Marshall and Schweizer)[18] would agree with Fitzmyer's conclusion that 'we are clearly confronted here with an abstract way of referring to the Eucharist, which was current in Luke's time'.[19] The view held by some (for example, Geldenhuys and Morris[20]), that Luke is merely describing an ordinary meal and intending no eucharistic associations, seems to be short-circuited by the generally accepted links between the fellowship meals which Jesus shared with his disciples during his ministry, the occurrence of several resurrection appearances in the context of meal times and the apostolic meals in which bread was broken with great joy.

The exact connection between the joyous meals recorded in Acts and the formal celebration of the Lord's Supper recorded by Paul has given rise to elaborate theories on the origins of the Eucharist. For example, Lietzmann, Lohmeyer, Bultmann and Cullmann[21] have claimed that there were originally two types of Church meals which, at a fairly early stage (pre-Pauline), were fused into one sacramental ritual. We do not need to be detained by an analysis of the accuracy of the two-meals theory.[22] The important point for our purposes is that the fellowship meals at which the early Christians broke bread, cannot be seen apart from the pre-resurrection meals with Jesus and the resurrection appearances which occurred at meal times. The intimacy of the disciples' table-fellowship – culminating in their profound experiences in the last of these – was the precondition for their recognition of his resurrection appearances in the context of a meal. Both were the precedents for their enjoyment of his presence as they broke bread with 'glad and generous hearts' (Acts 2: 46) in the early life of the Church. And all three were framed by the ultimate expectation of sharing in the fullness of the eschatological banquet at the Messiah's *parousia*. The question of whether these joyous meals recorded in Acts were theologically and liturgically related to the

Last Supper from the beginning, or whether the connection was made at a slightly later stage, is a relatively academic point. For all practical purposes, it seems difficult to deny that from the earliest moment, the breaking of bread would have been surrounded by associations which would have included the most significant meal the disciples shared with their Master on the night in which he was betrayed.

Having established the validity of treating the breaking of bread at Emmaus as a clear eucharistic reference we may now make two points about the implications of the story. First, it would seem that the Emmaus incident complements the narrative of the Last Supper. The death predicted by Jesus in the Supper has been overcome by the reality of the resurrection made known at Emmaus. There is now no need to look 'sad' (v. 17), for the one who had been 'condemned to death, and crucified' (v. 20) is known to be risen from the dead – not just on the basis of hearsay, but through personal historical contact. Secondly, the method of the contact is by an interdependent combination of word and act. The recognition of Christ in the breaking of the bread is based on a realization of the true nature of the Messianic mission as revealed by the unfolding of the Scriptures – 'Was it not necessary that the Christ should suffer these things and enter into his glory?' (v. 26). But although the word warmed their hearts it did not open their eyes. It was not until 'he took the bread and blessed, and broke it, and gave it to them' (vv. 30–1) that the stranger's real identity, and accordingly, the full reality of the Gospel of which he spoke, was grasped in the depths of their beings.

Morris speculatively suggests that they recognized Jesus when he broke the bread, not because of the sacramental associations of the action, but because they saw in his open hands the scars of his death.[23] His theory may owe more to poetic licence than to historical certainty, but it does capture something of the feel of the story. However, his distinction between the sacramental action and the sight of the scars seems to miss the point that the whole meaning of Jesus' action at the Last Supper was to present a tangible form of the reality of his death. Hence, as the four actions are repeated at Emmaus, the word of the Gospel spoken from Scripture is made concrete with the bread, so that (as Schweizer says) 'his word takes the form of visible gift'.[24]

The significance of these points is reinforced once critical questions are asked about the reasons for the form of the narrative and the

Not original
&
Morris.

' *the dear to know of his*
passion

redactional motives operating in Luke's way of telling the story. It is not possible to pursue these in any detail except to make the following two observations. First, it seems highly unlikely that the narrative has not been shaped by the apostolic experience of the Eucharist as the fulfilment of their pre-Easter times with Jesus around his table – particularly their memory of the last of these. The Eucharist therefore cannot be defined merely by reference to the Last Supper – it must include the joyous meals which celebrated the saving presence of the living Christ amongst them as they broke bread together. Secondly, the apostolic experience of God's saving grace in Christ was mediated by the interdependent function of Word and Sacrament. It seems difficult to deny that Luke's purpose is to underline the belief that although Christ's visible presence is no longer to be found amongst his people, he still makes himself known to their hearts and eyes by the proclamation of his Word in the Scriptures and the celebration of his action in the Eucharist. However, although Word and Sacrament are interdependently related, the making known of the risen Christ through them appears to be a cumulative process. Luke seems to be reflecting the experience that the fullest apprehension of the reality of God's grace in the crucified and risen Christ is to be expected when the proclamation of the Word is consummated in the breaking of the bread: 'the evidence of the Emmaus story suggests that the meal with the accompanying apostolic teaching was regarded as an occasion when the Lord was especially present'.[25]

John 6: 25–59: the discourse on the bread of life

As with the Emmaus story it has long been a matter of dispute as to whether the discourse on the bread of life actually refers to the Eucharist. However, it is now generally accepted that the discourse falls into two parts. In the first (vv. 25–50), symbolic and sapiential categories are prominent: Jesus is described as the bread of life in whom we must believe. In the second (vv. 51–9), sacramental categories are dominant: the bread is said to be Christ's flesh and we are told that his flesh is to be eaten.

Again, elaborate theories have been developed to explain this structure. Bultmann believed that the sacramental section is a later interpolation by an ecclesiastical editor who wanted to correct an (alleged) anti-sacramental strain in the Johannine Gospel.[26] Brown also argues against the unity of the passage but he claims that the sacramental section is an authentic Johannine discourse deriving from a later stage of the Johannine tradition.[27] Its insertion was designed to develop the implicit eucharistic references in the original discourse. Others have argued for the unity of the passage (for example, Hoskyns, Cullmann, Jeremias, Dunn, Lindars, Barrett, Marshall and Heron[28]), whilst Schnackenburg has preferred to present an impartial exegesis rather than dictate an answer to the question.[29]

Our concern is not so much with the validity of the various theories on the origin of the passage, as with the light its final form sheds on the relationship between the apostolic experience of the *kerygma* and the apostolic experience of the Eucharist. To this end, it is Hoskyns's conclusion that sapiential and sacramental themes interpenetrate throughout the discourse, which gives us our most helpful starting point. Dunn, Marshall and, to a lesser extent, Barrett, confirm his thesis in a negative way, by their claim that John's aim was to correct current automatic notions of sacramental efficacy by an emphasis on the necessity of faith. Schnackenburg, Dodd and, to a lesser extent, Lindars, confirm it in a positive way, by their claim that the discourse as a whole unites faith in Christ and reception of the Sacrament in a dialectical relationship so as to underline the necessity of both.

Clearly there is a strong temptation for critics to be drawn into a hermeneutical circle in which dogmatic presuppositions determine exegetical conclusions. However, I would suggest that Hoskyns, Brown and Schnackenburg do the greatest justice to the discourse as a whole. They see the discourse as reflecting the nature of the apostolic experience of the crucified and risen Christ: 'The two-fold form of the Bread of life Discourse represents a juxtaposition of Jesus' two-fold presence to believers in the *preached word* and the *sacrament* of the Eucharist.'[30] However, as Schnackenburg shows, the inter-penetration is even more complex than this suggests. The essential themes of the sapiential section – union with Christ by faith – are also the underlying themes of the sacramental section. Hence, as at Emmaus, the Word has priority because it makes known that in the initiative of the Father (v. 38) Christ's death is to be the source of salvation (v. 51) to those who participate in him by faith (v. 47).

Nevertheless, this Word does not exist alone. It finds (following Hoskyns) 'concretion' in the Eucharist. The same bread of life made known in his life-giving Word (v. 63) is so identified with the bread of the Eucharist that for those fulfilling the one contextual condition of faith the two become one. As they share in the earthly bread so they participate in the bread of heaven. And as they begin their part in the eschatological life of heaven in the present, so the fullness of their share in its complete manifestation in the future is assured – 'and I will raise [them] up at the last day' (v. 40). The interpenetration of the sapiential and the sacramental themes ensures that, on the one hand, the Eucharist is not seen as the only means of union with the saving presence of Christ but, on the other, it is seen as a particular form in which Christ makes himself available to those who are drawn to him by the Father.

We may go further and say that once the importance of the Eucharist is recognized in the weekly, even daily, life of the early Church, the internal movement of the discourse becomes clearer. Jesus' description of himself as the bread of life, who must be eaten, could not fail to be related by the first Christians to those times 'together ... with glad and generous hearts' (Acts 2: 46) when Jesus was known to be amongst them, not just as the one who breaks the bread, but as the one who is the bread: 'Now as they were eating, Jesus took bread, and blessed, and broke it, and gave it to the disciples and said. "Take, eat; this is my body"' (Matt. 26: 26). Hence, because of the Eucharist's liturgical centrality and experiential reality, it was inevitable and quite natural that all that Jesus said of himself as the bread of life should be applied to the Eucharist – and not merely in terms of 'a vivid picture of what it means to receive Christ by faith',[31] but as the context in which participation in him was found to be most fully realized.

WORD AND SACRAMENT

We are now in a position to examine the relationship between Word and Sacrament in a more systematic way. To this end it will be helpful first to compare the approaches of Edward Schillebeeckx and Karl Rahner to the question and, secondly, to explore the way the issue is handled in the theology of Thomas Torrance.

Schillebeeckx begins with a definition of Christ as the 'sacrament of the encounter with God'.[32] He means by this that, as 'the humanity of Jesus is concretely intended by God as the fulfilment of his promise of salvation',[33] it is only as we participate in that humanity that we meet the salvific grace of God and become '*filio in*

Filio.[34] However, because of the present invisibility of his body to us, the heavenly Christ works out that salvation through the presence and actions of the Church. The Church, therefore, may be said to prolong the 'function of the earthly body of Jesus',[35] both by being its 'visible manifestation'[36] and by doing a series of actions which are to be identified as the 'personal saving acts'[37] of the heavenly Christ in a visible, tangible and historical form. He defines these actions as the traditional seven sacraments of the Church. However, he sees the Eucharist as qualitatively superior for the reason that in the other sacraments 'Christ is present only in virtue of his redemptive *act* sacramentally embodied',[38] whilst in the Eucharist his person is really present by means of the change in the elements. This is not to say that Christ does not make himself present through the other sacraments, but that in the Eucharist Christ makes 'himself present *in* the gift of the holy bread'.[39] The result is that 'there is in the Eucharist, as distinct from the other sacraments, a specific earthly real presence of Christ',[40] In short, Christ is present in the Eucharist in a unique 'level of ontological density'.[41]

He regards the role of the Word in the sacramental event as decisive. It is only as the liturgical word is added to the liturgical action, that a 'sacramental realization of Christ's personal act of redemption'[42] actually occurs. However, the Word is defined in terms, on the one hand, of the corporate faith of the Church and, on the other, of the consecratory petition for the real action and – in the case of the Eucharist – the real presence of Christ; it is not seen as itself a dynamic act of God on the hearer.

In contrast, Rahner sets out to recover an understanding in Catholic theology of the Word as itself a revelatory event, that is, 'the presence of the act of God's salvation of men in the Church'.[43] This concept of the 'actualizing word' derives from Rahner's fundamental theological principle that God's uncreated self-communication has entered our history in the self-transcending humanity of Christ;[44] it also leads to his doctrines of the Church and the sacraments. The Church is defined as the 'primary sacrament'[45] because in its 'concrete reality' it is the 'permanent sign' of the offer and acceptance of that self-communication in grace.[46] In its life of prayer, preaching and sacraments, the 'word of salvation'[47] makes present the reality of God's self-communication in varying degrees of 'concentration and intensity'.[48] Its fullest forms of realization occur in the sacramental context, for it is here that the efficacious word of

God reaches its 'unambiguous, historical and ecclesiological presence' in its 'embodiment and eschatological absoluteness'.[49] However, both the non-sacramental word and the sacramental word
spoken outside the Eucharist are merely 'preliminaries and echoes'[50]
of the eucharistic Word of God, because it is this Word that makes, 'in
actual reality', 'the crucified and the risen Lord and his whole work
of salvation present in the Church'.[51]

Three comments could be made from the perspective of Evangelical theology on the understanding of the relationship between
Word and Sacrament presented by Schillebeeckx and Rahner. First,
Evangelical theologians would detect the use of artificial distinctions
both when Schillebeeckx distinguishes between the act of the person
of Christ through the sacraments and the reality of his presence in the
Eucharist, and when Rahner distinguishes between the partial self-
communication through the non-eucharistic word and the 'actual
reality' of his presence in the eucharistic Word. They would suspect
that an unnecessary distinction in the theological assumptions is
driving a wedge between the act of Christ and the presence of his
person. Indeed, they may even wonder whether the exclusiveness
posited to the Eucharist is derived from the dictates of the doctrines
of the real presence, rather than from the demands set by the
characteristics of the relationship between Christ and his people.
They would want to stress that the Word must be seen in all its
Christological and soteriological fulness. Its content is the Word who
was made flesh and who gave himself as a ransom for many. The
making known of this grace in preaching (and in the other ministries
of the Church) is the making known of Christ himself. And the
receiving of this grace by faith is the receiving of Christ himself.

Secondly, Evangelical theologians would question Schillebeeckx's
restriction of the identity between the act of Christ and the act of the
Church to the sacraments. They would agree with Rahner that the
Church's prayer and preaching also coincide with the eternal action
of the Son. However, they would want to question why the act of
preaching should not be included in his definition of a sacrament, in
that it is an ecclesial event, uttered in eschatological seriousness in a
historical context. They would say to both Schillebeeckx and Rahner
that, on the basis of their definition of a sacrament, they have not too
many but too few sacraments. In short, they would argue that their
understanding of a sacrament relates more to the spectrum of the
valid ministries of the Church than to its officially defined sacraments.

Thirdly, Evangelical theologians would also wonder whether, in the strong identity claimed between Christ and the Church (particularly in Schillebeeckx), the role of the vicarious humanity of Christ, as the bearer of our salvation, is being displaced by an over-emphasis on the institution of the Church and an under-emphasis on the Spirit as, in Calvin's phrase, the 'bond of connection' between ourselves and the distanced humanity of Christ.

Nevertheless, despite these reservations, the following elements in their analyses are helpful pointers to the solution of our immediate problem (that is, to explain and justify the experience of the Eucharist as the highest means of grace). The first is their concern to ground the Sacrament in the salvific event of Christ and, therefore, to ensure that the categories employed are fully personal ones. The second is their understanding of the Eucharist as a real act of the living Christ on the basis of his past history and in the context of our present history. The third is their appreciation that this happens in the Church and by means of the Church. The fourth is their insistence that because of the incarnational, historical and ecclesiological character of God's salvation, the event in which it meets us cannot be merely existential, inward and individual but must be manifested, experienced and expressed in tangible, visible and concrete forms. The fifth is Rahner's delineation of different phases in the life of God's gracious Word which involve it in varying degrees of realization and intensity.

These same five emphases are present in the theology of Thomas Torrance but they are framed in such a way as to avoid the criticisms noted above.[52] First, Torrance roots the Eucharist in the person of Christ in his saving act: 'the mystery of the Eucharist is not any mystery of the Eucharist itself but the paschal mystery of Christ which he set forth in the Eucharist for the participation of all who believe in him'.[53] Christ is the 'all-inclusive Sacrament'.[54] The Word has united himself to the world in the flesh of Christ and so provided a place in the spacio-temporal life of man where the eternal God can be met and known.

Secondly, Baptism and the Eucharist are the appointed contexts where God's interaction with time and space in the person and work of Christ are manifested in analogical expression. For example, just as the Word took flesh so, in the Eucharist, he makes use of an action with bread and wine to give a real participation in that flesh, hence 'we may say that as God and man are united in the God–Man in such a way that the two natures may not be identified with or separated from each other ..., so the sacraments involves [*sic*] on another plane, in conditions of this fallen world, a like union between divine action and human action'.[55]

Thirdly, this union between the '*actio* of Christ Jesus and the *re-actio* of the Church'[56] means that the Church is to be regarded as the 'visible counterpart of the resurrection-body of Christ'.[57] The Church embodies and ministers the *kerygma* of God's real presence with mankind in Jesus Christ. At the same time it must be underlined that the act of the ascended Christ in the life of the Church and in the chosen context of the Eucharist takes place in the power of the Spirit: 'the risen and glorified Christ, in accordance with his specific appointment in the Eucharist, comes to meet us in the Spirit'.[58]

Fourthly, the Incarnation decisively means that any hint of dualism between the spiritual and material is foreign to the Christian understanding of the relationship between God and the world. Reflexively, the Eucharist witnesses to God's real involvement with the creatureliness of man. As the miracles of Jesus acted out his words, so the sacraments manifest 'in deed and in power'[59] the reality of the Word made flesh.

Fifthly, it is this 'twofold event of *kerygma*'[60] in word and act which allows Torrance to define the uniqueness of, first, the sacraments (that is, Baptism and Eucharist), and then, because of its continuing rather than once-for-all character, the Eucharist. He says that the '*kerygma*' is in the fullest sense the sacramental action of the Church through which the mystery of the Kingdom concerning Christ and His Church, hid from the foundation of the world, is now being revealed in history'.[61] The 'mystery hidden' is the reality of God's ontological involvement with creation in the person of Christ. The kerygmatic word is the announcement of this ontological relationship with humankind in Christ by the preaching of the Church demanding the response of faith. But it is a word caught in eschatological tension – for it is not until the future that the content of the Word (that is, the real involvement of God with the world) will be fully manifested. The present is the time for 'repentance and decision'.[62] Nevertheless, just as Jesus gave signs of the Kingdom's presence in his earthly ministry, so he gives to us today signs or partial revelations (Baptism and Eucharist) of that same Kingdom present and active in our midst. Baptism, therefore, is the proleptic presence of the eschatological *kerygma* as 'real act in time, as Word–deed'.[63] Similarly, the Eucharist briefly and provisionally transcends the eschatological divide. And it allows us to participate in the future reality of the Kingdom, not just once, but repeatedly, for 'every time we communicate is eschatological time until we drink it anew in the Kingdom of God'.[64]

These five aspects of the sacramental theologies of Schillebeeckx and Rahner on the one hand, and Torrance on the other, help to explain the experience of the Eucharist as a unique moment of Christ's activity in the Church, and to justify the claim that it should be treated theologically as such. Essentially they are statements about God's relational and redemptive dealings with humanity in his Word who became flesh and who gave his life as a ransom for many. They may be summarized in the following way. First, God has saved us by assuming humanity and then living its life and dying its death: 'This is my body which is given for you' (Luke 22: 19). Secondly, salvation is applied by the ascended Christ in his presence amongst us by the power of the Spirit: 'Do this in remembrance of me' (Luke 22: 19) because 'You heard me say to you, "I go away, and I will come to you"' (John 14: 28). Thirdly, salvation is made known in and through the Church. Indeed, it is this very calling to hear and bear this salvation which constitutes the Church: 'Because there is one bread, we who are many are one body, for we all partake of the one bread' (1 Cor. 10: 17). Fourthly, salvation is manifested in act as well as in word:

When he was at table with them he took the bread and blessed, and broke it, and gave it to them. And their eyes were opened and they recognised him; and he vanished out of their sight. They said to each other, 'Did not our hearts burn within us while he talked to us on the road, while he opened to us the scriptures?' (Luke 24: 30–2).

Fifthly, salvation is the reality of the new age which is proleptically present in the old age: 'for I tell you that from now on I shall not drink of the fruit of the vine until the kingdom of God comes' (Luke 22: 18).

This correspondence between the soteriological event of Christ and the themes of the Eucharist has two consequences. First, the Eucharist may not be seen in exclusive terms. It is a function of God's relational and redemptive word of grace in Christ (the Word who became flesh and who gave his life as a ransom for many). It does not give a

different gift from the other functions of the word of grace – for, as
Torrance stresses, the gift cannot be separated from the giver. In all
the functions of the word, Christ is given to the receiving faith of the
participants. Even the sacramental and eschatological dimensions
cannot be restricted to the Eucharist. Baptism and other forms of
ministry and mission act out the Gospel. The signs of the eschatological Kingdom in Jesus' day may also be present in our own.
Indeed, following Rahner, we may see the preached word as both an
act and an eschatological sign. However, the second consequence is
that the Eucharist may be considered in inclusive and intensive
terms. It includes in 'awesome simplicity'[65] the essential features of
the Gospel. As such it may be described, with Gregory Dix, as the
representative Christian act.[66] Like the view from the peak of a
mountain, it tells the whole of the story which is assumed or told only
in part elsewhere. And like the hub of a wheel it is the centre from
which all else around draws strength. It may also be described (with
Leslie Houlden) as the expressive Christian act.[67] It is the appointed
place at which the past, present and future of God's dealing with man
in Christ come to clear, concrete and climactic expression.

   The Eucharist therefore may be compared with the hopes of a
playwright for the communication of his ideas. The play may be
experienced in its read form, or in its heard form or even in its
discussed and debated form, but the playwright intends it to reach
embodiment, tangibility and visibility on the stage before an
audience which does not merely spectate but is engaged by the action
in such a way that it truly participates, and even itself becomes part
of the action. The same ideas are there at each stage of the
presentation of the play, but it is only in the acted form that they reach
the fulfilment of expression for which they were intended. In a similar
way, a loving relationship may move from friendship to courtship to
marriage in an ever intensifying attempt to realize its own commitment to love. It is the same love present in the feelings of love and
in the affections of love but it is not until its consummation in the act
of love that it reaches its fullest expression.

   I am not therefore claiming that the Eucharist provides an
exclusive ontological reality but rather suggesting that it is given a
unique functional force and, thereby, a level of ontological intensity
not ordinarily to be found in the other moments of Christ's activity in
the Church. It is this understanding that both accounts for the
positive element in Evangelical eucharistic devotion from the

Reformers to the present day and coheres with the fundamental features of Evangelical theology. It is not a new contention. It was voiced in 1589 by the Scottish Presbyterian Robert Bruce:

It is certainly true that we get no new thing in the Sacrament; we get no other thing in the Sacrament, than we got in the Word. For what more would you ask than really to receive the Son of God Himself...If you get him, you get all things with him. Your heart cannot imagine any new thing beyond him. Why then is the Sacrament appointed? Not that you may get any new thing but that you may get the same thing better than you had in the Word...that we get a better hold of Christ than we got in the simple Word...That Christ might have more room in which to reside in our narrow hearts than he could have by the hearing of the simple Word, and that we may possess Him more fully, it is a better thing.[68]

CHAPTER 13

The Eucharist as presence

Christian faith rests on the reality of Christ's presence with his people: 'I shall not leave you as orphans; I shall come to you' (John 14: 18); 'For where two or three meet in my name, I am there among them' (Matt. 18: 20); 'And look, I am with you always; yes, to the end of time' (Matt. 28: 20); 'Look, I am standing at the door, knocking; If one of you hears me calling and opens the door, I will come in to share a meal at that person's side' (Rev. 3: 20).[1]

The tragedy of Evangelical eucharistic theology is that whilst it has used well its positive resources for affirming the reality of Christ's presence in other spheres of its spirituality, when it has approached the Eucharist it has, at times, turned those resources into polemical negations which have seemed to reduce the reality of the eucharistic presence. For example, the radical commitment to justification by faith in Evangelical theology has too often been used as a means of locating the heart of the eucharistic action in the subjective depths of response, and too seldom as a means of underlining that all the Eucharist requires of us is that we welcome the objectivity of God's grace in the gift of Christ's presence to us. Similarly, the seriousness with which it has taken the ascension, the stress it has laid on the role of the Spirit and the theological discipline with which it has awaited the *parousia*, have too often been used as devices for emphasizing the restrictions on the presence of Christ's humanity and too seldom as affirmations of the possibility of a real participation by all flesh in the humanity of Christ in anticipation of the fullness of the eschatological life.

What is needed is not an abandonment of the traditional axioms but rather their reorientation to that point at which they no longer function primarily as negative limitations but can be seen to be positive strengths – that is, strengths which are not merely stated (for that is not to rise above the polemic), but are actively developed in the direction of the fullest affirmation of the reality of the presence of the Christ who fulfils his promise to be with us always. In the limited space available I can do no more than indicate the lines along which the traditional Evangelical concerns for the role of faith in the eucharistic event and the place of the humanity of Christ in the eucharistic presence may be developed.

FAITH AND THE EUCHARISTIC EVENT

In chapter 12 we focused the fundamental character and content of the Eucharist in Christological and soteriological terms. As we turn to the nature of Christ's presence in the Eucharist – surrounded as it is by scholastic (Protestant as well as Catholic) controversy – it will be vital to carry this principle with us as the basic criterion of analysis. It is no more than the Pauline identification of the core of eucharistic theology and experience as 'participation in the body and blood of Christ'. As we saw in chapter 2 it is the route Calvin encouraged all sides of the Reformation debate to travel: 'the primary question in fact is: How does the body of Christ, as it was given for us become ours? In other words, how do we possess the whole Christ crucified and become partakers of all his blessings?'[2]

It is the emphasis to which modern Roman Catholic theology seeks to direct its own Church: 'the first truth of Eucharistic doctrine is, "This is my body", not "Here I am present"' (Rahner).[3] And in turn it is the key with which Reformed theology has tried to enter the inner chambers of the doctrine of transubstantiation: 'Reformed theology does better to recognise gladly what, with all its problematic aspects, [the doctrine of transubstantiation] is attempting to affirm – that in the Eucharist Christ makes himself present to us, and gathers us with him into the presence of the Father' (Heron).[4]

This is not to say that the problems have been resolved and that, for example, Rahner and Heron would agree over the nature of the eucharistic presence. Roman thought is merely seeking to re-express the doctrine of transubstantiation in categories which make contemporary sense; it does not want to abandon the doctrine. Reformed theology is still critical of the underlying philosophical and theological grammar which means that the literal (rather than analogical) identification of the sign and the signified is left intact in the new translation.[5] However, the shift in emphasis away from either the causal efficacy of the rite itself or its effect on the participants, towards the fact of the salvific encounter with Christ's presence in the Eucharist, means that there is a common concern to rediscover and re-express the real heart of both the doctrine of transubstantiation and the Reformers' reaction to it – that is, the reality of God's saving gift of Christ's presence to his people.

General framework : grace – faith – Church

How then (following Calvin) do we 'possess the whole Christ crucified'? At first sight the Evangelical answer appears quite simple – 'by faith'. However, as Wesley had to prove to the Moravians and as we saw in chapter 12, the dynamics of the Gospel are more complex than the exclusive reference to faith allows. In order for God's salvation in Christ to be received through faith it must be given by grace, that is its objective givenness precedes its subjective acceptance. It is not summoned by faith, it is a summons to faith. Further, in order for this exchange of giving and receiving to occur it must be contextualized in the being and activity of the Church. The gift of grace cannot be received until it is made known by the Church. And the receiving of the gift is identical with entry into the Church. As the epistle to the Ephesians makes clear, in God's work of salvation by grace through faith he is creating a holy temple in which he lives and acts, so that 'through the Church, the principalities and rulers should learn how many-sided God's wisdom is, according to the plan he had formed in all eternity in Christ Jesus our Lord' (Eph. 3: 10–11).

It is important to make clear that the saving presence of Christ is the content of each stage of the process – in the giving of the grace, in the receiving of the grace and in the contextualizing of the exchange in the being and act of the Church. As Torrance continually stresses, grace is not an intermediate realm of divine activity which bridges the gap between God and the world, but rather the gift of Jesus Christ, who is himself 'the one place appointed by God... where heaven and earth, eternity and time, God and man fully meet and are forever united'.[6]

The role of faith is to take us into this 'place' where we may meet with God's real presence and saving action. But Torrance underlines that faith is merely the way by which we enter into God's ontological relationship with humanity and humanity's ontological relationship with God which has been effected in Christ. It is the door, not the building; it is the wedding not the wife – for through the 'relation in faith' we move into the 'relation in being' with Christ. He appeals to Calvin's distinction between the act of faith and the union and communion with Christ which is the result of faith:[7] 'For even though the apostle teaches that "Christ dwells in our hearts through faith", no one will interpret this indwelling to be faith, for through this believers gain Christ abiding in them.'[8] In fact, Torrance takes us two stages further back. He claims that we have an ontological relationship with Christ through the fact of the Incarnation and that this is extended to us for our participation in the ways he has appointed. But he is clear that it is only when we receive that gift through faith that Christ dwells in our hearts and unites us in a personal participation in his new humanity.

This brings us back to the discussion in chapter 2 on Luther's understanding of faith. It was noted that for Luther faith is not in itself the medium between the individual and God but rather the willingness to acknowledge and accept Christ as that medium. Once it has been established that faith is the active recognition of the mediatorial role of Christ, the next step is to identify the ways in which he has chosen to communicate the reality of his mediation to our faith.

As Luther affirmed, the Church must be seen as the context in which this exchange takes place. The Epistle to the Ephesians describes the Church as Christ's body which is being built up by him through works of service so that it will attain the 'whole measure of [his] fulness' (4: 12–14). The Church is therefore constituted by an ongoing spiral of Christ's presence and act which will reach its culmination eschatologically when the Church's unity with him will be fully achieved. But in the mean time the principles on which this future reality rests are present and active: we are already seated with Christ in the heavenly places, already inhabited by him in his Spirit and already receiving his ministry and doing his work.

Eucharist: presence – form – faith

We are now in a position to relate this general framework more directly to the Eucharist. The ecumenical debate over the nature of Christ's presence in the Eucharist has been greatly helped by the recognition that – as it is put in the Lima Statement – 'Christ fulfils in a variety of ways his promise to be with his own even to the end of the world.'[9] Vatican II identified some of the modes in which Christ is present:

> Christ is always present in his Church, especially in her liturgical actions. He is present in the sacrifice of the Mass...By his power he is present in the sacraments, so that when a man baptises, it is really Christ himself who baptises. He is present in his Word, since it is he himself who speaks when the holy Scriptures are read in Church. He is present lastly, when the Church prays and sings for he promised 'where two or three are gathered together in my name, there am I in the midst of them'.[10]

Some of the 'non-liturgical' actions in which Christ is present in a specific way for a certain purpose may be seen as the missionary proclamation of the Word (Luke 10: 16; Matt. 28: 19–20); as the ministry of acceptance, love and compassion to the 'least of his brethren' (Luke 9: 41; Matt. 25: 31–46); as times of weakness, persecution and pain (Acts 7: 54–60; 2 Cor. 12: 7–10) and as the individual's prayer behind 'closed doors' in which his participation in the prayer of Christ brings him into a new intimacy with the Father (Matt. 6: 8; Rom. 8: 34; Heb. 4: 14–16).

The contemporary concept of the modes of Christ's presence is not dissimilar to Luther's relational understanding of God's omnipresence:

> It is one thing if God is present, and another if he is present for you. He is there for you when he adds his Word and binds himself, saying, 'Here you are to find me'...Just as I say of the right hand of God: although this is everywhere, as we may not deny, still because it is also nowhere, as has been said, you can actually grasp it nowhere, unless for your benefit it binds itself to you and summons you to a definite place.[11]

Luther identified this 'place' as the humanity of Christ – it is here that we will 'surely find him'. However, just as the right hand of God is ultimately to be defined in relational rather than spatial ways, so Christ's humanity is to be sought only in those settings where he has willed himself to be accessible. We may also detect a relationship between the contemporary notion of modes of presence and Wesley's defence of the means of grace as designated settings in which we are to 'wait' for the act of God's grace upon us: 'I exhorted the society to wait upon God in all his ordinances; and in so doing to be still, and suffer God to carry on His whole work in their souls.'[12] It is in the various contexts which God has set that he gives the saving presence of his Son to our receiving faith.

Luther's concept of multivolent presence, Wesley's commitment to

the means of grace and the current affirmation of the modes of
Christ's presence may be seen as ways of underlining the facts, first,
that grace precedes faith, (that is, it evokes apprehension and is not
evoked by apprehension, thus ensuring that the giving is really free
and not manipulated), and secondly, that the gift of grace is
contextualized in certain ecclesial settings (that is, the content of
grace is linked to a form in which it is made available).

Torrance defines the 'eucharistic form' of Christ's presence as the
'particular empirical form in which [Jesus] has promised as the risen
and glorified Christ to meet his people in the closest and most
intimate way'.[13] We have seen that his claim has a great deal of
support in the Evangelical tradition. We saw it eloquently expressed
in the Wesleyan hymn:

> It seem'd to my Redeemer good
> That faith should *here* His coming wait.
>
> The prayer, the fast, the word conveys,
> When mixed with faith, Thy life to me;
> In all the channels of Thy grace
> I still have fellowship with Thee:
> But chiefly here my soul is fed
> With fulness of immortal bread.[14]

However, we have also seen that when the anatomy of the
encounter has been dissected, certain potentially negative features
have at times emerged. First, the heart of the eucharistic action is
often located in the subjective depths of response (faith) rather than
the objective heights of gift (grace). For example, John Owen based
his sense of a 'special communion' with Christ on the Eucharist's
ability to activate faith in Christ's saving death in a particularly
intense way.[15] Similarly, for the eighteenth- and early-nineteenth-
century Evangelicals, the Eucharist involved a 'peculiar union with
Christ which no other means of grace is designed to convey',[16]
because it is 'peculiarly calculated to increase faith'.[17]

The problem is that when the critical action is seen to be occurring
subjectively, the specifically eucharistic form of God's grace may be
undermined as the mechanics of the saving exchange of grace to faith
are seen to be exactly the same as in any other context. By this we
mean that if the way the Eucharist works is by awakening faith in
Christ's broken body, then it may be asked how the Sacrament of
Christ's death differs from the sermon on the meaning of Christ's
death. To the traditional Reformed response that the one makes the

Gospel known in a visible way, whereas the other makes it known in an audible way, it may be asked how the eucharistic bread differs from the crucifix (or even the empty Cross), or from the mystery play (or a passion scene from Zeffirelli's *Jesus of Nazareth*), or from any other form of visual aid. After all even a hot cross bun refers the recipient to the Cross of Christ and may lead to feeding on Christ by faith with thanksgiving.

The liturgical implications are that for all the emphasis in Evangelical theory on reception as the high point in the Eucharist and on the Sacrament as a sign of grace, in practice, the giving of grace to faith may take place at whatever point in the rite at which the individual makes his own authentic, believing remembrance of Christ's death, and thus the Sacrament becomes in its essence an act of faith. This is exactly the problem Dix identified in Cranmer's theology and saw embodied in the 1552 rite – 'This is what it all came to in the end – the bread had nothing to do with the body.'[18] In other words, if the essential eucharistic action occurs as the individual remembers and believes in Christ's death, and thereby feeds on him by faith, then the external eucharistic rite and particularly the elements are ultimately superfluous, for the same action can take place without them. Dix went on to say that Cranmer's failure to create a rite in which the communion in Christ's body and blood was intrinsically related to the receiving of the elements was not a fault of his liturgical skill, which was of the highest order, but of his commitment to the doctrine of justification by faith, which simply made the attempt to do so inherently impossible.

It needs to be said that Dix did not appreciate that Cranmer and Calvin were clear that the Sacrament is grounded in the objectivity of God's grace and that this grace is contextualized by Christ's promise that he will seal the grace of the Gospel by means of the Sacrament. Nevertheless, whereas for Luther the promise was attached to the elements so that they became the place at which the ever present Christ could be 'caught and grasped',[19] for Cranmer and Calvin, the promise was directed to the participants, so that rather than changing the status of the elements, it preached the Gospel to those who would hear. Hence – and here we see the penetration of Dix's critique – the door was left open to the subjectivization of the eucharistic action and to the minimization of the specificity of the eucharistic form of God's grace. As was observed in chapter 4, if we believe the Word as it is preached by the liturgy, why do we need to bother with the bread? Indeed, if the Word can be heard outside the Eucharist, then why bother with the Sacrament itself, except perhaps for reasons of dutiful obedience?

In chapters 3 and 4 we saw how Anglican and Puritan theology did not rest content with the legacy it received from the Reformers. In an intuitive way it recovered the notion of an objective consecration and restored it to an essential role in the action. By the 'setting apart for a holy use' they saw the elements being taken into the purposes of God to be used by him as instruments of Christ's presence. As a result of the consecration they believed that the elements were united in a sacramental relationship with the body and blood of Christ so that – as Lewis Bayly put it – they became 'in the act of receiving ... one and the same thing'.[20] Similarly, Wesley was quite clear that the Spirit's work in the act of consecration made the elements 'glorious instruments Divine':

> The outward sign of inward grace
> Ordained by Christ receive:
> The sign transmits the Signified
> The grace is by the means applied.[21]

I would suggest that the notion of an objective consecration enables Evangelical theology to hold the bread and the body together, because it ensures that in this particular context faith cannot find a way to the content except through the form in which it is being communicated. In this way the role of the elements is not just to affect the individual's faith, it is to effect a union with him by communicating the gift of Christ's saving presence. They do not merely help the participant to meditate on the life-giving significance of the Cross, they actually mediate that reality to him. The bread has everything to do with the body because Christ has promised that in this context, the material of bread and wine will be the form through which he will give himself to his people and unite them with him in ever increasing degrees of depth. Therefore, with Torrance, we may say that 'apart from the specific form commanded and to which the promise has been attached we cannot conceive or receive the reality'.[22] This is not to fetter faith or control grace; it is simply to direct faith to that setting at which grace is being given.

Having established the objectivity and contextualization of the eucharistic reality we must now move on to consider in more detail the way in which the gift given becomes the gift received. To do so is not to undermine the objectivity of the gift or its givenness in this particular context; it is rather to underline that the content of the gift is the person of Christ and not an intermediate influence or effect which he extends to us. If, therefore, Christ does not greet us from afar but actually comes to meet us in the Sacrament, then we cannot fail to ask relational questions about how we respond to that meeting.

Roman Catholic theology has been involved in a reconsideration of the relational dimension of the Eucharist as a result of its recognition that the natural philosophical categories in which the doctrine of transubstantiation has been expressed are no longer coherent in the contemporary age. Charles Davies regards the 'basic defect of Scholastic theology' to be that it 'considers transubstantiation simply as an event in the physical world, even though not at the perceptible level, without reference to the interpersonal and sacramental encounter with Christ to which it properly belongs'.[23] Although Scholastic theology did not actually define Christ's presence in spatial terms, its first and major concern was to prove the presence of Christ in the elements as an independent datum, rather than to consider the purpose of Christ's action in the Eucharist and then from that develop an understanding of the reality of his presence. It is a methodology which, as Schillebeeckx shows, contemporary Catholic theology has tried to reverse: 'We no longer say, "Christ is there", without saying for whom he is present.'[24] Indeed, Catholic theologians have accused the doctrine's traditional presentation of producing various spatial ramifications in theology, liturgy and devotion.[25] For example, it implied a disjunction of Christ's presence in the elements from his presence in the Church and the individual; it led to the emphasis on the consecration to the neglect of the communion; and it encouraged a piety of the Tabernacle and so deflected attention away from the real purpose of the presence, which is to develop the believer's union with Christ.

Therefore, in their attempt to re-express the inner meaning of the doctrine of transubstantiation, modern Catholic theologians have emphasized the difference between a spatial and a personal presence, noting that 'mere physical proximity, for example, of one human being to another does not constitute personal presence'.[26] Piet Schoonenberg has drawn attention to the 'lonely crowd' experience in which, though surrounded by people, one may be quite isolated and alone. The relational absence of one person to another, despite their spatial contiguity, can be overcome only if the individuals move towards each other to interact on a personal level. The movement must be reciprocal in order for an authentic personal exchange to take place. The willingness of subject 'A' to be known will be frustrated if subject 'B' is not open to the possibilities of the encounter, for 'the complete personal presence is that which is both given and accepted'.[27]

Schoonenberg also makes the point that whereas spatial presence either occurs or does not occur (that is, either one is there or one is not), personal presence involves degrees and gradations – and, further, it may be effectively communicated by various signs. He defines the Eucharist as the way in which Christ unfolds his personal presence with the Church in its corporate whole and individual parts, through signs which, in their deepest reality, become the gift of Christ's presence: 'The Eucharist begins with a *praesentia realis* ... and its aim is to make this presence more intimate.'[28] But for this process both to occur and to reach its intended completion, the assent of the Church and of the individual is required. This is not to say that the faith of the Church or of the individual creates the reality but that, as Schillebeeckx shows, the new meaning that Christ attaches to the elements and the use he makes of them can be perceived only by the faith of the Church and received only by the faith of the individual:

What, then the 'faith of the Church' realises in the coming about of Christ's eucharistic presence as a sacramental offer, the faith of the individual realises in his personal acceptance of this offered presence. The Church's relationship within the Covenant with Christ realises the 'sacramental sign', whereas the individual's personal attitude in faith within the believing community realises his personal involvement with the Covenant.[29]

Thus, as the Church gathers around the Lord's Table in remembrance of him, believing that this is no ordinary meal in which bread and wine are for the nourishment of the body, but is truly the Lord's Supper, in which bread and wine are a 'participation in the body and blood of Christ', we are confronted with the ontological reality of Christ's gift of himself which we may either welcome by faith or reject to our judgement. To welcome the gift by faith means that we must be open to the unconditional terms on which the gift is given – to come 'not with any works, or powers, or merits of one's own, but by faith alone',[30] as Luther said. And as we do so Christ will dwell in our hearts.

THE HUMANITY OF CHRIST AND THE EUCHARISTIC EVENT

Participation in Christ's humanity

If the Epistle to the Ephesians unambiguously affirms that we are saved by grace through faith, and if it shows that this happens as grace is contextualized in the life of the Church, it is no less clear that a real participation in the permanent humanity of Christ is the beginning, middle and end of the salvation which God graciously gives to our receiving faith in the life of the Church.

It is the beginning because in his body and through his death Christ has created a new humanity which is reconciled to God and at peace with itself (2: 13–18). It is the middle because by the renewal of the Spirit we are enabled to 'put on the New Man that has been created on God's principles' (4: 22–6). We are now 'parts of his Body', united to his flesh and being looked after and fed by him with the same affectionate intimacy with which a husband cares for his wife (5: 28–33). It is the end because God's purpose will be finally fulfilled when we 'reach unity in faith and knowledge in the Son of God and form the perfect Man fully mature with the fullness of Christ himself' (4: 12–13).

The radical and absolute way God has committed himself to working out our salvation through the Incarnation means that the presence of his fullness to us (3: 19) is a consequence of the presence of Christ's fullness to us (1: 22–3). And what is true of God's relation to people is true of his relation to the whole cosmos. It is through Christ's filling of all things that 'everything in the heavens and everything on earth' will be brought together to the praise of God's glory (3: 10; 1: 10).

As we saw in chapter 2, the passion of Luther's eucharistic theology stemmed from his incarnational theology which refused to allow humanity any point of access to God except through the man Jesus Christ, and him crucified: 'I do not know of any God except him who was made flesh, nor do I want to have another. And there is no other God who could save us, besides the God Incarnate.'[31] If the discussion had remained on this soteriological level the Lutheran–Reformed divide may have been avoided. But it went beyond the soteriological statement to spatial speculation, from grace to geography, from the open road of the question 'What is Christ's humanity doing now?' to the cul-de-sac of 'where is Christ's humanity now?' It led to the

Lutheran use of the *communicatio idiomatum* to prove the omnipresence of Christ's humanity and to the Reformed *extra Calvinisticum* to distinguish the fixed proportions of the human Christ from the omnipresence of the divine Word. The tragedy of the divide is that they were not in fact disagreeing over the permanent significance of the Incarnation; they were just debating the theological parameters of the doctrine. The result was that they deflected theological attention and theological resources from their agreement over the central beliefs that we cannot come to the Father except through the Son, and that we cannot receive the Spirit except through the Son, and that we cannot participate in the Son except by being incorporated into his new humanity.

It is out of these central beliefs that the doctrine of the eucharistic presence must be developed. It needs to be stated with absolute clarity that we deal with the whole Christ in the Eucharist. We relate to the person of Christ in his divine humanity, his deified corporeality and his God–man entirety. To try to identify the metaphysical characteristics of that participation and to isolate the conditions differentiating the mode by which the humanity is present to us from the mode in which the divinity is present to us belongs to scholastic schematizing, not to Evangelical reflection on the Gospel of the Word who became flesh and gave his life as a ransom for many. We do better to align ourselves with the reluctance of seventeenth-century Anglicanism to plumb the depths of the mystery of Christ's presence to us: 'Do not say with the Capernaites, Master, how comest Thou hither? But with the disciples be glad thou dost enjoy him.'[32]

However, there are certain soteriological characteristics which do need to be respected and reflected in our understanding of the nature of our participation in Christ's humanity. They tend to be stated negatively and so cloud the reality of Christ's presence with us by a series of qualifications such as 'It is not like it was' and 'It is not like it will be'. Our task will be to agree fully with the truth of both of these statements but in such a way that their positive value – that is, their capacity for affirming the reality of Christ's presence with us in the time between the ascension and the parousia – can be seen clearly.

The three characteristics we shall examine correspond to the three moments (beginning, middle and end) of our participation in the humanity of Christ which were identified in the Epistle to the Ephesians. The first is the ascension. The Christ who fills all things is also the one seated at the right hand of the Father in heaven (Eph. 1 : 20). The authentic human presence of the crucified and risen Christ before the Father must be expressed in any doctrine of his presence with us. The negative side of this is that clearly Christ is not present with us now in the same way as he was with the disciples – even in the resurrection appearances. That dimensional presence cannot be diffused into an omnipresence without compromising the authentically human characteristics of the risen Christ, and so displacing the presence of the new humanity before the Father by the presence of a new being who no longer coheres with us because he no longer shares the distinguishing features of what it means to be human.

However, the positive side is that the distance between us and the dimensional presence of Christ is not intended to take Christ from us but to give Christ to us. The new humanity may still have dimensional characteristics consistent with the old, but it has participatory potential far exceeding the old. Whereas we had a racial relationship with the first Adam through our common humanity, we have an ontological and personal relationship with the second Adam. He not only assumes our humanity but actually lives in us and unites us with him in the new humanity he has created. Whereas the old man takes us out of the garden of God's presence, the new man fills us 'with the utter fullness of God' (Eph. 3: 19). That Christ might live in us and that we might participate in his oneness with the Father was the prayer he could pray only on the eve of his going away, because it is only through his glorification in the Cross, resurrection and ascension, that we can be with him where he is (John 17: 24). In his early ministry he could show the disciples the Father only through his presence. In his heavenly ministry he unites us to the Father in his presence.

All this, of course, would not be possible without the second characteristic of our participation in the humanity of Christ, which is that he lives in us by the Father's Spirit (Eph. 3: 16). This is to say that the mysterious unity by which we are made one flesh with Christ does not rest on the proximity of the physical contact between Christ's dimensional presence and ours, but on the transcendent initiative of the Father in which he gives him to us through the immanent action of his Spirit. It is by the work of the Spirit that we may 'put on the New Man that has been created on God's principles' (Eph. 4: 24) and so participate in an intimacy with Christ's flesh that not even the beloved disciple knew as he reclined on Jesus' chest – for why else would he have told him and the others that their sadness at his leaving at the Cross would be overtaken by their joy at his coming in the Spirit (John 14: 18; 16: 22)?

The third characteristic of Christ's presence with us is set by the eschatological perspective of Christian experience between the ascension and the *parousia*. We have not yet reached the 'unity of the Son of God' and so have not yet been formed into 'the perfect Man fully mature with the fullness of Christ himself' (Eph. 4: 13). We have not yet grown completely into Christ by being built up in love (Eph. 4: 15–16), because we are not yet in the age of the rule of love. Indeed, although all things have been put under Christ's feet, he has not yet brought them together under his headship (Eph. 2: 22; 1: 10). We must therefore distinguish between the form of Christ's presence with us now from the form of Christ's presence with us at the *parousia*. But this is not to doubt the reality of his presence with us now; it is merely to say that there is more to come.

The *parousia* must not be seen only in terms of the fullest manifestation of Christ's presence but also in terms of the effect that it will have on us. In Romans 8 Paul pictures the Church groaning with the whole of creation for the revealing of the children of God, for then our bodies will be set free to share fully in the pattern of humanity which Christ, our elder brother, has set. In 1 Corinthians 15 he pictures our natural (mortal) bodies 'putting on' the spiritual (immortal) body of the heavenly man. The end, therefore, will manifest Christ's humanity to us in the fullest way not only because, at his *parousia*, we will see him 'face to face' but because we ourselves will be changed in the 'twinkling of an eye'.

Participation in Christ's humanity at the Eucharist

The participation in the humanity of Christ which we are given at the Eucharist must be seen from the perspective of the connection between the Cross and the ascension: 'But God, being rich in faithful love, through the great love with which he loved us, even when we were dead in our sins, brought us to life with Christ... and raised us up with him and gave us a place with him in heaven, in Christ Jesus' (Eph. 2: 4–6). The dual reference which the Eucharist has to the Cross and the ascension has been inscribed in the eucharistic liturgy from its earliest days. Thanksgiving is made for the death of Christ by the people whose hearts and minds are with Christ's ascended presence in heaven. The dialectic is clearly present in Calvin's theology. For him the Eucharist both 'sends us to the Cross'[33] and directs us to the real presence of Christ before the Father. Similarly the two themes are woven closely together in Torrance's thought. He sees Christ coming to us in the 'form of his humiliation' because 'it is precisely there, at the Cross, that the risen and ascended Lord comes to meet us that we, united with him through communion in his body and blood, may be lifted up with him into the highest in the power of the resurrection and exaltation, and worship the Father with, in and through him'.[34]

However, there is a tendency amongst Anglican Evangelicals to focus on the Cross rather than the ascension – on proclaiming his death as the beginning of our salvation rather than on celebrating and deepening our participation in his presence before the Father as the ongoing experience of our salvation. Hence, the elements are seen as symbols of the crucified body and blood of Christ rather than as the gift of his glorified presence. Of course, it must be said that to be confronted by the Cross in such a way that we grasp its meaning is no less than to receive the whole person of Christ in all the fullness of what he is doing for us now. Nevertheless, it still needs to be said that Christ's death makes sense only from the perspective of the ascension. The death of the man on the Cross could have been a death for our sins only if that same man now lives for ever with God (Rom. 6: 10). Accordingly, we proclaim Christ's death in the Eucharist in order to announce that the old humanity has died its God-forsaken death and that a new humanity has been perfected which has the right to live in the presence of the Father. The proclamation tells us that the place we have before the Father has been paid for by Christ's death but that it must be occupied by a participation in his ascended life. It is therefore Christ's presence that we meet in the Eucharist as he comes to us, in the *anamnesis* of his crucified form, to show us that we 'being dead to sin' are 'alive to God' in his glorified form (Rom. 6: 11). The eucharistic gift is then a real participation in the glorified life of Christ which he lives in the presence of the Father. It is to be met by the response of Thomas who, after he had touched the body that was once broken and the side from which blood once flowed, cried 'My Lord and my God'. The one difference is that our response is made in the confidence that we are more blessed than he because we have believed without seeing. In other words, we have not just met the dimensional presence of the risen Christ; we have been indwelt by his personal presence as the ascended Lord.

Our participation in the ascended Christ at the Eucharist is made possible by the work of the Spirit. In saying this, there is no implication that the Spirit is a substitute for the presence of Christ. Rather, as Calvin said, he is the 'bond of our participation' with Christ, the one who conveys the full reality of the ascended Christ to us, and as the Epistle to the Ephesians states, the one who enables us to 'put on the New Man...created on God's principles, in the uprightness and holiness of truth' (Eph. 4: 24).

Calvin's emphasis on the role of the Spirit effecting our participation in Christ's humanity helps to explain why he was so dissatisfied with the Augustinian equation – which had been exploited by Zwingli – between believing in Christ's death and eating Christ's flesh. Calvin wanted to distinguish the act of faith in Christ's death and the ongoing participation in his life, which he saw as the result of faith:

In this way, the Lord intended, by calling himself the 'bread of life', to teach not only that salvation for us rests on faith in his death and resurrection, but also that, by a true partaking of him, his life passes into us and is made ours – just as bread when taken as food imparts vigor to the body.[35]

His concern was to avoid the juridical and external description of our relationship with God to which the doctrine of justification by faith is prone. He wanted to show that, as well as being put right with God by faith in his crucified body and blood, we are gradually recreated by him through an ongoing participation in depth with the glorified body and blood of Christ.

In chapter 3 we saw the same concern operating in Hooker's theology. He experimented with ways of integrating Catholic notions of imparted righteousness with the Reformation principle of imputed righteousness. Whereas justifying righteousness is applied through our faith in Christ's crucified body and blood, sanctifying righteousness is created in us as we are united more and more to the living humanity of Christ. It is here that the Eucharist plays its vital part because its function is to unite the whole being of the believer to the whole being of Christ, for 'these holy mysteries received in due manner impart unto us even in true and real though mystical manner the very Person of our Lord himself, whole, perfect and entire'.[36]

In chapter 5 we found a similar concern at work in Wesley's refusal to isolate justification from sanctification. He believed that accompanying the sinner's justification by faith is the different but complementary gift of the new birth. In the former one's status is changed through faith in Christ; in the latter one's state is changed through the work of the Spirit: 'Justification implies only a relative, the new birth a real change. God in justifying us does something for us, in begetting us again, he does the work in us.'[37] However, although Wesley saw the new birth as simultaneous with justification, he was clear that the real change which it creates is not a realized change until the believer is so united with Christ that he loses the desire to sin. Wesley believed that the Eucharist exposes us to the grace and demand of the Cross with such intensity that it unites us to Christ in a unique degree of intimacy. He therefore regarded it as the most effective means available not only for maintaining the state of justification but for realizing the fullness of the new life into which we have been born.

The Charismatic delineation of a further experience – or series of experiences – of the Spirit subsequent to initiation into Christ and its holistic concept of salvation are an articulation of the same belief that Christian existence involves a change from one degree of glory to another as the Spirit leads us into a deeper and fuller participation in the life of Christ. Hence, the heightening of eucharistic spirituality amongst Evangelical Charismatics, which was identified in chapter 11, should be seen as an experiential discovery of the same participation in depth in the humanity of Christ that caused Calvin to 'break forth in wonder at this mystery' and to advise us rather to 'feel' than expect to understand Christ's eucharistic gift of himself.[38]

The eucharistic participation which we have in the ascended Christ through the power of the Spirit must be understood from the perspective of the eschatological kingdom which is both present in our midst and also to come in its full manifestation. Again this dual reference was felt and articulated in the first experiences of the Eucharist. Paul told the Corinthians to proclaim the Lord's death until he comes. In the earliest liturgies the people rejoiced at the presence of Christ amongst them ('The Lord is here') but yearned for the completion of his coming in the future ('Even so, come Lord Jesus'). As Lietzmann said, 'in the eucharistic experience of the first Church present and future were interwoven into a single fabric'.[39]

The eschatological character of the Eucharist may have been obscured by medieval Scholasticism and Reformation dispute but it was revived in the hymnody of the Wesley's ('that, that is the fulness, this is the taste'[40]), and has received considerable attention in contemporary scholarship as well as in recent liturgical revision. Geoffrey Wainwright, in his study of the eschatological character of the Eucharist, argues that it should be seen as an embodiment of the tension between the 'now' and the 'not yet'. It is a 'real expression of the divine kingdom'[41] but it is limited in the degree to which it can manifest the fullness of the Kingdom because it is a periodic event, involving only a portion of creation and only a part of humanity and is celebrated by a still sinful people.

In my more general discussion of the *parousia* I suggested that it should be seen in two dimensions. The first is the way in which it will bring the fullest revelation of Christ's presence to us and the second is the way in which it will free us to share fully in his new humanity. The fact that the Kingdom which lies in the future is already present amongst us means that there is a continuity both between Christ's presence to us at the Eucharist and his presence at the *parousia*, and between the effect that his presence has on us now in the Eucharist and the effect it will have on us at the *parousia*. As Torrance says, 'the New Testament emphasis upon the future is not so much the future of the reality but the future of its full manifestation'.[42]

One way of describing this continuity is in terms of the place before the Father which we have in the ascended Christ. Although this 'place' is an eschatological reality and therefore belongs to the future, it has even now broken into our present. In short, we participate already in the eschatological salvation which Christ won for us on the Cross and will fully bring at his *parousia*. In 2 Corinthians 3 Paul defines this 'place' in terms of an experience of the divine glory. He describes how, because we are in Christ, we can stand confidently before the Father with 'unveiled faces'. He goes on to show that we are made to reflect the glory of God in increasing degrees by the work of the Spirit as he transforms us more and more into the likeness of Christ. Hence, the eucharistic experience of a participation in depth with Christ by the power of the Spirit is both a real experience of our eschatological future and a real glimpse of the complete manifestation of God's glory which the visible presence of Christ will bring at the *parousia*.[43]

Christ comes to us in the Eucharist, as Wainwright implies,[44] as much clothed with his *parousia* as with his death. This does not mean that his coming in the Eucharist is identical with his coming at the *parousia*, just as it does not mean that his eucharistic presence is identical with the event of his death. But it does mean that, just as in the *anamnesis* of his death, the power of his past is present and active amongst us, so in the anticipation of his *parousia* the power of his future is also present and active amongst us. Therefore, as Torrance says, because Christ's presence in the Eucharist is a presence of Christ as he really is, the Eucharist must also involve 'the real presence of the *Eschatos*'.[45] Hence, as he goes on to say, 'the future supper of the Kingdom of God interpenetrates the present action of the Church'.[46] This means that in the Eucharist we are, again to use Wainwright's words, 'thrown forward'[47] as the eschatological Christ comes to us in the power of the Spirit to take us further (though not completely) into our eschatological place in his presence before the Father.

CHAPTER 14

The Eucharist as sacrifice

The Reformation rejection of the medieval understanding of the Mass as a sacrifice may be seen as a sustained exegesis of Paul's statement in the letter to the Romans that we 'are justified by [God's] grace as a gift, through the redemption which is in Christ Jesus, whom God put forward as an expiation by his blood, to be received by faith' (Rom. 3: 24). On the Cross Christ offered a perfect sacrifice and thereby effected a complete Atonement. His sacrifice does not need to be offered by the priest in the Mass as a propitiatory sacrifice for the remission of sins; rather, its efficacy needs to be received by faith.

It is remarkable, therefore, to find that when describing the process through which the effects of Christ's sacrifice are received by faith, the Reformers, the Puritans and the Wesleys at times talked in terms of offering Christ to the Father:

I also offer Christ, in that I desire and believe he accepts me and my prayer and praise and presents it to God in his own person (Luther).[1]

It is necessary that each of us should *offer Christ to the Father*. For, although He only, and that but once, has offered Himself, still a daily offering of Him, which is effected by faith and prayers, is enjoined to us (Calvin).[2]

For he hath ordained that ... by faith and prayer, they might, as it were, *offer him to God*, that is might shew the Father that sacrifice, once made for sin, in which they trust, and for which it is they expect all acceptance of their persons with God (Baxter).[3]

And this directs us also, in our devotions to God, how to carry ourselves in prayers and services, *to offer Christ to God* (Sibbes).[4]

> Do as Jesus bids us do,
> Signify his Flesh and Blood,
> Him in Memorial shew,
> *Offer up the Lamb to God* (Wesley).[5]

> Ye royal priests of Jesus, rise,
> And join the daily sacrifice
> Join all believers, in his Name
> *To offer up the spotless Lamb* (Wesley).[6]

This is more than merely an ironic semantic coincidence between Evangelical devotion and Catholic dogma; it is an indication that at the heart of the Catholic doctrine of the sacrifice of the Mass, with its emphasis on the propitiatory value of Christ's death, there lies the basic evangelical truth that we are saved by Christ's sacrificial work alone. The difference between the Catholic and Evangelical attempts to defend and express that truth revolve around two fundamental soteriological questions. The first has a Christological character: how is the effect of Christ's past sacrifice for sins maintained and communicated by him in the present? The second has an ecclesiological character: what part does the Church play in this maintenance and communication? Therefore, in order to identify the relationship between the Church's action in the Eucharist and Christ's sacrificial work on the Cross, we must consider these two questions in some detail.

THE MINISTRY OF CHRIST

Because of the historical nature of Christian faith we cannot bypass the dilemma created by the distance in time and space between Christ's crucifixion and our present experience. Christianity is not a mythological religion in which salvation consists in eternal realities which may or may not be manifested in history by way of illustration. The salvation of which it speaks was forged in a historical event and cannot be known except in relation to that historical event. The attempt to make Christ's death contemporary with us in the Eucharist has traditionally taken two forms. The first assumes some sort of renewal, reiteration or repetition of Christ's death in which its atoning action is somehow continued in the present. The second assumes some form of recollection of Christ's death in order that its atoning significance may be appropriated in the present.[7]

The problem with both approaches is that they view Christ's death in abstraction from his ascension. As a result, the event of the Cross is in a sense locked in history awaiting its release by either a cultic act or an intellectual process. However, the inner connection between the Cross and ascension means that the efficacy of Christ's sacrifice is maintained by his eternal presence before the Father and is communicated by his presence with us. Karl Barth argued that the problem raised by the distance between Christ's sacrifice and our present is dissolved when we recognize that the Cross and the resurrection are twin moments in the one redemptive event: 'It is the power of the event of the third day that the event of the first day – as something that happened there and then – is not something which belongs to the past…but is as such a present event, the event which fills and determines the whole present.'[8]

Barth shows that the contemporaneity of the Cross involves a Godward and a manward aspect. On the one hand, the resurrection (followed as it is by the ascension) means that Christ is present before the Father as 'our Representative who there [that is, on the Cross] suffered and died for us and therefore speaks for us'.[9] And, on the other, the resurrection (followed as it is by the ascension) means that Christ is present with us 'here and now in the full efficacy of what…He was and did there and then'.[10]

Descriptions of the heavenly ministry and eternal priesthood of Christ must preserve the dialectic between the Cross and the ascension. On the one hand they must express the unity between them – the Lamb looks as though he has been slain; the risen Christ still bears the scars of his death; and the Priest in heaven '*is* the expiation for our sins' (1 John 2: 2; my emphasis). And on the other hand they must also express their differentiation, that is, they must show with Barth that the resurrection and the ensuing ascension is the verdict of the Father that his Son has justly borne his judgement on sin. The resurrection is not merely the continuation of the life lived and died, it is the birth of a new humanity out of the death of the old. Therefore, Christ's ascended life is the living proof that relations between God and humankind have permanently altered. They must show also, with Moltmann, that the resurrection is the contradiction of the Cross.[11] It is the promise of the transformation of present reality in its God-forsaken experience into the new creation which will live in the eschatological presence of God. And they must show with Paul that Christ has endured God's curse in order that we may know his blessing – the blessing which is no less than adoption into the Trinitarian relationship: 'because you are sons, God has sent the Spirit of his Son into our hearts, crying, "Abba! Father!"' (Gal. 4: 6).

The connection between the Cross and ascension in the eternal
priesthood of Christ was well expressed by Wesley:

> Live our Eternal Priest,
> By men and angels blest!
> Jesus Christ the Crucified,
> He who did for sins atone,
> From the cross where once He died,
> Now He up to heaven is gone.
>
> He ever lives, and prays
> For all the faithful race;
> In the holiest place above
> Sinners' Advocate He stands,
> Pleads for us His dying love,
> Shows for us His bleeding hands.[12]

Wesley was able to combine a clear concept of the completeness of the
Atonement with a vivid sense of Christ's continuing work. Christ
pleads his death to the Father – though not for it to be accepted but
for it to be applied. Its acceptance is proven by his ascended presence
– 'That all-sufficient sacrifice subsists eternal as the Lamb.'[13]
However, its application depends on the ongoing prayer of Christ
that we might be included under the mantle of his death ('cover'd
with th' atoning blood'[14]) and be united in his ascended life ('Rise,
ye worms, to priests and kings; / Rise in Christ, and reign with
God'[15]). It is here that our first question of how the efficacy of Christ's
sacrifice is maintained and communicated by him impinges on our
second question, regarding the part the Church plays in this process.

THE MINISTRY OF THE CHURCH

In chapter 13 it was argued that the giving and receiving of God's
grace is contextualized in the being and action of the Church. This
means that the plea which is made by the presence and prayer of the
ascended Christ for the application of the salvific effects of his death
coincides with the plea made by the presence and prayer of the
Church for the giving of God's grace in Christ. Reformed theology in
Scotland during this century has made much use of the idea of
pleading Christ's sacrifice. Thomas Torrance pictures the relationship between the ministry of Christ and the ministry of the Church in
the following way: 'There in heaven is the ascended Lamb Himself

ever before the Face of the Father; here on earth is the waiting
Church of sinners, with all saints, showing forth His death and
pleading his sacrifice.'[16]

In the light of this interest in Reformed theology, it is significant
that in his analysis of the debates and decrees of the Council of Trent,
the Roman Catholic theologian David Power has identified the
presence of two understandings of the way in which the Mass was
thought to unite the Church with the sacrifice of the Cross. He admits
that the first – *per modum satisfactionis* – became the dominant one at
Trent and in post-Tridentine theology. However, he is critical of the
propitiatory categories with which this understanding works and
argues that the second – *per modum suffragii* – with its broader concept
of a prayer for reconciliation, should be recovered and used as the
controlling model. There is a clear correspondence between his
thought and the Reformed idea of pleading Christ's sacrifice:

the prayer of remembrance, which is known as a prayer of thanksgiving and
praise, is also a prayer for forgiveness, reconciliation and nourishment. It is
the pleading of the blood of Christ for mercy, the Church's part in the
intercession that Christ makes at God's right hand.[17]

Power believes that this approach enables the (Roman Catholic)
Church to be faithful both to the substance of Tridentine dogma and
to the new theological and ecumenical context in which it now finds
itself. For example, he points to the emphasis which the Lima
Statement places on the union between the Church's intercession at
the Eucharist with the 'continual intercession of the risen Lord'[18]
and argues for its consistency with the underlying theological concern
of the Council of Trent.

Whatever the use made of pleading Christ's sacrifice on the
ecumenical theological scene, Anglican Evangelicals have found the
whole notion somewhat alien.[19] They are cautious over any implication that the Eucharist is a sacrificial action which somehow
renews or releases the efficacy of Christ's death. Their underlying
concern is to avoid any implication that the Church must do
something in the Eucharist in order to affect or move God to give his
grace. However, it is difficult to see any dynamic function in the
activities of the Church – from prayer to preaching – unless there is
some form of interaction and mutuality between God and his people.
Further, although God does not need to be manipulated to give his
grace, he does want us to ask for his grace in the settings he has

appointed. It is not a case of trying to affect God, but rather of allowing him to affect us. There is an active side in which we ask and plead and there is a passive side in which we trust and receive. Just as we found that personal categories are determinative for our understanding of the gift of Christ's presence in the Eucharist, so must we see the same relational categories as determinative for our understanding of the connection between the Eucharist and Christ's sacrifice: 'Ask, and it will be given you; seek, and you will find; knock, and it will be opened to you. For every one who asks receives, and he who seeks finds, and to him who knocks it will be opened' (Luke 11: 9).

The notion of pleading Christ's sacrifice has raised misgivings amongst Evangelicals beyond these rather general hesitations regarding the interactive effect of the Eucharist. These centre on the fear that ideas of pleading Christ's sacrifice may imply that it has not been fully accepted by God.[20] In chapter 6 we saw that whilst Edmund Knox objected to the concept of pleading the Sacrifice he was quite happy with the idea of pleading by the Sacrifice.[21] His distinction is a helpful one. The Church does not pray for the acceptance of Christ's sacrifice but rather for the acceptance of itself in Christ's accepted sacrifice. To plead by Christ's sacrifice is therefore the essence of Christian existence because it is the acknowledgement that we have nothing in our hands to bring and therefore can cling only to the Cross of Christ. To plead by Christ's sacrifice is to appeal to it as the only ground of our salvation. It is to stand at the foot of the Cross and ask that we may be seen in its shadow.

The acknowledgement of the sole sufficiency of Christ's sacrifice, and the recognition of the exclusive mediatorial ministry of Christ on the basis of his sacrifice, lie behind the references to offering Christ in the Evangelical tradition which are quoted at the beginning of the chapter. The doctrine of justification by faith assumes a displacement of the individual in his sin by Christ in his righteousness. This is what Calvin meant by the 'wonderful exchange'. God does not see us as we are in ourselves but as we are in Christ.[22] Hence, when Luther, Calvin, Baxter, Sibbes and Wesley spoke of offering Christ to God, they were simply affirming that Christian existence begins and ends with the acknowledgement and acceptance of Christ crucified as, in Wesley's words, the 'only ground of all our Hope'.[23] There is a sense, therefore, in which the *anamnesis* at the Eucharist is made before God as well as made for man. Indeed, the test of whether the proclamation has penetrated to our hearts is whether we are prepared to proclaim before God that we know in the deepest recesses of our being that Christ has died for us and for our salvation and are therefore prepared to accept him as the 'one mediator between God and men' (1 Tim. 2: 5).

In a detailed structural analysis of the sacrificial dimension present in the liturgical history of the Eucharist, Kenneth Stevenson has argued that it is appropriate to describe the Eucharist as a sacrifice because – amongst other reasons – the story of our salvation which it tells is a story which has a claim on us. It is not a neutral narrative which we recount out of historical interest; it is the history of our salvation which we recount because we believe it to be true. In this sense it is quite appropriate to call the Eucharist – as Stevenson does – a sacrifice of proclamation.[24] The Church acknowledges that it is not its own but has been bought with a price and therefore signals its willingness to be led deeper into this new life of sonship and further away from its old life of slavery.

To describe the Eucharist as a sacrifice of proclamation is the same as calling it a sacrifice of thanksgiving. It is a thanksgiving for the completeness of the Atonement and consequently an intercessory plea that we may fully participate in this new age where God has forgiven our wickedness (Jer. 31: 34) and where there is no longer any sacrifice for sin (Heb. 10: 18). In this sense, therefore, it is not a cultic act. It is a joyous acknowledgement, a eucharistic proclamation of the completion of the cult. This is why the Reformers made such a radical distinction between the propitiatory sacrifice of Christ and the eucharistic sacrifice of the Church. However, Alasdair Heron has argued that, just as there was a very real danger that the sacrifice of the Mass – despite all its technical safeguards – could be seen as something additional to Christ's sacrifice, something which we do in order to renew or release the efficacy of Christ's death, so in the Reformers' absolute contrast between Christ's expiatory sacrifice and the Church's sacrifice of thanksgiving there is the corresponding danger that our response in the Eucharist becomes something additional to Christ's sacrificial action in the sense that it is offered to him rather than with him:

If our sacrifice is only that of thanks and praise for what Christ has objectively done, that can only mean that at the very heart and core of Christian worship, *anamnesis* and offering, he stands over against us, apart from us, rather than with us – and that our offering of ourselves is something *we* bring in response to his offering of himself for us.[25]

He claims that while the disjunction may express the vicarious and substitutionary character of the Atonement, it fails to express its inclusive and incorporative character and, therefore, gives insufficient weight both to the intimacy which the doctrine of the Incarnation assumes between ourselves and Christ, and to the mediatorial ministry of Christ.

Clearly the immense Christological and soteriological issues which are involved here demand the sort of systematic treatment which lies far beyond the limitations of this study. However, the relationship between the death and ascension of Christ, which has been developed earlier, may give some clues as to the way an answer may develop on the nature of our participation in Christ's self-offering.

Although Paul describes Christ as the one whom God put forward as an expiation of our sins (Rom. 3: 25), he can also say that he himself has been crucified with Christ (Gal. 2: 20). Similarly, although he claims to boast in nothing but the Cross of Christ, he also says that he has been crucified to the world on that same Cross (Gal. 6: 14). And although he is quite clear that through the act of the one, the many will be made righteous, he is just as clear that we too have died with Christ (Rom. 5: 19–6: 8). Here we see quite starkly the substitutionary and incorporative aspects of the Atonement to which Heron is referring. However, the simple fact that we are here dealing with the historical event of the death of Jesus of Nazareth means that our involvement in the Cross is of a quite different kind from Christ's. In order to help us distinguish between the forms of involvement, I shall draw heavily on Karl Barth's approach to the question.

Barth reflects the Pauline paradox. On the one hand, he is quite radical in his emphasis on Christ's death as something done for us and without us, involving no contribution from us. On the other hand, he maintains that to say that Christ has taken our place in death does not mean that he has removed the need for us to die, but rather that – actually and ontologically – he has taken mankind to a universal death: 'we have died in Him and with Him ... we have been done away and destroyed'.[26]

Barth defines Christ's death as an act of obedience in which he assumes the role of our representative by taking responsibility for our sin and willingly entering the court of God's justice, and there confessing the rightness of God in judging sin. In this way he acts for us by freely bearing the consequences of our sin, that is, God's judgement on sin. The fact that his death was for us means that we are indeed absent from the Cross in that he takes our place, but it also means that we are present on the Cross in the sense that the place he has taken is ours: 'we were there, for there took place there the dying of the Son of God for us'.[27] In other words we have died because, as the representative man he has died the death of all: 'For the love of Christ controls us, because we are convinced that one has died for all; therefore all have died' (2 Cor. 5: 14).

As noted earlier, Barth holds Christ's death and resurrection together in a dialectical relationship. The death which is God's 'No' to humanity in its sin is followed by his 'Yes' to humanity in his approval, acknowledgement and acceptance of Christ's act of obedient sacrifice demonstrated by his raising of Jesus Christ from the dead. Just as Christ's death in our place involved the most profound implications for us, so does his resurrection. It must be seen as 'the word of the divine assent, as God's permission and command that as sinners we are and should be there with Him ... Because Jesus Christ the Crucified is risen again and lives there is room for us.'[28] By means of the Cross and resurrection God has permanently altered the relationship between himself and humankind. In the person of his Son and through his Incarnation, crucifixion and resurrection, he has created a new humanity which, forever reconciled to him, will never die again.

However, the salvation which the act of the representative man has effected is not our salvation until we accept and agree to the representation. In Barth's terms it is not until I acknowledge, recognize and confess that Christ's death for us was his death for me that

I also am reached and found and seized by Him – by His being and activity, and therefore that I discover and confirm myself as the subject also intended and envisaged in His being and activity, as a man whom His existence as the Saviour of the world and Head of His community also concerns, who is also bound and committed to Him as the Saviour and Head.[29]

Here we can begin to see that there is a very real difference between our involvement with Christ's death and our involvement with his ascended life. We are involved with his death by way of identification. Christ identifies with us by agreeing to be our representative and so takes our place in death. We identify with him by accepting that he is the representative who takes our place to endure what we should endure and to effect what we could not effect. But we are involved with his ascended life by way of participation. Christ dies our death in order that we may share in his life beyond death: 'And you, who were dead in trespasses and the uncircumcision of your flesh, God made alive together with him' (Col. 2: 13). He takes our place under God's judgement so we may join him in his place in God's glory: 'He who did not spare his own Son, but gave him up for us all – will he not also give us all things with him?' (Rom. 8: 32). Christ becomes what we are in order to make us what he is: 'But when the time had fully come, God sent forth his Son, born of a woman, born under the law, to redeem those who were under the law, so that we might receive adoption as sons' (Gal. 4: 4).

The essence of the matter, therefore, is that though we died because Christ died for us, we live because Christ lives in us and we in him. This is why the modes of our involvement in his death and ascended life are different. In the one, the judgement of our slavery to sin was borne for us; in the other, the status of sonship is experienced by us. In the one, as Barth says, his blood and not a drop of ours was shed[30] but in the other, we are born again into the new creation. In the one God transferred his judgement on us on to himself, in the other, he adopts us into the Trinitarian relationship whereby we call him Abba by the power of Christ's Spirit within us.

The consequences for the Eucharist are that on the one hand we proclaim the sacrifice of Christ in such a way that we accept that it was made for us and, on the other hand, we move deeper into our participation in the life which the ascended Christ lives before the Father in the power of the Spirit. That is, we both acknowledge that Christ offered himself once for us all and we share in his eternal movement of love, worship and prayer to the Father. All this, of course, is not our own work. It is the work of the Spirit amongst us – the Spirit who first opens our eyes to the meaning of the death of Christ and so creates in us the act of faith to identify with his death in Baptism (Acts 8: 26–40); the Spirit who goes on reminding us of all that Christ did and said (John 14: 26); the Spirit who unites us in the relationship of loving dependence and obedience which the Son eternally has with the Father (Rom. 8: 12–16: 26–27).

To summarize, it has been shown that our involvement in the event of Christ's death is by the way of the mutual identification whereby Christ, representing us, dies our death and we receive and accept his representation for us through Baptism and by faith. It has also been shown that the result of the mutual identification is that we are involved in the effects of his death by way of a participation in his ascended life – the new humanity living as children of the Father and indwelt by the Spirit. On the one hand, this conclusion heeds Barth's warning that 'the ultimate and the penultimate things, the re-demptive act of God and that which passes for our response to it, are not the same. Everything is jeopardised if there is confusion in this respect.'[31] On the other hand, by recognizing the following points it expresses something of what the Scottish heirs of the Barthian tradition (such as Thomas and James Torrance and Alasdair Heron) mean when they say that we are united to Christ's self-presentation to the Father.[32] First, our response is itself evoked by the Spirit of Christ. Secondly, it derives its validity from Christ's obedient and representative response to the Father which he makes in our humanity on the Cross. Thirdly, it is taken into the relationship which the Son eternally shares with the Father and is thus made through him and with him and in him.

In this way we may define the Eucharist as the dominically appointed context both for the renewal of our identification with Christ's death and for the intensification of our participation in his life. In the body broken for us and in the blood shed for us, the remembrance of Christ's act of representation with the state of the old humanity is made and the acknowledgement and acceptance of his representative act for us is evoked. In the praise and thanks, the eating and drinking, the offering of one's life and love, we experience the reality of the new humanity in greater degrees of depth. Both dimensions are sacrificial moments. The one is a sacrifice of identi-fication, or as it was described earlier, a sacrifice of proclamation, in which we acknowledge that Christ's death was died for us. The other is a sacrifice of participation in which we give up our claims to independent self-existence and ask that we may share more fully in the life of Christ within his Church.

CONCLUDING ISSUES

There are complex and contentious areas of liturgical theology that have not so far been addressed. One, which touches on the consecratory as well as the sacrificial aspect of the Eucharist, is the question of the relationship between the people and the person who presides over the eucharistic celebration. Another is the question of how the sacrificial dimension of the Eucharist should be expressed in relation to the elements.

As we made clear at the beginning, the intention of this study has not been to attempt answers to all the vexing liturgical questions surrounding the actual celebration of the Eucharist. The aim has been to concentrate on the classic areas of theological dispute in the hope that reflection on these will shed light on other related issues. However, given the contemporary discussion on matters of priesthood and eucharistic presidency and given the traditional impasse over the placing and focusing of the oblation, it is worth turning our attention to both issues in order to see whether the resources provided by the Evangelical tradition can help to clarify the questions and even shift perspectives.

Sacrifice, priesthood and eucharistic presidency

Luther's emphasis on the priesthood of all believers played a key role in his thinking and in his programme of reform. Although Christ is the one priest of the new covenant, those who are united to Christ by Baptism and through faith share in his priestly work of intercession and instruction, praise and proclamation. There is one spiritual estate in which all have freedom of access to God's presence to pray and praise and all have the right to communicate the Word of God in service and speech.

Even though the doctrine of the priesthood of all believers did not figure so prominently in the writings of the other mainstream Reformers, the theological content of the doctrine was a foundational part of all Reformation theology. It was the essential theological equality of Christians which the Reformers believed to be undermined, even denied, by Roman theology and practice. Its doctrine of the priest's power to consecrate and offer created a mediatorial priesthood which not only dissolved the corporate priesthood of the Church but debased the perfect priesthood of Christ. Although contemporary Roman theologians and statements (including the encyclical *Mysterium Fidei* (1965)) are more careful to make clear that the whole Church participates in the sacrificial action of the Eucharist than their forebears appeared to be, the issue has not been fully resolved. In their irenic studies both the Reformed theologian Alasdair Heron and the Roman Catholic theologian David Power, conclude that the way in which the sacrificial movement is focused on the priest in Roman doctrine remains a point where difficulties and dangers persist.[33]

By concentrating too much theological weight on the priest, Catholic theology has always run the risk of shifting the locus of the praying, praising and proclaiming in the Eucharist away from the sacrificial activity of the Church to the sacrificial action of an individual. Evangelical theology can remain most alert to this danger by not merely stating the theological equality of all believers but by emphasizing the corporate character of the Christian priesthood. Even though Luther delighted in saying that all Christians are priests by definition, he did so not in order to encourage individualistic ideas of independence but to stress the fact of our corporate interdependence. As B. A. Gerrish says, for Luther 'to be a priest is to be a priest *for others*',[34] and, we might add, with others.

Because of the corporate character of the Christian priesthood, Luther drew a distinction between personal status and public office. As the priesthood belongs to all, it cannot be exercised in a public context without the consent of all. The theological equality amongst Christians does not mean that there can be no liturgical differentiation. In order to function effectively as the priesthood, the believers call out individuals to minister in Word and Sacrament. This distinction between status and function was maintained by the other mainstream Reformers. For example, Cranmer made it clear that the 'difference between the priest and the layman in this matter is only in the ministration; that the priest, as a common minister of the Church, doth minister and distribute the Lord's Supper unto other and the other receive it at his hands'.[35]

Calvin worked with the same distinction but at the same time emphasized the corporate dimension of both the common priesthood of all and the called ministry of the few. In terms of the Eucharist, Calvin underlined that as together we proclaim Christ's death, so together we offer the sacrifice of praise and lay our gifts on the altar of Christ.[36] Out of this common priesthood are those who are 'set apart over the Church...by the doctrine of Christ to instruct the people to true godliness, to administer the sacred mysteries and to keep and exercise upright discipline'.[37] It is, therefore, through the ministry of the few that Christ creates and maintains the whole. Their ministry of preaching, Sacrament and discipline both directs the Church and preserves its unity: 'The Lord has therefore bound his Church together with a knot that he foresaw would be the strongest means of keeping unity.'[38] For Calvin the corporate interdependence of the Church is most fully expressed and performed in the function of the ordained ministry by which 'the believers are held together in one body'.[39]

The evangelical case which the Reformers made for restricting the ministry of the Sacrament to appointed ministers rested ultimately on their understanding of the Church being constituted by the Word of God and therefore in constant need of the authorized ministry by which the Word is made available and applied to the life of the Church. Indeed, in a derived way, Calvin saw the ordained ministry itself as constitutive of the Church: for without the making known of the Word by those appointed to do so, the Church would cease to exist.

In itself this brief reference to the Reformers does not contribute anything decisive to the current debate on who exactly should preside at the Eucharist, for it still leaves open the question of what represents an authentic calling and authorization of ministers. However, it may serve to show that even within Evangelical theology, the questions surrounding the issue of eucharistic presidency have been found to touch directly and deeply upon the identity, unity and ministry of the Church, and have been found too complex to be solved merely by an appeal to the equality of Christians as defined in the doctrine of the priesthood of all believers. It may also show that, certainly in Calvin's mind, the issue of eucharistic presidency is integrally related to the matter of presidency in the community, for the 'human ministry' is the means which 'God uses to govern the Church'.[40]

Sacrifice and the elements

Kenneth Stevenson's structural analysis of the Eucharist has shown the implicit tendency for the elements to be involved – in some degree of directness – in the expression of the sacrificial dimension of the Eucharist. In the terms of his definitions: entwined in the themes of 'story' (the '*context*' of the Eucharist) and 'response' (the '*action*' of the Eucharist), there is the theme of 'gift' (the '*material*' of the Eucharist). On the one hand, this is entirely to be expected and, of itself, quite uncontroversial. It would be strange if the sacramental media were not involved in the proclamation of the Gospel and in the response that takes place there. On the other hand, there is a history of complex and controversial liturgical questions surrounding the way this involvement is expressed in word and action. As the following words of Edmund Knox show, it is these questions which often divide even when a level of theological agreement has been reached:

Is it not possible to [see] in the Eucharist a Godward aspect as well as a manward – a Sacrifice as well as a Sacrament? Undoubtedly it is possible to see both aspects in the same service ... The opposition is not in these beliefs, but in their relation to the consecrated elements.[41]

Clearly it was this issue which caused the dissension and division over Series Two's proposed *anamnesis* ('we offer unto thee this bread and this cup') and which remained in the background throughout the period of revision. However, the resolution of the problem that emerged with Series Three and was developed with the ASB was a creative one which proved influential in later revisions in various parts of the Communion. It was simply a 1549 type of affirmation that the celebration of the saving events in Christ is being made with this bread and this cup. This sort of formula shows that the elements have a real role to play in terms not just of receiving but also of proclaiming our salvation, whilst at the same time avoiding direct language of offering with all its loaded historical overtones.[42]

The relationship between the self-oblation and the elements also provoked heated debate between Evangelicals and others during the period of revision. Evangelicals were generally convinced that Cranmer's placing of the self-oblation after the recital of and reception of the Gospel was correct. However, as we have discovered, there is some evidence in the Evangelical tradition that suggests that whilst the Cranmerian surface structure expresses the essential theological structure of the Christian confession, it may do so at the cost of disrupting the deep structures (liturgical and experiential) operating in the internal movement of the Eucharist itself. For example, in chapter 4 we saw that the heart of the Puritan experience of the Eucharist lay in first the fraction and libation, and then in the self-presentation for communion, followed by the reception itself: we are to 'present ourselves to this table' to receive of God's 'free mercy and grace'.[43] Similarly, in chapter 5, we saw how the early Anglican Evangelicals found themselves expressing their self-oblation at the point of reception: it is here that having heard the Gospel message we must 'desire to give up [our] souls to God'.[44]

In many ways this is where we would expect the self-oblation to be located in Evangelical spirituality. It fits with the structure present in evangelistic meetings and evangelistic literature, where acceptance of Christ is seen as contemporaneous with commitment to Christ. Hence, the story of God's grace which is made known again in the Eucharist brings us afresh to the point at which we can do nothing else than to receive God's gift to us and give our lives to him in one unified and climactic response:

> When I survey the wondrous cross
> On which the Prince of Glory died.
> My richest gain I count but loss,
> And pour contempt on all my pride.
>
> Forbid it, Lord, that I should boast,
> Save in the death of Christ my God:
> All the vain things that charm me most,
> I sacrifice them to his blood.
>
> See from His head, His hands, His feet,
> Sorrow and love flow mingled down:
> Did e'er such love and sorrow meet,
> Or thorns compose so rich a crown?
>
> Were the whole realm of nature mine,
> That were an offering far too small,
> Love so amazing, so divine,
> Demands my soul, my life, my all.[45]

It is here, in the interplay between the demands of theology, liturgy and spirituality, that the future not only of this issue, or even of other liturgical issues related to the eucharistic sacrifice, but of Evangelical eucharistic life itself will be determined.

Notes

1 It should be noted at the outset that we are studying Anglican Evangelicalism within the Church of England rather than throughout the Anglican Communion. However, for the sake of simplicity and in line with standard procedure, I shall refer to the Evangelical movement within the Church of England as 'Anglican Evangelicalism'. The views of some overseas Anglican Evangelicals will be used as source material when their comments may be relevant.

Recent studies on the history of Evangelicalism can be found in D. W. Bebbington, *Evangelicalism in Modern Britain* (London: Unwin Hyman, 1989); K. Hylson-Smith, *Evangelicals in the Church of England 1734–1984* (Edinburgh: T. & T. Clark, 1989); R. Manwaring, *From Controversy to Co-existence: Evangelicals in the Church of England 1914–1980* (Cambridge: CUP, 1985).

2 J. I. Packer, *'Fundamentalism' and the Word of God* (London: IVF, 1958), p. 38. Such a claim can be seen as a point of difference between Conservative and Liberal Evangelicals: see L. E. Binns (a Liberal Evangelical), *The Evangelical Movement in the English Church* (London: Methuen, 1928), p. x.

3 See G. W. Stroup, *The Promise of Narrative Theology* (London: SCM, 1981).

4 P. L. Berger and T. Luckman, *The Social Construction of Reality* (Harmondsworth: Penguin Books, 1971), p. 153.

5 John Stott's closing address at the second National Evangelical Anglican Congress (NEAC) held at Nottingham in 1977, reported in B. T. Lloyd, *Evangelicals, Obedience and Change* (Bramcote: GB, 1977), p. 8.

6 J. C. Ryle, *Knots Untied* (London: William Hunt, 1886), p. 22.

7 Quoted by R. H. Bainton, *Here I Stand* (New York: New American Library, 1955).

8 H. Wace, 'The first principles of Protestantism', in *Church and Faith*, edited by H. Wace (Edinburgh: Blackwood, 1899), p. 25.

9 See Ryle, *Knots Untied*, pp. 4–10: T. C. Hammond, *What is an Evangelical?*, CPAS Fellowship Paper 219 (London: CPAS, 1959), pp. 6–13; J. I. Packer, *The Evangelical Anglican Identity Problem* (Oxford: LH, 1978), pp. 20–2; J. R. W. Stott, *Essentials for Tomorrow's Christians* (London: Scripture Union, 1978).

227

10 M. A. C. Warren, *What is an Evangelical?* (London: CBRP, 1944), p. 23.

11 See Stott's closing address at the NEAC in Nottingham in 1977: 'Every aspect of our tradition as Evangelicals needs to come constantly under the scrutiny of Scripture... I believe we need to be radical in our approach to tradition, so that we become biblically-radical–conservative–evangelicals!' Quoted by E. Neale, 'Nottingham '77', in E. Neale, M. Smout and C. Bedford, *77 Knots Untied* (London: Lakeland, Marshall, Morgan, Scott, 1977), pp. 1–19 (pp. 16–17).

12 Ryle, *Knots Untied*, p. 21.

13 Quoted by B. L. Woolfe, *Reformation Writings of Martin Luther* (London: Lutterworth, 1952), vol. I, p. 231.

14 H. Sasse described the motivating force behind the Reformers' attack as 'a manifestation of the longing for the pure Sacrament, so deeply rooted in the souls of Christian people on the eve of the Reformation. No one can understand the controversies of the Reformation on the Sacrament of the Altar unless he has understood that longing, so inconceivable to modern man' (*This is my Body* (Adelaide: Lutheran Publishing House, 1977), p. 61).

15 Declaration 1553; quoted by D. Stone, *A History of the Doctrine of the Holy Eucharist* (London: Longmans, Green, 1909), vol. II, p. 181.

16 From the rite, The Communion of the Sick, in the 1662 Prayer Book.

17 J. Calvin, 'Treatise on the Lord's Supper', in *Calvin: Theological Treatises*, edited by J. K. S. Reid (London: SCM, 1954), p. 158.

18 M. A. C. Warren, *Strange Victory: A Study of the Holy Communion Service* (London: Canterbury Press, 1946), p. 120.

19 A discerning rather than sectarian view of Anglican history has always been present within Evangelicalism. Ryle made a distinction between the Tractarians/Ritualists, whom he felt were latent Roman Catholics, and other Anglicans, past and present, who whilst not definable Evangelicals, were none the less anxious to distinguish themselves from Roman thought and practice (*Principles for Churchmen* (London: William Hunt, 1899), pp. 31–45).

The same approach can be seen specifically in terms of eucharistic doctrine amongst the Evangelical High Churchmen of the nineteenth century (see P. Toon, 'Evangelicals and Tractarians then and now', *Churchman*, 93 (1979), 29–38 (p. 35)). It was also the approach of the two architects of the scholarly evangelical response to the Tractarian eucharistic theology – William Goode, *The Nature of Christ's Presence in the Eucharist* (London: T. Hatchard, 1856), vol. I, p. ix; vol. II, pp. 955–72; and Nathaniel Dimock, *The History of the Book of Common Prayer*, memorial edition (London: Longmans, Green, 1910), p. xxxiii.

Again, in 1933 W. H. Mackean surveyed Anglican eucharistic theology from Laud to Waterland and concluded that despite the use of occasional exaggerated language, the representatives of the period held to a Reformed doctrine of the Eucharist ('Anti-Roman apologetics', in *The Evangelical Doctrine of Holy Communion*, edited by A. J. Macdonald

(London: SPCK, 1936), first published 1933, pp. 152–263). Further, in 1962 J. I. Packer dissociated the eucharistic theology of the 1958 Lambeth Statement from that of pre-Tractarian Anglican history and in so doing implied his general sympathy with that tradition (*Eucharistic Sacrifice* (London: CBRP, 1962), p. 3). For a similar position see R. T. Beckwith, *Priesthood and Sacraments*, (Abingdon: MMP, 1964), pp. 62–7. In the 1970s the policy of the Grove Booklet series was to 'quest for a scriptural "high" churchmanship' (C. O. Buchanan and D. Pawson, *Infant Baptism under Cross-Examination* (Bramcote: GB, 1974), p. 3), and was therefore prepared to learn from sources that might be considered closer to Catholic interests. Other Evangelical theologians have been also explicitly attempting to integrate key Evangelical and Catholic emphases (see P. Toon, *The Anglican Way: Evangelical and Catholic* (Wilton, Conn.: Moorehouse–Barlow, 1983); G. L. Carey, *The Meeting of the Waters* (London: H & S, 1985)).

20 See Packer, *Evangelical Anglican Identity Problem*: Lloyd, *Evangelicals, Obedience and Change*; C. O. Buchanan, 'The role and calling of an Evangelical college in the 1980's', *Churchman*, 94 (1980), 26–42; N. T. Wright, *Evangelical Anglican Identity* (Oxford: LH, 1980); W. H. Hopkinson, 'Changing emphases in self-identity among Evangelicals in the Church of England, 1960–1980' (M.Phil. thesis, University of Nottingham, 1983); *Restoring the Vision: Anglican Evangelicals Speak Out*, edited by M. Tinker (Eastbourne: MARC, 1990); and G. L. Bray, *Churchman* editorials 1988–91.

21 R. Goldmann, *Religious Thinking from Childhood to Adolescence* (London: Routledge & Kegan Paul, 1965), *Readiness for Religion* (London: Routledge & Kegan Paul, 1965); J. W. Fowler, *Stages of Faith* (San Francisco: Harper & Row, 1981); J. H. Westerhoff III, *Will our Children have Faith?* (New York: Seabury Press, 1976). It is worth noting that Berger and Luckman's description of a child's acquisition of knowledge within the language of the Sociology of Religion is along comparable lines (*Social Construction of Reality*, pp. 149–82).

22 Fowler, *Stages of Faith*, pp. 197–8.

23 e.g. D. N. Samuel, 'Roots and Reformations', *Churchman*, 104 (1990), 197–212.

24 e.g. *Restoring the Vision*, edited by Tinker.

25 See Carey, *Meeting of the Waters*.

2 THE REFORMERS' BEQUEST

1 M. Luther, 'Treatise on the New Testament, that is the Holy Mass, 1520', in *Works*, vol. xxxv, *Word and Sacrament*, vol. 1, edited by E. T. Bachmann and H. T. Lehmann (Philadelphia: Fortress Press, 1960), pp. 75–112 (p. 99).

2 J. Calvin, *Institutes*, bk. iv, xviii. 1. Quotations here and below are from

the translation of the 1559 *Institutes* in *Calvin: Institutes of Christian Religion*, vol. II, edited by J. T. McNeill (London: SCM, 1951).

3 T. Cranmer, edited by J. E. Cox (Cambridge: CUP, 1844), vol. I, p. 346.

4 Luther, 'The Babylonian captivity of the Church', in *Works*, vol. XXXVI, *Word and Sacrament*, vol. II, edited by A. R. Wentz and H. T. Lehmann (Philadelphia: Fortress Press, 1959), pp. 11–126 (p. 44).

5 Ibid., pp. 38–9.

6 A transcript of the Colloquy can be found in Sasse, *This is my Body*, pp. 180–220 (quotations from p. 203).

7 See J. Stephenson, 'Martin Luther and the Eucharist', *SJT* 36 (1983), 447–61 (455).

8 W. P. Stephens, *The Theology of Huldrych Zwingli* (Oxford: Clarendon Press, 1986), p. 188.

9 Ibid., p. 190.

10 Colloquy, in Sasse, *This is my Body*, p. 194.

11 Zwingli, 'On the Lord's Supper', in *Zwingli and Bullinger*, introduced by G. W. Bromiley, Library of Christian Classics, vol. XXIV (London: SCM, 1953), pp. 185–238 (p. 205).

12 *Opera Selecta* (Berth and Niesel), vol. I, p. 139, quoted by T. H. L. Parker, *John Calvin: A Biography* (London: J. M. Dent & Sons, 1975), p. 52.

13 'Short Treatise on the Lord's Supper', v, in *Calvin: Theological Treatises*, pp. 165–6.

14 Depite Calvin's use of substantial language his meaning was that Christ's life, not his material, is shared:

Meanwhile, I frankly confess that I reject their teaching of the mixture, of transfusion, of Christ's flesh with our soul. For it is enough for us that, from the substance of his flesh Christ breathes life into our souls – indeed, pours forth his very life into us – even though Christ's flesh itself does not enter us (*Institutes*, bk. IV, XVII. 32).

Nevertheless, it would be wrong to label Calvin as a virtualist, for his qualifications of substantialist language were designed not to separate the effect from the body, but to reject scholastic concepts of substance in terms of material, in favour of personal and soteriological categories:

Calvin's concern then is not to define what is given in the Eucharist in terms of substance, though he uses the term frequently, but rather to disengage us from the philosophical notion of substance and lead us to the notion of person. To receive his person is to receive the whole Christ – body, blood, and divinity. To receive Christ is not to receive an abstraction (K. McDonnell, *John Calvin, the Church and the Eucharist* (Princeton: Princeton University Press, 1967), p. 246).

15 *Institutes*, bk. IV, XVII. 19.

16 Ibid. XVII. 12.

17 Ibid. XVII. 19.

18 Ibid. XVII. 28.

19 Ibid. XVII. 10.

20　Sermon on Titus 1: 1–5, quoted by F. Wendel, *Calvin* (London: Collins, 1963), p. 354.

21　*Institutes*, bk. IV, XVII. 10.

22　Ibid. XVII. 5.

23　Ibid. XVII. 4. See also: 'Here then is the peculiar consolation we receive from the Supper, that it directs and conducts us to the cross of Christ and to his resurrection' ('Short Treatise on the Holy Supper of our Lord and only Saviour Jesus Christ', II, in *Calvin: Theological Treatises*, p. 145).

24　Quoted by McDonnell, *Calvin, Church and Eucharist*, pp. 283–4.

25　*Institutes*, bk. IV, XVII. 1.

26　Ibid. XVII. 35.

27　Ibid. XVII. 7.

28　See P. Brooks, *Thomas Cranmer's Doctrine of the Eucharist* (London: Macmillan, 1965), pp. 54–60; R. F. Buxton, *Eucharist and Institution Narrative* (Great Wakering: Mayhew–McCrimmon, 1978), pp. 60–1.

29　Parliamentary debate, quoted by Stone, *History of the Doctrine*, vol. II, p. 134.

30　'Defence of the true and catholic doctrine of the Sacrament' (1550), in *The Works of Thomas Cranmer*, edited by G. E. Duffield, Courteney Library of Reformation Classics (Appleford: Sutton Courtenay Press, 1964), vol. I, pp. 45–232 (p. 181).

31　See McDonnell, *Calvin, Church and Eucharist*, p. 230.

32　*PEER*, p. 178.

33　*Institutes*, bk. IV, XVII. 5.

34　Ibid. XVII. 33.

35　Last examination before the commissioners, 1555, quoted by Stone, *History of the Doctrine*, p. 193.

3 THE LEGACY IN THE ANGLICAN TRADITION

1　See R. J. Bauckham, 'Hooker, Travers and the Church of Rome in the 1580's', *Journal of Ecclesiastical History* 29 (1978), 37–50. Bauckham shows that Hooker's theological approach was not representative of Elizabethan Anglicanism.

2　Quoted by E. C. Ratcliff, 'The English usage of eucharistic consecration, 1548–1662 – II', *Theology* 60 (1957), 273–80 (p. 277).

3　Calvin, *Institutes*, bk. IV, XVII. 43.

4　See ibid., XVII. 39.

5　For supporting evidence from the contemporary Visitation Articles and Injunctions see Buxton, *Eucharist and Institution*, pp. 100–5; and from the 1559 Primer see E. G. C. F. Atchley, *On Epiclesis of the Eucharistic Liturgy and in the Consecration of the Font* (London: OUP, 1935), p. 193.

6　J. Jewel, 'Reply to M. Harding's Answer', in *Works* (Cambridge: CUP, 1845) vol. I, p. 123.

7　Ibid.

8　Jewel, *Apology*, quoted by Buxton, *Eucharist and Institution*, p. 93.

9 Hooker, *Laws of Ecclesiastical Polity* (London: J. M. Dent, 1940), bk. v, vol. II, p. 322.
10 Ibid., p. 331.
11 Ibid., p. 327.
12 Ibid., p. 322.
13 See Stone, *History of the Doctrine*, p. 208.
14 Ibid., pp. 213–19.
15 Jewel, 'Reply to Harding's Answer', p. 475.
16 Ibid., pp. 468–79.
17 Ibid., p. 473.
18 Ibid., p. 476.
19 Ibid., p. 478.
20 Ibid.
21 Ibid., p. 477.
22 Ibid., p. 475.
23 *Apology*, quoted by Buxton, *Eucharist and Institution*, p. 33.
24 Hooker, *Ecclesiastical Polity*, vol. II, p. 320.
25 Ibid., p. 201.
26 Ibid., p. 222.
27 Ibid., p. 220.
28 Ibid., p. 222.
29 Ibid., p. 228.
30 Ibid., p. 225.
31 Ibid., p. 322.
32 Ibid., p. 333.
33 Ibid., vol. I, pp. 37–40, 54–61.
34 Ibid., vol. II, p. 234.
35 Ibid.
36 Ibid., p. 236.
37 Ibid.
38 Ibid., p. 322.
39 Ibid., p. 331.
40 Jewel, 'Reply to Harding's Answer', p. 493.
41 Jewel, 'A Sermon preached at Paul's Cross', in *Works*, vol. I, p. 9.
42 Hooker, *Ecclesiastical Polity*, vol. II, p. 331.
43 For the reasons that justify the use of Anglican sources in this period see ch. 1, n. 19.
44 e.g. Cosin's attack on transubstantiation, in which he makes a sustained effort to show that he stands firmly in the Reformation tradition (*Works*, (Oxford: John Henry Parker, 1851) vol. IV, pp. 157–69).
45 For the different views on consecration during the period see Buxton, *Eucharist and Institution*, pp. 110–32; Atchley, *On Epiclesis of the Eucharistic Liturgy*, pp. 194–6.
46 Ussher, 'Sermon preached before the Commons House of Parliament' in *Works*, vol. II, quoted in *Anglicanism*, edited by P. E. More and F. L. Cross (London: SPCK, 1935), pp. 488–94 (p. 489).

47 Morton, *A Catholic Appeal for Protestants*, quoted by W. H. Mackean, 'Anti-Roman apologetics', in Macdonald, *Evangelical Doctrine of Holy Communion*, p. 229.

48 Cosin, *Works*, vol. IV, p. 171.

49 Richard Montague, 'A new gagg for the new Gospel? No a new gagg for an old goose', quoted by Stone, *History of the Doctrine*, p. 275.

50 Christopher Sutton, 'Goodly meditations upon the most holy Sacrament of the Lord's Supper', ibid., p. 291.

51 L. Andrewes, *Nintety-six Sermons* (Oxford: John Henry Parker, 1841), vol. II, p. 301.

52 See W. Laud, *Works*, vol. II, pp. 339–41.

53 Morton, 'Of the Institution of the Sacrament', quoted by Stone, *History of the Doctrine*, p. 288.

54 Taylor, 'Life of Christ', ibid., p. 303.

55 Richard Field, 'Of the Church', ibid., p. 303.

56 Thomas Jackson, 'Commentary on the Apostles Creed', ibid., p. 295.

4 THE LEGACY IN THE PURITAN TRADITION

1 See B. Hall, 'Puritanism: The Problem of Definition', in *Studies in Church History*, vol. II (London: Nelson, 1965), pp. 283–96.

2 P. Collinson, *The Elizabethan Puritan Movement* (London: Jonathan Cape, 1967), p. 27.

3 For a similarly wide definition see G. F. Nuttall, *The Holy Spirit in Puritan Faith and Experience* (Oxford: Blackwell, 1947), p. 9; Collinson, *The Elizabethan Puritan Movement*, p. 28; G. S. Wakefield, *Puritan Devotion* (London: Epworth, 1957), pp. 3–4; C. Hill, *Society and Puritanism in Pre-Revolutionary England* (London: Panther, 1964), p. 30. However, only Nuttall explores the connection between Puritanism and the Charismatic groups.

4 The complete text can be found in W. D. Maxwell, *The Liturgical Portions of the Genevan Service* (London: Faith Press, 1965), pp. 121–8. The central portions of the text can be found in *PEER*, pp. 179–81.

5 S. Mayor, *The Lord's Supper in Early English Dissent* (London: Epworth, 1972), pp. 11–18, provides the texts where they differ from Knox.

6 B. D. Spinks, *From the Lord and 'The Best Reformed Churches'* (Rome: Centro Liturgico Vincenziano, 1984).

7 The evidence from Scotland is provided by W. McMillan, *The Worship of the Scottish Reformed Church, 1530–1638* (London: James Clarke, 1930), pp. 170–7; G. Donaldson, *The Making of the Scottish Prayer Book of 1637* (Edinburgh: Edinburgh University Press, 1954), pp. 67–8; W. D. Maxwell, *A History of Worship in the Church of Scotland* (London: OUP, 1955), pp. 134–5. Buxton, *Eucharist and Institution*, p. 135, and B. D. Spinks, *Freedom or Order?* (Pittsburgh, Pa.: Pickwick Publications, 1984), p. 45, add their voices to the consensus; Spinks also provides evidence from England that the same practice was common south as well as north

of the border. Indeed, he disagrees with Ratcliff (and also, therefore, McMillan, pp. 176–7), that the inclusion of a direction to 'sanctify and bless' the elements in the Westminster Directory was merely a result of – even a concession to – Scottish pressure. Buxton (p. 142) identifies a parallel development in Anglicanism and Puritanism from a lower to a higher view of both consecration and the eucharistic presence during the period from Cranmer and Knox to the Caroline divines and Baxter and the Westminster Directory.

8 See Robert Browne in *The Writings of Robert Harrison and Robert Browne*, edited by A. Peel and L. H. Carlson (London: George Allen & Unwin, 1953), p. 284.

9 Westminster Confession XXIX. VI, in *Confession of the Faith* (Edinburgh: Blackwood, 1928), p. 44.

10 *PEER*, p. 190.

11 Ibid., p. 191.

12 *The Savoy Declaration of Faith and Order*, edited by A. Peel (London: Independent Press, 1939).

13 The other amendments can be found in Spinks, *Freedom or Order?*, pp. 53–6.

14 *PEER*, pp. 194–8 (p. 195).

15 Ibid., p. 195.

16 Quoted by Buxton, *Eucharist and Institution*, p. 141.

17 L. Bayly, *The Practice of Piety*, seventy-fourth edition (Exeter: J. Saunders, 1821), first published 1620, p. 320.

18 Ibid.

19 R. Baxter, 'The Poor Man's Family Book', in *Works*, vol. XIX, p. 517.

20 Quoted by Mayor, *Lord's Supper*, p. 58.

21 Bayly, *Practice of Piety*, p. 321.

22 Preston, 'A preparation to the Lord's Supper', p. 115, quoted by Wakefield, *Puritan Devotion*, p. 45.

23 Ibid.

24 J. Owen, 'The chamber of imagery in the Church of Rome laid open', in *Works* edited by W. H. Goold (Edinburgh: T. & T. Clark, 1862), vol. XVI, p. 62.

25 W. Marshall, *The Gospel Mystery*, p. 44, quoted by Wakefield, *Puritan Devotion*, p. 51.

26 W. Perkins, *Works*, vol. II, p. 81, quoted by Wakefield, *Puritan Devotion*, pp. 43–4.

27 J. Owen, 'Sacramental discourses' in *Works*, vol. IX, p. 521.

28 *PEER*, p. 180.

29 See McMillan, *Worship of the Scottish Reformed Church*, p. 166.

30 Westminster Confession, XXXI.

31 Savoy Declaration, XXX.

32 Baxter, 'Poor Man's Family Book', pp. 276–80.

33 *PEER*, p. 196.

34 See Spinks, *Freedom or Order?*, p. 63.

35 *PEER*, p. 196.
36 Ibid.
37 J. Owen, 'Greater Catechism', in *Works*, 1850–3 edition, vol. I, pp. 470ff.
38 Quoted by Mayor, *Lord's Supper*, p. 98.
39 For the consensus on this point see J. F. H. New, *Anglican and Puritan* (London: A. & C. Black, 1964), pp. 59–64; Stone, *History of the Doctrine*, pp. 308–12; Dix, *The Shape of the Liturgy* (London: A. & C. Black, 1945), p. 677; H. W. Roberts, 'Puritan and Separatist sacramental discourses', in *Union and Communion 1529–1979*, Westminster Conference Papers (London: Westminster Conference, 1979), p. 55; H. Davies, *Worship and Theology in England* vol. I (Princeton: Princeton University Press, 1970), pp. 62–4; Mayor, *Lord's Supper*, p. 15; and Buxton, *Eucharist and Institution*, p. 142.
40 See Collinson, *Elizabethan Puritan Movement*, p. 26.
41 For example, Donaldson, *The Making of the Scottish Prayer Book*, p. 72, cites the Presbyterian John Row criticizing the Book of Common Order for not having a consecratory petition and denouncing the 1637 Scottish liturgy for including one.
42 'An Admonition to Parliament', in *Puritan Manifestos*, edited by W. H. Frere and C. E. Douglas (London: SPCK, 1907), pp. 1–55.
43 See Whitgift, *Works*, Parker Society Edition (Cambridge: CUP, 1853), vol. III, p. 22.
44 J. F. H. New, *Anglican and Puritan* (London: A. & C. Black, 1964), pp. 66–9.
45 Hooker, *Ecclesiastical Polity*, vol. II, bk. 5, LX. 2.
46 T. Brooks, *Heaven on Earth: A Treatise on Christian Assurance* (London: Banner of Truth, 1961), first published 1664; p. 14.
47 G. Fox, *Journal*, edited by N. Penny, vol. I pp. 325, 253–4, quoted by Nuttall, *The Holy Spirit*, pp. 100–1.
48 Ibid., p. 100.
49 See H. G. Hageman, *Pulpit and Table* (London: SCM, 1962), pp. 13–35.
50 Quoted by Roberts, 'Puritan and Separatist sacramental discourses', p. 57.
51 Thomas Goodwin, in *Works* (Edinburgh: James Nichol, 1861–5), vol. XI.
52 Quoted by New, *Anglican and Puritan*, p. 70.
53 H. Davies, *The Worship of the English Puritans* (London: Dacre, 1948), p. 183.
54 Quoted by Roberts, 'Puritan and Separatist sacramental discourses', p. 66.
55 T. Goodwin, 'Gospel holiness', in *Works*, vol. VII, p. 312.
56 'The chamber of imagery in the Church of Rome laid open', quoted by Mayor, *Lord's Supper*, p. 107.
57 Ibid. It would seem that Puritan sacramental experience somewhere between the negative sacramentalism ascribed to it by New, *Anglican and Puritan*, and Marlowe, *The Puritan Tradition in English Life* (London:

Cresset Press, 1956), and the very positive impression given by a survey which merely looks at the liturgies and sacramental writings and fails to set the eucharistic comments in the context of the general theology and spirituality of the movement.

58 *PEER*, p. 180.

59 Ibid., p. 191.

60 J. Owen, 'Sacramental discourses', VII, in *Works*, vol. IX, p. 556.

61 Ibid., pp. 180–1.

62 From an optional prayer in the Book of Common Order, quoted by McMillan, *Worship of the Scottish Reformed Church*, p. 146.

5 THE TRADITIONS IN THE REVIVAL

1 Quoted by Stone, *History of the Doctrine*, p. 490.

2 Ibid.

3 Buxton, *Eucharist and Institution*, pp. 159–93.

4 For the texts with commentary see W. J. Grisbrooke, *Anglican Liturgies of the Seventeenth and Eighteenth Centuries* (London: SPCK, 1958).

5 D. Waterland, *A Review of the Doctrine of the Eucharist* (Oxford: Clarendon Press, 1880), first published 1736–40.

6 J. Johnson, 'The Unbloody Sacrifice and Altar, in *Theological Works* (Oxford: John Henry Parker, 1847), first published 1714, vol. I.

7 See E. W. Baker, *A Herald of the Evangelical Revival* (London: Epworth, 1948); J. B. Green, *John Wesley and William Law* (London: Epworth, 1945); *George Whitefield's Journal* (London: Banner of Truth, 1960), pp. 63, 105, 144, 254; *The Life and a Selection of the Letters of the Late Rev. Henry Venn M.A.*, edited by Henry Venn, fifth edition (London: John Hatchard & Son, 1837), pp. 19–20; *Memoirs of the Life of the Rev. Charles Simeon, M.A.*, edited by W. Carus, second edition (London: Hatchard, 1847), p. 9; J. H. Overton, *The Non-Jurors, their Lives, Principles, and Writings* (London: Smith, Elder, 1902), p. 387.

8 I shall examine John's rather than Charles's eucharistic thought on the grounds that, as John is generally considered to be the theological force in the fraternal combination and as I am seeking to relate Wesleyan thought on the Sacrament to other emphases in the Wesleyan Revival, John would seem to be the obvious choice. However, it would seem that their theology of the Eucharist was in essence the same. Therefore, the reference to John throughout this chapter may be seen as a convenient and conventional way of describing the theology of them both.

Following J. C. Bowmer, *The Sacrament of the Lord's Supper in Early Methodism* (London: Dacre Press, 1951), pp. 166–7; O. E. Borgen, *John Wesley on the Sacraments* (Nashville and New York: Abingdon Press, 1972), pp. 26–8; and J. E. Rattenbury, *The Evangelical Doctrine of Charles Wesley's Hymns* (London: Epworth, 1941), pp. 188–203, 215–34 (hereafter cited as *Ev.H.*), I shall treat John Wesley's hymns and translations and, more significantly, Charles Wesley's hymns, as valid expressions of

John's doctrine. I shall refer in particular to the eucharistic hymns first published in 1745 (*Hymns of the Lord's Supper*). The issue quoted hereafter is that published in J. E. Rattenbury, *The Eucharistic Hymns of John and Charles Wesley* (London: Epworth, 1948; hereafter cited as *EH*).

This method has been mildly challenged by J. R. Parris, *John Wesley's Doctrine of the Sacraments* (London: Epworth, 1963), pp. 70–1, and Beckwith, *Priesthood and Sacraments*, p. 61, has warned against viewing them from the perspective of nineteenth- and twentieth-century Anglo-Catholic rather than seventeenth-century Anglican theology. Nevertheless, it would seem that the method is justified on the following grounds. First, John used the method himself by scattering his sermons and writings, e.g. *A Plain Account of Christian Perfection* (London: Epworth Press), with hymnodic material. Second, John's Journals and sermons were originally published with appropriate hymnal appendices (see *The Journal of the Rev. John Wesley, A.M.*, edited by N. Curnock, second edition (London: Robert Culley, 1909–16), vol. II, p. 500). Third, despite the doctrinal differences between the brothers (see Parris, *John Wesley's Doctrine*, p. 71), John always exercised a doctrinal editing function before authorizing and publishing them (see Rattenbury, *Ev.H.*, pp. 64–6). Fourth, the prefaces to the hymn books always strongly commended their use as expressions of 'Scriptural Christianity' (*The Works of John Wesley* (Grand Rapids: Zondervan, [1958])), vol. IX, pp. 319–45. Fifth, his commendation of *The Hymns of the Lord's Supper* was particularly enthusiastic and survived the test of time (Borgen, *John Wesley on the Sacraments*, pp. 28–9; *EH*, pp. 67–8). Sixth, Wesley published an extract from Dean Brevint's 'The Christian Sacrament and Sacrifice' as a preface to *The Hymns of the Lord's Supper*. Borgen (*John Wesley on the Sacraments*, pp. 26–9) has established that Wesley adapted Brevint's work at several key points, thus proving that the version of Brevint published with the hymns is expressive of John's own eucharistic thought. The hymns are divided into sections comparable to those in the treatise and are in many ways poetic renderings of the text. Accordingly, there is an *a priori* case for treating the hymns as a primary source for John's thought.

Of course, following Parris, we must recognize that the hymns are in a poetic genre and, therefore, need to be approached in an appropriate way. Accordingly, I have (in a similar way to Parris), treated the hymns as illustrative rather than innovative examples of Wesley's thought.

9 Wesley, *Journal*, vol. I, p. 472.

10 Ibid.

11 Wesley's own account of his break with the Moravians can be found in his *Journal*, vol. II, pp. 307–500.

12 See ibid., pp. 314, 329ff, 314, 488ff; vol. III, 28 Nov. 1750.

13 Sermon XIV, part ii, sec. 1, 'Means of grace'.

14 See Sermon XII, 'On sin in believers'; Sermon XIV, 'The repentance of believers'; Sermon LXXXV, 'On working out your own salvation';

Sermon v, 'Justification by faith'; Sermon xix, 'The great privilege of those that are born again'; Sermon xlv, 'The new birth'.

15 Wesley, *Plain Account*, p. 52.

16 *HLS* 54.

17 *Journal*, vol. ii, p. 320.

18 Quoted by Rattenbury, *EH*, p. 49.

19 Quoted by Bowmer, *Sacrament of the Lord's Supper*, p. 47.

20 *HLS* 8.

21 Sermon xxvi, part iii, sec. 11, 'Sermon on the Mount – IV'.

22 *HLS* 81.

23 Ibid. 91.

24 Ibid. 54.

25 Ibid. 99; see 4, 9, 13, 25, 30, 42, 57, 60, 62, 81, 86, 90, 126, 141.

26 Ibid. 73; see 22.

27 Ibid. 59; see 57.

28 J. Wesley, *Notes on New Testament*, 1 Cor. 10:16; see 'A Roman catechism and a reply thereto', in *Works*, vol. x, p. 118.

29 *HLS* 72.

30 Ibid. 59.

31 Ibid. 28.

32 Ibid. 71.

33 J. Wesley, 'Roman catechism and reply', p. 118; see *Notes on New Testament*, 1 Cor. 11:24; Matt. 26:26; Mark 14:22; Luke 22:19–20.

34 *HLS* 76; see 56, 57, 58, 66, 72, 73, 76, 89, 92, 166; Sermon xvi, 'The means of grace'; Sermon civ, 'On attending church service'; 'Roman catechism and reply', p. 113; 'Popery calmly considered', in *Works*, vol. x, p. 149.

35 *Notes on New Testament*, 1 Cor. 11:25.

36 *HLS* 126.

37 This hymn describes the high vocation of preachers and is quoted by Bowmer, *Sacrament of the Lord's Supper*, p. 153.

38 *HLS* 126.

39 Ibid. 116.

40 Ibid. 26; cf. 124.

41 Ibid. 3.

42 Ibid. 140.

43 See 'Roman catechism and reply', p. 121; *Notes on New Testament*, Heb. 10:15.

44 *HLS* 126.

45 Ibid. 14; see *MHB* 188. On the general theme of Christ's intercession see *HLS* 5, 30, 104, 117, 126, 129, 137, 140, 148; *Plain Account*, pp. 73, 75; Sermon xiv, 'The repentance of believers'.

46 *HLS* 131.

47 See Rattenbury, *Ev.H.*, p. 190; *HLS* 131.

48 *HLS* 124. See *Notes on New Testament*, 1 Cor. 11:26.

49 See 'Letter to Revd. John Gambold 24 May 1738' and 'Letter to

Richard Viney 22 Nov. 1738', in *Works: Letters 1731–39*, edited by F. Baker, pp. 550–1, 583–4; J. E. Rattenbury, *The Conversion of the Wesleys* (London: Epworth, 1938), pp. 168–73.

50 *Plain Account*, pp. 29–30; see Sermon XLV, part ii, sec. 5, 'The new birth'.

51 *HLS* 54.

52 Ibid. 131.

53 *Plain Account*, p. 30.

54 *HLS* 123; see 3, 131, 134, 137, 140, 141, 142, 147, 153.

55 Ibid. 147.

56 Ibid. 130.

57 Ibid. 147.

58 *Plain Account*, p. 51.

59 *HLS*, 93, 103; *MHB* 407.

60 *Whitefields Journal*, p. 56.

61 See W. J. C. Ervine, 'Doctrine and diplomacy: some aspects of the life and thought of the Anglican Evangelical clergy 1797–1837' (Ph.D. thesis, University of Cambridge, 1979), pp. 21–2.

62 *Memoirs*, edited by Carus, p. 9. It is interesting that not only was Simeon's conversion experience intimately related to the Sacrament but his call to evangelism began on the same morning, together with a concern for the renewal of worship.

63 J. Bateman, *The Life of the Right Rev. Daniel Wilson* (London: Murray, 1860), vol. I, p. 25.

64 Ibid., p. 29. Wilson's experience in the Sacrament displays several classic features of Evangelical conversion: 'a brokenness of heart', a 'step' of faith and experience of grace. His call to evangelism was even more directly related to the Eucharist than was Simeon's – he dated his call to missionary work from the point of his first communion (see ibid.).

65 This is seen most clearly in T. Haweis, *The Communicant's Spiritual Companion* (London: Samuel Swift, 1812). Haweis outlined the aim of his manual in explicitly evangelistic terms, and claimed that a return to the Gospel would inevitably lead to a revival of the Sacrament (p. 2).

66 Ibid. p. 138.

67 D. Wilson, 'A practical address to the communicant', in *Sermons and Tracts*, seventh edition (London: George Wilson, 1825), vol. II, p. 384.

68 Ibid., p. 362.

69 E. Bickersteth, *A Treatise on the Lord's Supper* (London: L. B. Seeley & Son, 1824), p. 90.

70 Ibid., p. 92.

71 C. Simeon, *Works*, vol. XVI, pp. 292–3.

72 W. Romaine, *The Scriptural Doctrine of the Sacrament of the Lord's Supper Briefly Stated* (London: J. Worrall, 1756), p. 14.

73 Ibid., p. 15.

74 e.g. 'I find my not being in Priest's orders as a great hindrance to my ministry' (*Journal*, p. 146).

75 Ibid., p. 136.

76 Bateman, *Life of Wilson*, p. 55.
77 Haweis, *Spiritual Companion*, p. 27.
78 D. Wilson, 'Practical address', p. 366.
79 Haweis, *Spiritual Companion*, p. 77.
80 D. Wilson, 'Practical address', p. 390.
81 Bickersteth, *Treatise*, p. 119.
82 See ibid., p. 133.
83 Haweis, *Spiritual Companion*, p. 12. The vividness of the symbolism was seen as an important aspect of the Sacrament by the Evangelicals. In a similar way to the Puritans, Wilson and Bickersteth appealed to the fraction and libation as powerful representations of the events of the Cross.
84 Bickersteth, *Treatise*, p. 61. He does not name his source.
85 Ibid., p. 117.
86 D. Wilson, 'Practical address', p. 391.
87 Haweis, *Spiritual Companion*, p. 19.
88 D. Wilson, 'Practical address', pp. 392, 387.
89 Haweis, *Spiritual Companion*, p. 65.
90 Bickersteth, *Treatise*, p. 133.
91 Haweis, *Spiritual Companion*, p. 18.
92 Hugh McNeile, *Seventeen Sermons* quoted by E. J. G. Rogers, 'The Holy Communion in the Evangelical tradition', *Churchman*, 67 (1953), 11–18 (p. 18).
93 D. Wilson, 'Practical address', pp. 387–8.
94 See Bickersteth, *Treatise*, pp. 114–16; D. Wilson, 'Practical address', p. 406.
95 Simeon, *Works*, vol. XI, p. 554.
96 Ibid., p. 556.
97 D. Wilson, 'Practical address', p. 365.
98 See Warren, *Strange Victory*.
99 Haweis, *Spiritual Companion*, p. 17.
100 D. Wilson 'Practical address', p. 368.
101 Romaine, *Scriptural Doctrine*, p. 15.
102 Bickersteth, *Treatise*, p. 132.
103 Ibid.
104 Haweis, *Spiritual Companion*, p. 48.
105 D. Wilson, 'Practical address', p. 393.
106 Bowmer, *Sacrament of the Lord's Supper*, pp. 187–205.
107 See Rogers, 'Holy Communion'; 'The Evangelical Fathers and the Liturgy (with special reference to the Holy Communion)', *Churchman*, 60 (1946), 177–83.
108 *EH*, p. 3.
109 *Whitefield's Journal*, p. 195.

6 EVANGELICALS, THE TRADITION AND THE TENSION

1 W. Goode, *The Nature of Christ's Presence in the Eucharist* (London: T. Hatchard, 1856).
2 Ibid., vol. II, p. 6.
3 Ibid., p. 156.
4 Ibid., p. 215.
5 Ibid., p. 179.
6 Ibid., pp. 195, 599.
7 Ibid., p. 210.
8 N. Dimock, *The History of the Book of Common Prayer*, memorial edition (London: Longmans, Green, 1910), p. 94.
9 See Dimock, *Papers on the Doctrine of the English Church concerning the Eucharistic Presence*, memorial edition (London: Longmans, Green, 1911), vol. II, pp. 283–312.
10 Dimock, *Testimonies of English Divines* (London: Elliot Stock, 1896), p. 2.
11 Dimock, *The Doctrine of the Lord's Supper*, memorial edition (London: Longmans, Green, 1910), p. 23.
12 Dimock, *The Christian Doctrine of Sacerdotium*, memorial edition (London: Longmans, Green, 1910), p. 28.
13 *Eucharistic Presence*, vol. II, p. 312.
14 *Lord's Supper*, p. 51.
15 Dimock, *The Doctrine of the Sacraments in relation to the Doctrines of Grace*, new edition (London: Longmans, Green, 1908), p. 5.
16 Dimock, *The Sacerdotium of Christ*, memorial edition (London: Longmans, Green, 1910), p. 129. Dimock was here using the language of Heb. 13:20.
17 *Doctrine of the Sacraments*, p. iv.
18 Ibid., p. 19.
19 Ibid.
20 *Eucharistic Presence*, vol. I, p. viii.
21 The title of Ryle's address to the seventeenth Liverpool Diocesan Conference in 1898 was 'The Present Distress'; see J. C. Ryle, *Charges and Addresses* (Edinburgh: Banner of Truth, 1978), first published 1881–92, pp. 354–66, and a recurring description of the character of the age in Ryle's writings.
22 Ryle, *Knots Untied*, p. 199 – quoting the Church Catechism.
23 Ibid., p. 201.
24 Ibid., p. 239.
25 A clear view of Ryle's perception of the historical situation can be seen in his addresses to his diocesan clergy, a selection of which can be found in *Charges*.
26 *Knots Untied*, p. 216.
27 Ibid., p. 198.
28 *Charges*, pp. 271, 252.

29 *Knots Untied*, p. 198.

30 Ibid., p. 214.

31 *Expository Thoughts on the Gospels: St. John* (London: William Hunt, n.d.), vol. i, p. 403.

32 Ryle, *Holiness* (London: James Clark, 1956), p. 360.

33 *Principles for Churchmen*, p. 262.

34 *Knots Untied*, p. 218.

35 *Holiness*, p. 456.

36 Ibid., p. 430.

37 See *HAL*, pp. 210–12; R. C. D. Jasper, *The Development of the Anglican Liturgy 1662–1980* (London: SPCK, 1989), pp. 73–112.

38 C. Gore, *The Body of Christ*, fourth edition (London: John Murray, 1907).

39 W. H. Frere, *Some Principles of Liturgical Reform* (London: John Murray, 1911). See *Walter Howard Frere: His Correspondence on Liturgical Revision and Construction*, edited by R. C. D. Jasper (London: SPCK, 1954), pp. 24–5.

40 E. A. Knox, *Sacrament or Sacrifice?* (London: Longmans, Green, 1911), p. vii.

41 Ibid., pp. 10–11.

42 Ibid., p. 92.

43 Ibid., pp. 91, 119.

44 W. H. G. Thomas, *A Sacrament of our Redemption*, second edition (London: Bemrose, [1905]). Thomas was not writing against Gore alone but he did refer to him frequently, describing *The Body of Christ* as 'the most important of recent books on the Holy Communion' (p. 96), and was concerned to show that Gore had not succeeded in establishing a half-way house between the Catholic and Protestant positions. Knox passed the same judgement on him (*Sacrament or Sacrifice?*, pp. 91, 108).

45 Gore, *Body of Christ*, p. 11.

46 Ibid., pp. 246, 72; see Thomas, *Sacrament of our Redemption*, p. 22.

47 Ibid., p. 35.

48 Gore, *Body of Christ*, pp. 249; 261; see Thomas, *Sacrament of our Redemption*, p. 97.

49 Gore, *Body of Christ*, p. 269.

50 Ibid., p. 70.

51 Thomas, *Sacrament of our Redemption*, p. 39.

52 Ibid., p. 111.

53 *Frere: Correspondence*, edited by Jasper, p. 63.

54 See correspondence between Frere and Drury, Nov. 1918 to Jan. 1920 (ibid., pp. 62–82). For Drury's more general theological and liturgical views see 'The Lord's Supper', in *Church and Faith*, edited by Wace, pp. 163–206; *Two Studies in the Book of Common Prayer* (London: Nisbet, 1901); *Elevation in the Eucharist* (Cambridge: CUP, 1907).

55 Drury, 'Lord's Supper', pp. 178–9.

56 *Frere: Correspondence*, edited by Jasper, p. 73.

57 Ibid., p. 78.

58 H. B. Gooding, 'The Church – the sacraments – the ministry', in H. A. Wilson *et al.*, *Liberal Evangelicalism: An Interpretation* (London: H & S, 1923), pp. 147–73; A. E. Hughes, 'The sacraments: the Lord's Supper', in *Evangelicalism: By Members of the Fellowship of Evangelical Churchmen* (London: Chas. J. Thyne, 1925), edited by J. Russell Howden, pp. 232–64.

59 Gooding, 'Church – sacraments – ministry', p. 173.

60 Ibid., p. 157.

61 Hughes, 'Sacraments: Lord's Supper', pp. 240, 258.

62 Ibid., p. 246.

63 'Church – sacraments – ministry', pp. 157, 165, 163.

64 W. Joynson-Hicks, *The Prayer Book Crisis* (London: Putnam, 1928); A. Mitchell, *The Holy Communion* (London: CBRP, n.d.), p. 143.

65 Ibid., p. 176.

66 A. Mitchell, 'A liturgical essay', *Churchman*, 43 (1929), 51–62.

67 Ibid., p. 53.

68 Mitchell, *Holy Communion*, pp. 51–2.

69 The more sympathetic environment arose out of the changing theological context, created by such factors as the rise of the Biblical Theology Movement from the mid-1930s, the war-time and post-war ecclesiastical recognition of the need for evangelism (as witnessed by the formation of the Commission on Evangelism in 1943 and Bishop Wand's Mission to London in 1949), and the national profile provided by the Billy Graham Crusade in 1954.

70 *The Evangelical Doctrine of Holy Communion*, edited by A. J. Macdonald (London: SPCK, 1936), p. 132.

71 J. Stafford Wright, 'The place of the Lord's Supper in Evangelical worship', *Churchman*, 48 (1944), 68–75 (p. 72).

72 Ibid.

73 Warren, *Strange Victory*; S. C. Neill, 'The Anglican tradition in liturgy and devotion', *Churchman*, 59 (1945), 99–111.

74 F. Colquhoun, 'The Parish Communion', *Churchman*, 67 (1953), 19–23. See D. E. W. Harrison, *The Book of Common Prayer* (London: Canterbury Press, 1946), pp. 14–16, and W. Leathem's call for the Eucharist to be the principal Sunday service ('Evangelical Catholicity', *Churchman*, 58 (1944), 165–172 (p. 166)).

75 E. J. G. Rogers, 'Evangelical Fathers and the Liturgy'; Rogers, 'Holy Communion in the Evangelical tradition'; Warren, *Strange Victory*.

76 Colquhoun, 'Parish Communion', p. 21. See D. E. W. Harrison, *The Book of Common Prayer*, pp. 128–9.

77 Archbishops' Report, *The Fulness of Christ* (London: SPCK, 1950), p. 64.

78 R. Birch-Hoyle, 'The Holy Spirit in the Eucharist', *Churchman*, 31 (1945), 252–61 (p. 260).

79 Stafford Wright, 'Place of the Lord's Supper', p. 74.

80 Warren, *Strange Victory*, p. 7.

81 Ibid., pp. 82–3.

82 'Symbolism in the early middle ages', in *Evangelical Doctrine of Holy Communion*, edited by Macdonald, pp. 85–118 (p. 105).

83 See A. J. Macdonald, *Berengar and the Reform of Sacramental Doctrine*, pp. 413–14.

84 W. F. P. Chadwick, 'The Sacraments', in *Evangelicals Affirm in the Year of the Lambeth Conference* (London: CBRP, 1948), p. 160.

85 Ibid., p. 161.

86 *Fulness of Christ* p. 87.

87 Ibid., p. 68.

88 Ibid., p. 32.

89 *Fulness of Christ* pp. 79–81. See the reply: W. C. G. Proctor, 'The eucharistic sacrifice', *Churchman*, 65 (1951), 229–31.

90 S. C. Neill, 'The Holy Communion in the Anglican Church', in *The Holy Communion*, edited by H. Martin (London: SCM, 1947), p. 65.

91 C. F. D. Moule, *The Sacrifice of Christ* (London: H & S, 1956), p. 58.

92 Ibid., pp. 47, 48.

93 Ibid., pp. 54, 57.

94 L. W. Brown, *Relevant Liturgy* (London: SPCK, 1965), p. 45. Although Brown's thoughts were not formally published until 1965, it seems reasonable to surmise, both from the context of the discussion and from his influence on the Lambeth Conference of 1958, that he arrived at these views well before 1958.

THE NATURE OF ANGLICAN EVANGELICALISM IN THE RECENT PERIOD

1 The first National Evangelical Anglican Congress was held at Keele University in 1967. It is generally agreed that Keele was a watershed in modern Evangelical life. See John Stott, 'World-wide Evangelical Anglicanism', in *Evangelicals Today*, edited by J. C. King (Guildford and London: Lutterworth, 1973), pp. 176–99 (p. 181). The Congress issued a Statement to express its views, *Keele '67: The National Evangelical Anglican Congress Statement*, edited by P. Crowe (London: CPAS/Falcon Books, 1967). The Keele Statement has been described as 'one of the most important ecclesiastical documents, not only of the sixties but of this century' (A. Hastings, *A History of English Christianity 1970–1980*, third edition (London: SCM, 1991), p. 554).

2 The second National Evangelical Anglican Congress was held at Nottingham University in 1977. It also issued a Statement, *The Nottingham Statement: Statement of the Second National Evangelical Anglican Congress 1977* (London: CPAS/Falcon Books, 1977). It was at the Nottingham Conference that John King first voiced the contemporary problem of Anglican Evangelical self-identity. For the various attempts to address the question see ch. 1 n. 20.

3 The Caister Celebration in 1988 was the successor to the Keele and Nottingham Congresses. It was called in order to encourage the various

sub-groups within Evangelicalism to relate and, hopefully, to cohere. See P. Williams, 'Editorial', *Anvil*, 4 (1987), 2–7; 'NEAC 3 retrospect and prospect', *Anvil*, 5 (1988), 53–70; and G. Reid, 'Why NEAC 3?', in *Evangelical Roots*, edited by S. Henderson (Chippenham: CEEC, 1987), p. 4.

4 For an analysis of the movement during the period see Packer, *Evangelical Anglican Identity Problem*, pp. 24–32; G. J. C. Marchant, 'Through fire and water... to a place of liberty', *Churchman*, 93 (1979), 5–18; R. T. Beckwith, 'Keele, Nottingham and the Future', in *The Evangelical Succession in the Church of England, edited by D. N. Samuel* (Cambridge: James Clark, 1979), pp. 101–10; Buchanan, 'Role and calling' and 'Anglican Evangelicalism: the state of the party', *Anvil*, 1 (1984), 7–18; Manwaring, *From Controversy to Co-existence*, pp. 96–211; M. Saward, *The Anglican Church Today* (London: Mowbray, 1987), pp. 29–73; Hopkinson, 'Changing emphases in self-identity', p. 86; Bebbington, *Evangelicalism in Modern Britain:* Hylson-Smith, *Evangelicals in the Church of England*. For evidence of a similar movement in Evangelicalism in the USA see R. Quebedeaux, *The Young Evangelicals: Revolution in Orthodoxy* (New York: Harper & Row, 1974); *Evangelicals on the Canterbury Trail* edited by R. E. Webber (Waco, Tex.: Word Books, 1985).

5 See E. Troeltsch, *The Social Teaching of the Christian Churches* (London: George Allen & Unwin, 1931), vol. I, pp. 328–49.

6 Hopkinson, 'Changing emphases in self-identity', p. 86.

7 FEARING LITURGICAL REVISION: EVANGELICALS AND LAMBETH 1958

1 *The Lambeth Conference 1958* (London: SPCK and Seabury Press, 1958).

2 Ibid., pp. 83–5 (from which the following quotations are taken).

3 The Oxford Conference of Evangelical Churchmen in 1961 was dedicated to the question of eucharistic sacrifice and specifically to a refutation of Lambeth. See *Eucharistic Sacrifice*, edited by Packer. Stibbs, Green and Rodgers took up the theme of eucharistic sacrifice in the context of the debate arising from Lambeth. See A. M. Stibbs, *Sacrament, Sacrifice and Eucharist* (London: Tyndale Press, 1961); E. M. B. Green, 'The doctrine of Holy Communion', *Churchman*, 76 (1962), 90–8; J. H. Rodgers, 'Eucharistic sacrifice; blessing or blasphemy?', *Churchman*, 78 (1964), 248–54. Beckwith and Buchanan discussed the liturgical expression of Lambeth. See R. T. Beckwith, 'Lambeth 1958 and the "Liturgy for Africa" (I) and (II)', *Churchman*, 79 (1965), 248–54; 80 (1966), 33–40; *MAL*.

4 E. L. Mascall, 'A note on eucharistic sacrifice', in *Lambeth and Liturgy*, edited by A. H. Couratin (London: Church Union, 1959), pp. 12–16. It also received Roman Catholic criticism in F. Clark, *Eucharistic Sacrifice and the Reformation*, second edition (Oxford: Blackwell, 1967).

5 F. C. N. Hicks, *The Fullness of Sacrifice* (London: SPCK, 1946), first

published 1930. Evangelicals did recognize that Hicks was merely applying to the Eucharist the understanding of sacrifice which was accepted by many contemporary Old Testament scholars, but this increased rather than allayed their fears.

6 S. C. Gayford, *Sacrifice and Priesthood* (London: Methuen, 1924).

7 Dix, *Shape of the Liturgy*.

8 E. L. Mascall, *Christ, the Christian and the Church* (London: Longmans, Green, 1946), p. 112; see *Corpus Christi* (London: Longmans, Green, 1953).

9 J. I. Packer, 'Introduction to Lambeth 1958', in *Eucharistic Sacrifice*, edited by Packer, pp. 1–21 (p. 12).

10 R. J. Coates, 'The doctrine of eucharistic sacrifice in modern times', ibid., pp. 127–53 (p. 149).

11 Rodgers, 'Blessing or blasphemy?', p. 254.

12 Coates, 'Eucharistic sacrifice in modern times', p. 145.

13 Ibid., p. 146.

14 J. R. S. Taylor, 'The English Reformers' doctrine of the Eucharist', ibid., pp. 118–26 (p. 121).

15 e.g. E. M. B. Green, 'Doctrine of Holy Communion', pp. 91–2; Stibbs, *Sacrament, Sacrifice and Eucharist*, p. 81. The quotation is from Dix, *Shape of the Liturgy*, p. 672.

16 J. R. S. Taylor, 'The English Reformers' doctrine of the Eucharist', in *Eucharist Sacrifice*, edited by Packer, p. 122.

17 As Evangelicals defined the Sacrament's *raison d'être* in terms of the proclamation before men of Christ's death as the basis and source of the atonement, they were suspicious of Lambeth's suggestion that the Prayer of Consecration should not be focused exclusively on the Cross but should include 'thanksgiving for all the principal "mighty works of God"' (*Lambeth Conference*, p. 81).

18 Packer, 'Introduction to Lambeth 1958', p. 16.

19 For evidence of the position in the 1950s see D. R. Vicary, 'The revision of the Communion service', *Churchman*, 67 (1953), 23–9; T. Hewitt, 'Revision of the Communion Service', *Churchman*, 73 (1959), 163–7 (p. 166); 'Findings of the Oxford Conference of Evangelical Churchmen', in *Churchman*, 72 (1958). For evidence of the position in the early 1960s see Green, 'Doctrine of Holy Communion'; Stibbs, *Sacrament, Sacrifice and Eucharist*; Bromiley, 'Prayer Book development to 1662', *Churchman* 76 (1962), 7–15; J. A. Motyer, 'Principles of Prayer Book revision', *Churchman*, 76 (1962), 36–8; Beckwith, 'Lambeth 1958 and the "Liturgy for Africa" (1)'.

20 Bromiley, 'Prayer Book development to 1662'.

21 See *Studia Liturgica*, 3 (1964).

22 Motyer, 'Principles of Prayer Book revision', p. 38.

23 R. J. Coates, 'The ministry of the sacraments and the occasional offices', *Churchman*, 74 (1960), 31–6 (p. 33).

24 Beckwith, in 'The Pan-Anglican Document' and 'Lambeth 1958 and

the "Liturgy for Africa" (1)', claimed that the dominant influence on Anglican liturgical revision had been the Church of South India and 'the school of English neo-catholic liturgiologists represented by Dix, Ratcliff and Couratin' ('Pan-Anglican Document', in *MAL*, pp. 22–32 (p. 27)).

25 M. Parsons, *The Holy Communion* (London: H & S, 1961).

8 FACING LITURGICAL REVISION: EVANGELICALS AND SERIES TWO

1 'A Draft Order for Holy Communion', in the Church of England Liturgical Commission, *Alternative Services: Second Series* (London: SPCK, 1965), pp. 145–60 (p. 145).

2 Ibid.

3 *The Liturgical Conference 1966* (Oxford: CIO, 1966), pp. 70–87. A question mark was raised over the oblation by an Evangelical (Peter Johnston), but his was a lone voice.

4 *An Order for Holy Communion: A Report of the Church of England Liturgical Commission to the Archbishops of Canterbury and York April 1966* (London: SPCK, 1966).

5 Ibid. The wording of Buchanan's dissent had been slightly changed in the Report's version from his original note. For the original see C. O. Buchanan, *The New Communion Service: Reasons for Dissent* (London: CBRP, 1966), p. 3.

6 C. O. Buchanan, *Evangelical Anglicans and Liturgy* (Bramcote: GB, 1984), pp. 9–12.

7 They were (from summer 1962) F. D. Coggan (Chairman), D. E. W. Harrison, F. J. Taylor, C. W. J. Bowles.

8 Buchanan, *Evangelical Anglicans and Liturgy*, p. 10. During the debate Buchanan was writing a booklet designed to encourage Evangelicals (and others) to use the new service: *A Guide to the New Communion Service* (London: CBRP, 1966). In 1968 he followed this with an encouragement to use the authorized service: *A Guide to Second Series Communion Service* (London: CBRP, 1968).

9 Packer, 'Gain and loss', in *Towards a Modern Prayer Book*, edited by R. T. Beckwith (Abingdon: MMP, 1966), pp. 74–94 (p. 90). See Packer, *Tomorrow's Worship* Prayer Book Reform Series (Abingdon: MMP, 1965), pp. 19, 24–31.

10 See R. T. Beckwith, 'Introduction', in *Towards a Modern Prayer Book*, edited by Beckwith, pp. 4–6; G. E. Duffield, *Revision and the Layman* (London: CBRP, 1966), pp. 12–14.

11 For evidence in the mid-1960s see J. W. Charley, 'The Draft Order for Holy Communion', in *Towards a Modern Prayer Book*, edited by Beckwith, pp. 56–67 (p. 60); Buchanan, *Reasons for Dissent*, p. 4; *Keele Statement*, para. 66.

12 See J. A. Simpson, 'The new alternative services', *Churchman*, 80 (1966),

26–33 (pp. 31–2); Charley, 'Draft Order for Holy Communion', pp. 60–7; R. T. Beckwith and J. E. Tiller, *The Service of Holy Communion and its Revision* (Abingdon: MMP, 1972), pp. 28–9, 46–8; Packer, 'Gain and loss', p. 80.

13 See Charley, 'Draft Order for Holy Communion', p. 64.

14 See D. D. Billings, *Services on Trial* (London: CBRP, 1966), pp. 13–14; Packer, 'Gain and loss'; Packer, *Tomorrow's Worship*, pp. 19, 25–6; Simpson, 'New alternative services', p. 31; Beckwith, 'Lambeth 1958 and the "Liturgy for Africa" (II)', pp. 33–4.

15 All five points were raised and discussed by Colin Buchanan in correspondence with Eric Kemp in May and September 1966.

16 R. C. D. Jasper, 'Gore on liturgical revision', *Church Quarterly Review*, 166 (1965), 21–36 (p. 33). See also Packer, 'Gain and loss', pp. 88–9, and *Tomorrow's Worship*, p. 25; Beckwith and Tiller, *Holy Communion and its Revision*, p. 35.

17 See Charley, 'Draft Order for Holy Communion', p. 64; Simpson, 'New alternative services', p. 32.

18 See Charley, 'Draft Order for Holy Communion', p. 65; Simpson, 'New Alternative Services', p. 33; E. M. B. Green, 'Christ's Sacrifice and ours', in *Guidelines: Anglican Evangelicals Face the Future*, edited by J. I. Packer (London: CPAS/Falcon Books, 1967), pp. 87–118 (p. 112); *Keele Statement*, para. 68; Beckwith and Tiller, *Holy Communion and its Revision*, p. 32.

19 See Charley, 'Draft Order for Holy Communion', p. 65; *Keele Statement*, para. 68; Beckwith and Tiller, *Holy Communion and its Revision*, p. 31.

20 Charley, 'Draft Order for Holy Communion', p. 65.

21 e.g. Green, 'Christ's Sacrifice and ours'.

22 Buchanan, *Reasons for Dissent*, p. 4. See also Green, 'Christ's Sacrifice and ours', p. 113; Beckwith and Tiller, *Holy Communion and its Revision*, p. 27.

23 Buchanan, *Reasons for Dissent*, p. 4.

24 J. L. Houlden, 'Good liturgy or even good battlefield?', *Theology*, 69 (1966), 434–7 (p. 434).

25 See Beckwith and Buchanan, '"This Bread and This Cup"', *Theology*, 70 (1967), 265–71; Buchanan, 'Introductory Note', in C. H. B. Byworth and B. T. Lloyd, *A Eucharist for the Seventies* (Northwood: Northwood Christian Book Centre, 1968).

26 See E. C. Ratcliff: 'The Communion Service of the Prayer Book', and 'The principles governing liturgical reform', in *E. C. Ratcliff: Reflections on Liturgical Revision*, edited by D. H. Tripp (Bramcote: GB, 1980), pp. 12–19, 20–6; 'The eucharistic narrative of Justin Martyr's *First Apology*'; and 'The Sanctus and the pattern of the early Anaphora', in *Liturgical Studies*, edited by A. H. Couratin and D. H. Tripp, pp. 41–48, pp. 18–40; A. H. Couratin, 'Liturgy', in J. Daniélou, A. H. Couratin and J. Kent, *The Pelican Guide to Modern Theology*, vol. II (Harmondsworth: Penguin Books, 1969), pp. 131–240; Couratin, 'The Thanks-

giving: an essay', in *The Sacrifice of Praise*, edited by B. D. Spinks (Rome: Centro Liturgico Vincenziano, 1981), pp. 20–61; Couratin, 'Thanksgiving and thankoffering', *Studia Liturgica*, 3 (summer 1964), 53–7.

27 Ratcliff, 'Principles governing liturgical reform', p. 23.

28 Buchanan, *Reasons for Dissent*, p. 6; Buchanan, 'Introductory Note', in Byworth and Lloyd, *Eucharist for the Seventies*.

29 Buchanan, *Reasons for Dissent*, p. 13.

30 Ibid., pp. 6, 12–13; Beckwith and Buchanan, '"This Bread and This Cup"', p. 271.

31 The chairman of the group was H. J. Carpenter, the Bishop of Oxford, and its members were Leslie Brown, Eric Kemp, Leo Stephens-Hodge and Peter Johnston.

32 I am grateful to Colin Buchanan and Eric Kemp for permission to quote (here and in the above text) from their private correspondence from May and June 1966.

33 For the text agreed by the Bishop of Oxford's group see *MAL*, p. 142.

34 Ibid., p. 119; *Recent Liturgical Revision in the Church of England* (Bramcote: GB, 1973), pp. 24–7.

35 For the text see *MAL*, p. 142.

36 Ibid.

37 See Beckwith and Tiller, *Holy Communion and its Revision*, pp. 7–8; Buchanan, *Evangelical Anglicans and Liturgy*, p. 20 n. 3.

38 Buchanan, 'Introductory Note', in Byworth and Lloyd, *Eucharist for the Seventies*.

39 The *Keele Statement* (April 1967) identified the three different attitudes amongst Evangelicals towards liturgical revision, which could be characterized as conservative, progressive and radical. It did not indicate where the weight of opinion lay, but the following comments reveal the mood of the Congress: 'Liturgical Revision is long overdue'; 'to all [Evangelicals] the period of experiment is welcome' (para. 66).

40 D. A. Scales, *What Mean Ye by This Service* (Cambridge: Truth and Faith Society, 1969).

41 *Keele Statement*, para. 76.

9 WELCOMING LITURGICAL REVISION: EVANGELICALS AND SERIES THREE TO THE ASB AND BEYOND

1 References to Synodical debates have not been given as they can be traced in General Synod, *Report of Proceedings* (CIO), from the dates of the debates given in the text. However, where appropriate, references to individual speeches have been cited. For a history and analysis of the development of Series Three see *HAL*, pp. 214–19; Jasper, *Development*, pp. 308–69. The most detailed history is to be found in Buchanan's studies. As he admitted, he could 'not pretend to be a dispassionate historian writing definitive history'. Instead, he attempted to write

'*accurate* journalism' (*Recent Liturgical Revision*, p. 3). Clearly, for our purposes, he cannot be regarded as a theologically neutral observer. Nevertheless, the following works attempt to be factual records (and generally succeed) rather than evaluative discussions. Therefore, given appropriate allowances, they may be treated as valid sources: *FAL*, pp. 41–5; *Recent Liturgical Revision*, plus supplements A–C; *Latest Liturgical Revision in the Church of England 1978–1984* (Bramcote: GB, 1984), pp. 8–12. Buchanan also provided month-by-month accounts of the progress of liturgical revision in *NOL* 1975–80.

2 See E. M. B. Green with E. L. Mascall, 'Eucharistic sacrifice – some interim agreement', in C. O. Buchanan, E. L. Mascall, J. I. Packer and the Bishop of Willesden, *Growing into Union: Proposals for Forming a United Church in England* (London: SPCK, 1970), pp. 186–92.

3 Buchanan, *Evangelical Anglicans and Liturgy*, p. 12. It should be noted that the crucial verb in the *anamnesis* – 'celebrate' – was included after a suggestion from outside the Commission and so was not a product of the dialogue between Jasper, Ross and Buchanan; see *FAL*, p. 41.

4 CELC, *A Report to the Archbishops of Canterbury and York. Alternative Services Series 3: An Order for Holy Communion* (London: SPCK, 1971).

5 *An Order for Holy Communion: Alternative Services Series 3* (London: SPCK, 1973).

6 Buchanan, *Reasons for Dissent*, p. 6; 'Editorial', *NOL* 42 (June 1978), 1–2 (p. 2); 'Anglican Evangelicalism', p. 14.

7 Beckwith and Tiller, *Holy Communion and its Revision*, pp. 86–92; R. T. Beckwith, *The Revised Series Three Communion: A Way Forward* (Oxford: LH, 1979), pp. 13–19. He welcomed the changes made from Series Two but felt that they did not go far enough in the Reformed direction.

8 'The approaching revision of Series Three', *Churchman*, 90 (1976), 289–93 (pp. 289, 291); *Revised Series Three Communion*, pp. 6, 13, 21, 39.

9 C. O. Buchanan, *Patterns of Sunday Worship* (Bramcote: GB, 1972), p. 3.

10 Buchanan and Pawson, *Infant Baptism under Cross-Examination* (1974), p. 3. The same was repeated in the second edition, 1976.

11 Titles in the first two years of the Series' life offered a guide to Series Three Holy Communion, a justification of its language, detailed accounts of its evolution and ideas for its setting to music. Grove Books also published the following aids to the use of the new service: *Collects for use with the New Lectionary* (1972), *Series 3 for the Family* (1973), *Series 3 for Children* (1974).

12 Beckwith, 'Approaching revision of Series Three', p. 291.

13 Beckwith and Tiller, *Holy Communion and its Revision*, pp. 47–8.

14 Buchanan, 'The Order for Holy Communion', in *Anglican Worship Today*, edited by C. O. Buchanan, B. T. Lloyd and H. Miller (London: Collins Liturgical Publications, 1980), pp. 115–51.

15 Beckwith, 'A turning point in Prayer Book revision', *Churchman*, 89 (1975), 120–9 (p. 126).

16 Buchanan, *Reasons for Dissent*, p. 6.

17 See D. D. Billings, *Alternative Eucharistic Prayers* (Bramcote: GB, 1973), pp. 3–8; D. G. Kibble, 'The Reformation and the Eucharist', *Churchman*, 94 (1980), 43–57.

18 D. A. Scales, 'The theology of the English Reformers: a survey of some important themes', in *Evangelical Succession*, edited by Samuel, pp. 5–29 (p. 16).

19 Beckwith, 'Do the alternative services legalize reservation?', *Churchman*, 85 (1971), 203–15 (p. 213).

20 See Buchanan, *Liturgy for Communion* (Bramcote: GB, 1979), p. 19; 'Editorial', *NOL* 55 (July 1979), pp. 1–2. Colin Buchanan did join with Roger Beckwith and James Packer in a contribution to the debate which sought to analyse the issue of reservation in relation to the communion of the sick. Both Beckwith and Packer were prepared to allow communion of the sick by extended administration provided that perpetual reservation and extra-liturgical practices were explicitly excluded. Buchanan went on to discuss the practical means by which this could be organized so as to 'obviate any alleged need for reservation' ('Communion of the sick: a new approach', in C. O. Buchanan, R. T. Beckwith, J. I. Packer and C. O. Buchanan, *Reservation and Communion of the Sick* (Bramcote: GB, 1972), pp. 22–8).

21 Beckwith, 'Approaching revision of Series Three', p. 292. Beckwith's suggested changes were as follows: *Prayers for the dead*: to excise 'that in them your will may be fulfilled' from the commendation; *eucharistic sacrifice*: to remove 'accept through him, our great high priest, this our sacrifice of thanks and praise' from the eucharistic prayer and to insert it into the post-communion Prayer of Oblation; *reservation*: to change the rubric from the present tense ('Any consecrated bread and wine which is not...') to the perfect tense ('Any consecrated bread and wine which has not been...').

22 Beckwith recorded their findings in *Revised Series Three Communion*, pp. 23–4. For Buchanan's reaction see 'A cross wind', *NOL* 36 (Dec. 1977), pp. 1–3.

23 *Nottingham Statement*, para. F.3(d).

24 Ibid., para. F.3(e).

25 Samuel, 'The challenge of the twentieth century', in *Evangelical Succession*, edited by Samuel, pp. 82–100 (p. 98).

26 See Buchanan, *Liturgy for Communion*, pp. 15–16.

27 Buchanan, *The End of the Offertory* (Bramcote: GB, 1978), p. 29; see also pp. 4, 38–9.

28 *GS 364 Alternative Services Holy Communion Series Three Revised* (London: SPCK, 1978).

29 Beckwith, *Revised Series Three Communion*, p. 24.

30 See ibid., pp. 31–8. For the text of the Hippolytan-inspired prayer see 'Proposals for an Alternative Thanksgiving', *NOL* 47 (Nov. 1978), pp. 7–8.

31 Buchanan, 'Series 3 Holy Communion Revised Revised', *NOL* 49 (1979), 3–4.
32 Beckwith, *Revised Series Three Communion*, p. 33.
33 Saward, *Evangelicals on the Move*, p. 51.
34 *GS 364A Alternative Services – Series 3: The Order for Holy Communion* (London: SPCK, 1979).
35 Beckwith, *Revised Series Three Communion*, pp. 41–2. For Buchanan's reaction to Beckwith's approval of *GS 364A* see his review of Beckwith's *Revised Series Three Communion* in *NOL* 50 (Feb. 1979), p. 7.
36 Dix, *Shape of the Liturgy*, p. 720.
37 Published as *Ministry to the Sick* (1983) by the publishers of the ASB 1980.
38 *Patterns for Worship* (London: Church House Publishing, 1989).

10 EVANGELICALS AND ECUMENICAL STATEMENTS ON THE EUCHARIST

1 'An open letter concerning the Anglican–Methodist relations', February 1964, in *All in Each Place*, edited by J. I. Packer (Abingdon: MMP, 1965), pp. 15–16.
2 *All in Each Place* is the title of a compendium of Evangelical essays, referred to in n. 1, which suggested alternative proposals for reunion in England to those upon which the Anglican–Methodist Conversations (1963) were based.
3 'Open letter: Anglican–Methodist relations'. see *All in Each Place*, edited by Packer; *Keele Statement*, para. 81; *Unity on the Ground*, edited by C. O. Buchanan (London: SPCK, 1972); *Nottingham Statement*, para. L.1.
4 See M. Harper, 'Christian unity: the growing fact', *Renewal*, 30 (1970–1), pp. 2–5; *This is the Day: A Fresh Look at Christian Unity* (London: H & S, 1979).
5 See G. E. Duffield, 'Agreeing in the truth', in *Evangelicals and Unity*, edited by J. D. Douglas (Abingdon: MMP, 1964), pp. 82–94; James Atkinson, 'The Gospel and reunion', in *All in Each Place*, edited by Packer, pp. 41–56; *Keele Statement*, para. 66; *Nottingham Statement*, para. L.1.
6 The issues of intercommunion and open communion absorbed a lot of Evangelical energy during the 1960s and early 1970s. However, I do not propose to deal with the debate, as it reflected more the psychology of the Ecumenical Movement and the Church of England at a particular period in history than a real engagement with the substantial theological themes of the Eucharist. The arguments can be traced in G. E. Duffield, 'Intercommunion and the ministry', *Churchman*, 77 (1963), pp. 235–43; Duffield, *Admission to Holy Communion* (Abingdon: MMP, 1964); R. T. Beckwith, *Priesthood and Sacraments*, pp. 100–12; J. P. Hickinbotham, *The Open Table: Christian Hospitality at the Lord's Table*, Christian Foundations Series 13 (London: H & S, 1966); C. O. Buchanan with the Bishop of Willesden, 'Intercommunion – some interim agreement', in Buchanan

et al., *Growing into Union*, pp. 176–85; G. E. Duffield, *A Guide to Intercommunion Today* (London: CBRP, 1970).

7 *Conversations between the Church of England and the Methodist Church: A Report* (London: CIO/Epworth Press, 1963). For the section on the Eucharist, see pp. 21–33.

8 'A Dissentient view', in *Conversations*, pp. 57–63.

9 Beckwith, *Priesthood and Sacraments*, p. 76.

10 *Conversations*, p. 32.

11 Beckwith, *Priesthood and Sacraments*, p. 82.

12 Ibid.

13 Ibid., p. 77.

14 Beckwith, 'The Gospel and Sacraments', in *The Church of England and the Methodist Church*, edited by J. I. Packer (Abingdon, MMP, 1963), pp. 18–23 (p. 84).

15 Ibid., p. 90.

16 Ibid. Beckwith developed this theme in 'The doctrine of Holy Communion', in *The Oxford Conference 1975: Agreement in the Faith* (London: CBRP, 1975), pp. 73–80 (pp. 76–8).

17 Beckwith, *Priesthood and Sacraments*, p. 91.

18 See *Prospects for Reconciliation*, edited by C. O. Buchanan (Northwood: Northwood Christian Book Centre, 1967), pp. 1–3 (p. 2).

19 Anglican–Methodist Unity Commission, *Towards Reconciliation: An Interim Statement* (London: SPCK/Epworth Press, 1967). For the section on the Eucharist see pp. 19–21.

20 Beckwith, 'Priesthood and Holy Communion', ibid., pp. 10–13 (p. 13).

21 Anglican–Methodist Unity Commission, *Anglican–Methodist Unity*, part 2, *The Scheme* (London: SPCK/Epworth Press, 1968), pp. 30–2.

22 See James Packer's dissension from the Commission's proposed Service of Reconciliation (Anglican–Methodist Unity Commission, *The Scheme*, pp. 182–3) and Buchanan's and Packer's objections and alternative to the scheme in *Growing into Union*.

23 The work, *Growing into Union*, was published in 1970 but it was discussed and written in 1969.

24 Ibid., pp. 59–60. Julian Charley described *Growing into Union* as 'an auspicious preliminary' to the meeting of Anglican–Roman Catholic International Commission at Windsor in 1971 to discuss the Eucharist (*The Anglican Roman Catholic Agreement on the Eucharist*, (Bramcote: GB, 1971), p. 8). He quoted this passage as an expression of the meaning of the disputed clause in the Statement which talked of the Church entering into the 'movement of [Christ's] self-offering' (ibid., p. 18).

25 E. M. M. Green and E. L. Mascall, 'Eucharistic sacrifice – some interim agreement', *Growing into Union*, appendix 4, pp. 186–92 (p. 191).

26 Ibid., p. 188.

27 Ibid.

28 Ibid.

29 For a complete catalogue of Evangelical response to each stage of the

ARCIC process in relation to the Eucharist see C. J. Cocksworth, 'A study of Evangelical eucharistic thought – in the Church of England with special references to the period *c.* 1960–*c.* 1980' (Ph.D. thesis, University of Manchester, 1989), p. 398 n. 32.

30 *Keele Statement*, para. 96.

31 *Nottingham Statement*, para. M1(b).

32 Julian Charley saw himself as representing the Evangelical wing of the Church of England. As a member of the sub-commission dealing with the Eucharist he had a significant role in drafting the Statement and also in criticizing its early versions (see *Anglican Roman Catholic Agreement*, p. 7; *Rome, Canterbury, and the Future* (Bramcote: GB, 1982), p. 17). When describing ARCIC's reception at Nottingham, Trevor Lloyd records how Charley's participation with 'integrity…inspired confidence' in the Statement (*Evangelicals, Obedience and Change*, p. 21).

33 Buchanan claimed that he 'shadowed the Anglican–Roman Catholic Agreement on the Eucharist (1971)' ('Editorial Introduction', in *Essays on Eucharistic Sacrifice in the Early Church*, edited by Buchanan (Bramcote: GB, 1984), p. 2).

34 'The ARCIC Agreed Statements are not agreeable to Scripture and the 39 Articles. For the motion: David Samuel. Against the motion: George Carey', *Churchman*, 102 (1988), pp. 151–65.

35 D. N. Samuel, *Agreeing to Differ* (Grimsby: Harrison Trust, 1981), pp. 14–17; R. T. Beckwith (on behalf of the Evangelical Anglican–Roman Catholic Dialogue Team), *Christ's Presence and Sacrifice* (London: CBRP, 1973), pp. 18–19; Beckwith, 'The ecumenical quest for agreement in faith', *Themelios*, 10 (1984), 28–30 (p. 30).

36 Beckwith, 'Relations with Rome: the present situation and the immediate prospects', *Churchman*, 94 (1980), 315–19 (p. 318).

37 Samuel, *Agreeing to Differ*, p. 17.

38 Buchanan, *ARCIC and LIMA on Baptism and the Eucharist* (Bramcote: GB, 1983), pp. 12–13.

39 Beckwith, *Christ's Presence and Sacrifice*, p. 19.

40 *Evangelical Anglicans and the ARCIC Final Report*, drafted by John Stott on behalf of the CEEC (Bramcote: GB, 1982), pp. 6–7. See also Stott, *The Cross of Christ* (London: IVP, 1986), pp. 267–73.

41 CEEC, 'Open letter concerning the eucharistic Statement', *CEN* 18 Feb. 1972, p. 4; 'An open letter: on relations between the Anglican Churches and the Roman Catholic, Eastern Orthodox, Old Catholic and Ancient Oriental Churches, June 1977', in R. T. Beckwith, G. E. Duffield and J. I. Packer, *Across the Divide* (Basingstoke: Lyttelton Press, 1977), pp. 4–13; G. L. Bray, *Sacraments and Ministry in Ecumenical Perspective* (Oxford: LH, 1984).

42 Buchanan, 'The Order for Holy Communion', in *Anglican Worship Today*, edited by Buchanan, Lloyd and Miller, pp. 115–51 (p. 124). See Buchanan, *ARCIC and LIMA on Baptism and the Eucharist*, p. 14 n. 3.

43 Charley, *Rome, Canterbury, and the Future*, p. 18.

44 Samuel, *Agreeing to Differ*, p. 18.
45 Beckwith, *Christ's Presence and Sacrifice*, pp. 19–20; Beckwith, 'The ecumenical quest for agreement in faith', p. 29. He did not feel that *Elucidations* sufficiently remedied the situation ('Relations with Rome', p. 318).
46 'Open letter: 1977'; 'An open letter to the Anglican Episcopate: ARCIC' (Bramcote: GB, 1988), para. 5. See also 'Open letter: 1972'.
47 Stott, *Assessment and Critique*, p. 7.
48 Charley, *Anglican Roman Catholic Agreement*, p. 20.
49 Ibid., p. 21.
50 Buchanan, *ARCIC and LIMA on Baptism and the Eucharist*, pp. 15–16.
51 *Baptism, Eucharist and Ministry*, Faith and Order Paper 111 (Geneva: WCC, 1982).
52 T. Price, *Evangelical Anglicans and the Lima Text* (Bramcote: GB, 1985), p. 92.
53 Ibid., pp. 16, 23–4.
54 Beckwith, 'The ecumenical quest for agreement in faith', p. 30.
55 Price, *Evangelical Anglicans and the Lima Text*, p. 12.
56 Buchanan, *ARCIC and LIMA on Baptism and Eucharist*, p. 15.
57 Beckwith, 'The Ecumenical quest for agreement in faith', p. 29. For other Evangelical support on this see D. Gregg, *Anamnesis in the Eucharist* (Bramcote: GB, 1976), p. 26; A. C. Thiselton, *Language, Liturgy and Meaning*, GLS 2 (Bramcote: GB, 1975), p. 31; Bray, *Sacraments and Ministry*, pp. 4–25; Price, *Evangelical Anglicans and the Lima Text*, p. 12.
58 Ibid., p. 12; see also Buchanan, *ARCIC and LIMA on Baptism and Eucharist*, pp. 12–14.
59 *Anglican–Lutheran International Conversations: The Report of the Conversations 1970–1972 authorized by the Lambeth Conference and the Lutheran World Federation* (London: SPCK: 1973).
60 *Anglican–Lutheran Dialogue: The Report of the Anglican–Lutheran European Regional Commission* (London: SPCK, 1983).
61 *Anglican–Lutheran Conversations*, paras. 68, 69, 63.
62 *Anglican–Lutheran Dialogue*, paras. 28, 27.
63 *Anglican–Orthodox Dialogue: The Moscow Agreed Statement*, edited by K. Ware and C. Davey (London: SPCK, 1977).
64 *Anglican–Orthodox Dialogue: The Dublin Agreed Statement* (London: SPCK, 1984).
65 *Moscow Statement*, paras. 31, 30.
66 See K. Ware, 'The Moscow Conference 1976', in *Moscow Statement*, pp. 39–81 (pp. 71–2).
67 'Thessaloniki Meeting 1977', in *Moscow Statement*, pp. 92–3.
68 Ibid., p. 93.
69 See Ware, 'The Moscow Conference 1976', pp. 72–3.
70 'Thessaloniki Meeting 1977', p. 93.
71 *Dublin Statement*, para. 111.
72 Ibid., para. 109.

73 Ibid., para. 111; see also *Moscow Statement*, para. 25.
74 Beckwith, 'The Ecumenical quest for agreement in faith', p. 29.
75 *God's Reign and our Unity: The Report of the Anglican–Reformed International Commission 1981–1984* (London: SPCK, 1984).
76 Ibid., para. 68.
77 Ibid., paras. 65, 63.
78 Bray, *Sacraments and Ministry*.
79 Charley, *Anglican Roman Catholic Agreement*, p. 17.
80 Buchanan, *ARCIC and LIMA on Baptism and Eucharist*, p. 12.
81 Ibid., p. 12.
82 Bray, *Sacraments and Ministry*, p. 8.
83 Ibid., p. 9.
84 Buchanan, *ARCIC and LIMA on Baptism and Eucharist*, p. 14.
85 Gregg, *Anamnesis in the Eucharist*, pp. 4, 24–5. For a similar analysis see Thiselton, *Language, Liturgy and Meaning*, pp. 25–32.
86 Gregg, *Anamnesis in the Eucharist*, p. 25.
87 Ibid., p. 24.
88 Packer, 'Reservation: theological issues', in Beckwith, Packer and Buchanan, *Reservation and Communion of the Sick*, pp. 15–21 (p. 20).
89 Bray, *Sacraments and Ministry*, p. 18; see also pp. 15–17, 22–3.
90 Charley, *Anglican Roman Catholic Agreement*, p. 19.
91 Ibid., p. 21.
92 Ibid., p. 20.

11 EVANGELICALS, THE EUCHARIST AND SPIRITUALITY

1 J. R. W. Stott, *Your Confirmation* (London: H & S, 1958), p. 97. See also *Basic Christianity* (London: IVF, 1958), p. 142.
2 *Keele Statement*, para. 76.
3 C. H. Hutchings, 'The Church and Holy Communion', in *Evangelical Essays on Church and Sacraments*, edited by C. O. Buchanan (London: SPCK, 1972), pp. 62–73 (p. 68).
4 Buchanan 'Liturgy', in *Evangelicals Today*, edited by King, p. 68.
5 Hutchings, 'Church and Communion', p. 65.
6 Buchanan, *Patterns of Sunday Worship*, p. 15.
7 Hopkinson, 'Changing emphases in self-identity', p. 182.
8 Buchanan and Pawson, *Infant Baptism under Cross-Examination*, p. 3.
9 T. Lloyd, 'The life of the local Church', in *Obeying Christ in a Changing World*, edited by Cundy (London: Collins, 1977), vol. II, pp. 42–66 (p. 56).
10 *Nottingham Statement*, para. F.3.
11 Buchanan, 'Role and calling', p. 35.
12 Buchanan, *The Heart of Sunday Worship*, GWS 121 (Bramcote: GB, 1992), p. 22.
13 Y. M. J. Congar, *I Believe in the Holy Spirit* (London: Geoffrey Chapman, 1983), vol. II, p. 168.

14 E. Troeltsch, *The Social Teaching of the Christian Churches* (London: George Allen & Unwin, 1931), vol. I, p. 232.

15 Roman Catholic Church International, 'The Charismatic Renewal and Ecumenism', in *Presence, Power, Praise: Documents on the Charismatic Renewal*, edited by K. McDonnell (Collegeville, Minn.: Liturgical Press, 1980), vol. III, pp. 175–279.

16 Ibid., pp. 251–2.

17 See various Roman Catholic and Lutheran Reports, ibid., vols. II and III.

18 J. B. Hillyer, 'Liturgical change in Cambridge; attitudes to liturgy with special reference to charismatic gifts' (M.Phil. thesis, King's College, University of London, 1977), pp. 52–5.

19 J. Bax, *The Good Wine: Spiritual Renewal in the Church of England* (London: Church House Publishing, 1986), p. 175.

20 e.g. C. O. Buchanan, *Encountering Charismatic Worship*, (Bramcote: GB, 1977).

21 Lutheran Church in America, 'The Charismatic Movement in the Lutheran Church in America' (1974); Presbyterian Church, Canada, 'The Work of the Spirit, (1976), in *Power, Presence, Praise*, edited by McDonnell, vol. I, pp. 547–73; vol. II, pp. 221–55; J. Gunstone, 'Spirit and Eucharist: experience and doctrine', *Renewal*, 64 (1976), pp. 11–13.

22 See various Roman Catholic Reports in *Power, Presence, Praise*, edited by McDonnell, vol. II.

23 'The Charismatic Movement in the Church of England', p. 37.

24 S. Tugwell, 'The speech-giving Spirit', in *New Heaven? New Earth?*, edited by S. Trigwell, P. Hocken, G. Every (London: DLT, 1976) pp. 119–59 (p. 151).

25 'The Charismatic Movement in the Church of England', p. 37.

26 As well as in definitions of worship by Charismatics, the sacrificial emphasis in Charismatic worship is most clearly seen in its songs and hymns.

27 Peter Hocken, 'A survey of the worldwide Charismatic Movement', in *The Church is Charismatic*, edited by A. Bittlinger (Geneva: WCC, 1981), pp. 117–46 (p. 127).

28 Hopkinson, 'Changing emphases in self-identity', pp. 91–124.

29 Ibid., p. 111.

30 D. C. K. Watson, *I Believe in Evangelism* (London: H & S, 1976), p. 43.

31 M. Harper, 'These stones cry out', in *Open to the Spirit: Anglicans and the Experience of Renewal*, edited by C. Craston (London: Church House Publishing, 1987), pp. 18–30.

32 See D. C. K. Watson, *Be Filled with the Spirit* (Eastbourne: Kingsway, 1982), p. 13.

33 Watson, *I Believe in Evangelism*, pp. 53–5; *I Believe in the Church* (London: H & S, 1978), p. 244.

34 E. M. B. Green, *I Believe in Satan's Downfall* (London: H & S, 1981).

35 D. Pytches, *Come Holy Spirit* (London: H & S 1985), p. 260.

36 Watson, *I Believe in the Church*, pp. 210–11.

37 See Watson, *I Believe in Evangelism*, pp. 115–33; *Discipleship* (London: H & S, 1981), pp. 95–116.

38 Watson, *I Believe in the Church*, p. 225.

39 D. Gregg, 'New-found sacramentalism', *Renewal*, 75 (1978), pp. 14–16.

40 M. Harper, *Walk in the Spirit* (London: H & S, 1968), p. 22.

41 Green, *I Believe in Satan's Downfall*, p. 135.

42 A. Stibbs, 'Putting the gift of tongues in its place', *Churchman*, 80 (1966), 295–303; J. R. W. Stott, *The Baptism and Fulness of the Holy Spirit* (London: IVF, 1964), p. 28.

43 J. I. Packer, 'Theological reflections on the Charismatic Movement', *Churchmen*, 94 (1980), pp. 7–25, 103–25.

44 J. R. W. Stott, *Your Mind Matters: The Place of the Mind in the Christian Life* (London: IVP, 1972), p. 31; *I Believe in Preaching* (London: H & S, 1982), p. 325.

45 Green, *I Believe in Satan's Downfall*, p. 142; see also M. Harper, *Spiritual Warfare* (London: H & S, 1970), p. 106.

46 M. Harper, *This is the Day* (London: H & S, 1979), p. 50.

47 Watson, *One in the Spirit* (London: H & S, 1973), p. 111; *I Believe in Evangelism*, pp. 156–67; *I Believe in the Church*, p. 179.

48 Stott, *Your Mind Matters*, p. 25; see also A. Bennett, *Table and Minister* (London: CBRP, 1963), p. 117.

49 Watson, *You are my God* (London: H & S, 1983), p. 109; see also *I Believe in the Church*, pp. 179–98.

50 J. Gunstone, *Pentecostal Anglicans* (London: H & S, 1982), p. 80.

51 Watson, *I Believe in Evangelism*, p. 156.

52 M. Harper, *Love Affair* (London: H & S, 1982), p. 214.

53 See Harper, *This is the Day*, pp. 50–1; Watson, *I Believe in the Church*, p. 344; Gregg, 'New-found sacramentalism', p. 14.

54 Watson, *I Believe in Evangelism*, p. 50.

55 Watson, *Discipleship*, pp. 62–4.

56 Watson, *I Believe in the Church*, p. 244.

57 See M. Searle, 'New tasks, new methods: the emergence of pastoral liturgical studies', *Worship*, 57 (1983), pp. 291–308.

58 Buchanan, 'Role and calling', p. 27. In 1959 T. C. Hammond defended the Evangelical liturgical symbols and clearly regarded adherence to them as a natural and, indeed, necessary part of being an Evangelical (*What is an Evangelical?* (London: CPAS, 1959), pp. 21–4). The relationship between the recognition symbols and the Evangelical sense of identity is analysed by Hopkinson, 'Changing emphases in self-identity', pp. 181–90.

59 Bennett, *Table and Minister*; J. A. Motyer, A. M. Stibbs and J. R. W. Stott, *Why I Value the North Side Position*, CPAS Fellowship Paper 238 (London: CPAS, 1963).

60 For CPAS's policy before 1966 see Hopkinson, 'Changing emphases in self-identity', pp. 44, 70 n. 6.

61 *Keele Statement*, para. 78.

62 See Buchanan, *Evangelical Anglicans and Liturgy*, pp. 14–15. Hopkinson conducted a survey at the 1980 Eclectics Conference ('Changing emphases in self-identity', pp. 253–64). The replies showed that only 39% still used North Side and that 10% of these would have preferred the westward position.

63 See Hillyer's research into a Charismatic Church in Cambridge, 'Liturgical change in Cambridge', p. 75. Hopkinson reveals that some curates wanted to introduce the stole to that bastion of Evangelicalism, All Souls, Langham Place ('Changing emphases in self-identity', p. 94).

64 Ibid., pp. 185–9. His claims are based on a detailed word analysis comparing the new services with the 1662 rite (appendix D, p. 276).

65 Two out of the four main liturgies compiled by Evangelicals during the period used 'Eucharist' as a title – 'An Evangelical Eucharist' (1964), 'Eucharist for the Seventies' (1968).

66 See D. Robinson, 'Eucharist and Offertory: the Anglican tradition', *Churchman*, 75 (1961), 31–40; P. E. Dale, *A Guide to Series 3* (Bramcote: GB, 1972), pp. 10–11; More, *Freedom in a Framework* (Bramcote: GB, 1975), pp. 17–18; T. Lloyd, *Ceremonial in Worship*, (Bramcote: GB, 1981), pp. 21–2.

67 Buchanan, *The End of the Offertory*.

68 See J. R. K. Fenwick, *Eucharistic Concelebration* (Bramcote: GB, 1982).

69 A. Kavanagh, *On Liturgical Theology* (New York: Pueblo Publishing Company, 1981), p. 76.

70 On extended communion see Buchanan, 'Communion of the sick', in Beckwith, Packer and Buchanan, *Reservation and Communion of the Sick*, pp. 22–8; *Pastoral and Liturgical Ministry to the Sick*, edited by M. Botting (Bramcote: GB, 1978); D. Smethurst, *Extended Communion* (Bramcote: GB, 1986).

   On child communion see *Keele Statement*, para. 75; C. O. Buchanan, 'An Anglican Evangelical looks at sacramental initiation', *Faith and Unity*, 12 (1968), pp. 44–8; Buchanan, *Children in Communion*, GWS 112 (Bramcote: GB, 1990); C. H. B. Byworth, *Communion, Confirmation and Commitment*, revised edition (Bramcote: GB, 1977); *Nottingham Statement*, para. G.4; D. Young, *Welcoming Children to Communion* (Bramcote: GB, 1983).

71 On extended communion see Beckwith, 'Extended communion: one parish's experience: a response', *Churchman*, 100 (1986), 335–8. But for an earlier and more sympathetic view see Beckwith 'Reservation: history and law', in Beckwith, Packer, and Buchanan, *Reservation and Communion of the Sick*, pp. 5–14 (p. 14).

   On child communion see 'The age of admission to communion', *Churchman*, 85 (1971), 13–31. *The Nottingham Statement* showed that Beckwith's disquiet over child communion clearly represented that of a substantial proportion of Evangelicals: 'We are divided on the advisability of admitting children to Communion' (para. G.4). However, significantly, Trevor Lloyd records that the arguments in favour were felt most strongly by Evangelicals in Parish Communion parishes (*Evangelicals, Obedience and Change*, p. 17).

72 As reported in C. O. Buchanan, 'Some Anglican historical perspectives', in *Lay Presidency at the Eucharist?*, edited by T. Lloyd (Bramcote: GB, 1977), pp. 11–19 (p. 19).

73 Lloyd, 'Life of the local Church', in *Obeying Christ in a Changing World*, edited by Cundy, p. 59.

74 *Lay Presidency at the Eucharist?*, edited by Lloyd.

75 R. Bowen, 'The Church of the Province of Tanzania', in *FAL*, pp. 234–46 (p. 239).

76 The story is recounted by Alan Hargrave in *But Who Will Preside?* (Bramcote: GB, 1990); I am indebted to a private conversation with Brian Skinner for further details.

77 B. Skinner and D. Pytches, *New Wineskins* (Guildford: Eagle, 1991), p. 32.

12 THE EUCHARIST AS SACRAMENT

1 Calvin, *Institutes*, bk. III, XI, 1.

2 Augustine, 'Homilies on the Gospel of John', Tract XXI, in *Nicene and Post-Nicene Fathers*, edited by P. Shaff, vol. VII (Grand Rapids: Eerdmans, 1956).

3 Luther, 'Babylonian captivity', in *Works*, vol. XXXVII, p. 44.

4 Zwingli, 'On the Lord's Supper', p. 199.

5 Calvin, *Institutes*, bk. IV, XVII. 39.

6 'The Communion of the Sick', *Book of Common Prayer* (1662). This part of the rubric is quoted by various Evangelical theologians, e.g.; Ryle, *Knots Untied*, pp. 210, 191; Thomas, *Sacrament of our Redemption*, pp. 47, 118; Stibbs, *Sacrament, Sacrifice and Eucharist*, pp. 51–2.

7 Bickersteth, *Treatise*, p. 119.

8 Calvin, *Institutes*, bk. IV, XVII. 7.

9 Owen, 'The chamber of the Church of Rome laid open', quoted by Mayor, *Lord's Supper*, p. 107.

10 Ryle, *Knots Untied*, p. 239.

11 Calvin, *Institutes*, bk. IV, I. 4.

12 Dimock, *Doctrine of the Sacraments*, p. iv.

13 See Kavanagh, *On Liturgical Theology*.

14 G. Wainwright, *Doxology: The Praise of God in Worship, Doctrine and Life* (London: Epworth, 1980), p. 242.

15 Ibid., p. 247.

16 Review of Kavanagh's *On Liturgical Theology* in *Worship*, 61 (1987), pp. 183–6.

17 A. Schmemann, *Introduction to Liturgical Theology* (London: Faith Press, 1966).

18 O. Cullmann, *Early Christian Worship* (London: SCM, 1953); Cullmann, 'The meaning of the Lord's Supper in primitive Christianity', in *Essays on the Lord's Supper*, edited by J. G. Davies and A. R. George (London:

Lutterworth Press, 1958), pp. 5–23; A. R. C. Leaney, *A Commentary on the Gospel according to St. Luke* (London: A. & C. Black, 1958); J. Jeremias, *The Eucharistic Words of Jesus* (London: SCM, 1966), pp. 120–1; E. J. Tinsley, *The Gospel according to Luke* (Cambridge: CUP, 1969); I. H. Marshall, *The Gospel of Luke: A Commentary on the Greek Text* (Exeter: Paternoster, 1978); Marshall, *Last Supper and Lord's Supper* (Exeter: Paternoster, 1980), pp. 124–30; E. Schweizer, *The Good News according to Luke* (London: SPCK, 1984).

19 J. A. Fitzmyer, *The Gospel according to Luke X–XXIV* (New York: Doubleday, 1985), p. 1569.

20 N. Geldenhuys, *The Commentary on the Gospel of Luke* (London: M. M. Scott, 1950); L. Morris, *Luke* (London: IVP, 1974). For older support see A. Plummer, *A Critical and Exegetical Commentary on the Gospel According to Luke*, third edition (Edinburgh: T. & T. Clark, 1900).

21 H. Lietzmann, *Mass and the Lord's Supper* (Leiden: E. J. Brill, 1979), first published 1926; Cullmann, *Early Christian Worship*; Cullmann, 'The Meaning of the Lord's Supper'. For the views of Lohmeyer and Bultmann see Marshall, *Last Supper and Lord's Supper*, pp. 130–3.

22 For such a critique see A. J. B. Higgins, *The Lord's Supper in the New Testament*, Studies in Biblical Theology 6 (London: SCM, 1952), pp. 156–63; Marshall, *Last Supper and Lord's Supper*, pp. 130–3.

23 Morris, *Luke*, p. 340.

24 Schweizer, *Good News according to Luke*, p. 373.

25 Marshall, *Last Supper and Lord's Supper*, p. 130.

26 R. K. Bultmann, *The Gospel of John: A Commentary* (Oxford: Blackwell, 1971).

27 R. E. Brown, *The Gospel according to John: I–XII*, second edition (New York: Doubleday, 1966).

28 *The Fourth Gospel by the Late Edwyn Clement Hoskyns*, edited by F. N. Dayey (London: Faber & Faber, n.d.), vol. I; Cullmann, *Early Christian Worship*, pp. 93–102; Jeremias, *Eucharistic Words of Jesus*, pp. 106–37; J. D. G. Dunn, 'John VI – a eucharistic discourse?', *NTS* 17 (1971), 328–38; B. Lindars, *The Gospel of John* (London: Oliphant, 1972); C. K. Barrett, *The Gospel according to St. John*, second edition (London: SPCK, 1978); Marshall, *Last Supper and Lord's Supper*, pp. 133–9; Heron, *Table and Tradition*, pp. 42–53. In addition, Dodd assumes the unity of the passage; see *The Interpretation of the Fourth Gospel* (Cambridge: CUP, 1953).

29 R. Schnackenburg, *The Gospel according to St. John* (London: Burns & Oats, 1980), vol. II.

30 Brown, *Gospel according to John*, p. 290.

31 Barrett, *Gospel according to St. John*, p. 297.

32 E. Schillebeeckx, *Christ the Sacrament of our Encounter with God* (London: Sheed & Ward, 1963), p. 16.

33 Ibid., p. 14.

34 Ibid., p. 46.

35 Ibid., p. 75.
36 Ibid., p. 54.
37 Ibid., p. 110.
38 Ibid., p. 71.
39 Schillebeeckx, *The Eucharist* (London: Sheed & Ward, 1968), p. 81.
40 Ibid.
41 Ibid., p. 81.
42 Schillebeeckx, *Christ the Sacrament*, p. 120.
43 K. Rahner, 'Word and the Eucharist', in *Theological Investigations* (London: DLT, 1966), vol. IV, pp. 253–86 (p. 260).
44 Ibid., p. 261.
45 His fundamental principles can be traced in *Foundations of Christian Faith* (London: DLT, 1978).
46 Rahner, 'Word and the Eucharist', p. 272.
47 Ibid., p. 274.
48 Ibid., p. 265.
49 Ibid., p. 280.
50 Ibid., p. 282.
51 Ibid.
52 A thorough treatment of Torrance's eucharistic theology can be found in R. J. Stamps, '"The Sacrament of the Word made Flesh": the eucharistic theology of Thomas F. Torrance' (Ph.D. thesis, CNAA St John's College Nottingham/University of Nottingham, 1986).
53 T. F. Torrance, *Theology in Reconciliation* (London: Geoffrey Chapman, 1975), p. 107.
54 Quoted by Stamps, 'Eucharistic theology of Thomas F. Torrance', p. 229.
55 Torrance, 'Eschatology and the Eucharist', in *Intercommunion*, edited by D. Baillie and J. Marsh (London: SCM, 1952), pp. 303–50 (p. 311).
56 Ibid.
57 Ibid., p. 310.
58 Torrance, 'The Paschal mystery of Christ and the Eucharist: general thesis', *Liturgical Review*, 6 (1976), 6–12 (p. 8).
59 Torrance, 'Eschatology and the Eucharist', p. 313.
60 Ibid., p. 307.
61 Ibid.
62 Ibid., p. 308.
63 Ibid., p. 313.
64 Ibid.
65 L. Weil, *Sacraments and Liturgy: The Outward Signs* (Oxford: Blackwell, 1983), p. 88.
66 Dix, *Shape of the Liturgy*, p. 254.
67 See Houlden, 'Sacrifice and Eucharist', in I. T. Ramsey, J. R. Lucas and A. R. Peacocke, *Thinking about the Eucharist* (London: SCM, 1972), pp. 81–98 (p. 96).
68 R. Bruce, 'First sermon on the Sacrament in general', in *The Mystery of*

the Lord's Supper, translated and edited by T. F. Torrance (London: James Clarke, 1958), pp. 63–4.

13 THE EUCHARIST AS PRESENCE

1 All biblical references in this chapter are taken from the *Jerusalem Bible*, second edition.
2 *Opera Selecta*, translated by P. Barth (Munich, 1926), vol. I, p. 139, quoted by T. H. L. Parker, *John Calvin: A Biography* (London: J. M. Dent & Sons, 1975), p. 52.
3 Rahner, 'The presence of Christ in the Sacrament of the Lord's Supper', in *Theological Investigations*, vol. IV, pp. 287–311 (p. 309).
4 Heron, *Table and Tradition*, p. 167.
5 e.g. Torrance, 'Eschatology and the Eucharist', pp. 803–4.
6 Torrance, 'Paschal mystery', p. 121.
7 See 'Eschatology and the Eucharist', pp. 334–6; 'The legacy of Karl Barth (1886–1986)', *SJT* 39 (1986), 289–308 (pp. 306–8).
8 Calvin, *Institutes*, bk. IV, XVII. 5. See also Calvin's comments on Eph. 3:17 in *Commentaries on the Epistles of Paul to the Galations and Ephesians* (Grand Rapids: Eerdmans, 1957), pp. 262–3.
9 'Eucharist', in *Baptism, Eucharist and Ministry* (Geneva: WCC, 1982), para. 13.
10 The Constitution of the Liturgy, article 7; quoted by N. Lash, *His Presence in the World* (London: Sheed & Ward, 1968), pp. 140–1.
11 Luther, 'That those words of Christ, "This is my Body", etc., still stand firm against the Fanatics, 1557', in *Works*, vol. XXXVII, *Word and Sacrament*, vol. III, edited by R. H. Fischer and H. T. Lehmann (Philadelphia: Muhlenberg Press, 1961), pp. 3–150 (pp. 68–9).
12 Wesley, *Journal*, vol. III, p. 320.
13 Torrance 'Paschal Mystery', p. 120.
14 HLS 54.
15 Owen, 'Sacramental discourses: II–III', in *Works*, vol. IX, pp. 521–622.
16 D. Wilson, 'A practical address to the communicant', in *Sermons and Tracts*, p. 390.
17 Bickersteth, *Treatise*, p. 117.
18 Dix, *Shape of the Liturgy*, p. 674. A similar argument runs through R. I. Wilberforce's *The Doctrine of the Holy Eucharist* (London: Mozley, 1854).
19 Luther, '"This is my Body"', p. 68.
20 Bayly, *Practice of Piety*, p. 320.
21 HLS 71.
22 Torrance, 'Towards a doctrine of the Lord's Supper', in *Conflict and Agreement in the Church* (London: Lutterworth, 1960), vol. II, pp. 133–54 (p. 141).
23 C. Davies, 'Understanding the Real Presence', in *Word and History*, edited by T. P. Burke (London: Collins, 1966), pp. 154–78 (p. 174).
24 Schillebeeckx, *Eucharist*, p. 104.

25 See Rahner, 'Presence of Christ'; Schillebeeckx, *Eucharist*; Davies, 'Understanding the Real Presence'; J. Powers, *Eucharistic Theology* (London: Burns & Oats, 1968).
26 Lash, *His Presence in the World*, p. 110.
27 Quoted by Schillebeeckx, *Eucharist*, pp. 118–19.
28 Ibid., p. 120.
29 Ibid., pp. 143–4.
30 Luther, 'Babylonian captivity of the Church', in *Works*, vol. XXXVI, pp. 38–9.
31 Luther, 'Transcript of the Marburg Colloquy', in Sasse, *This is my Body*, p. 203.
32 Christopher Sutton, 'Godly meditations upon the most holy Sacrament of the Lord's Supper', quoted by Stone, *History of the Doctrine*, p. 291.
33 Calvin, *Institutes*, bk. IV, XVII. 5.
34 Torrance, 'Paschal mystery', pp. 120–1.
35 Although Calvin believed that the Johannine discourse referred to the believer's general relationship with Christ rather than to his specific eucharistic experience, he was quite happy to apply it to the Eucharist on the grounds that the Sacrament is the 'sign and confirmation' of all that Christ said of himself and of our relation to him in the sermon (*Commentary on the Gospel according to John* (Grand Rapids: Eerdmans, 1956), p. 166).
36 Hooker, *Ecclesiastical Polity*, bk. V, p. 325.
37 Wesley, Sermon XIX, part 1, section 2, 'The great privilege of those that are born again'.
38 Calvin, *Institutes*, bk. IV, XVII. 5.
39 H. Lietzmann, *A History of the Early Church* (London: Lutterworth, 1961), p. 64.
40 *Methodist Hymn Book*, 406, quoted by Rattenbury, *EH*, p. 74.
41 G. Wainwright, *Eucharist and Eschatology* (London: Epworth, 1971), p. 104. See also Torrance, 'Eschatology and Eucharist'.
42 Ibid., p. 312.
43 See Wainwright's suggestive use of the biblical category of God's glory in *Eucharist and Eschatology*, pp. 102–4.
44 Ibid., p. 67.
45 Torrance, 'Eschatology and the Eucharist', p. 327.
46 Ibid.
47 Wainwright, *Eucharist and Eschatology*, p. 92.

14 THE EUCHARIST AS SACRIFICE

1 'Treatise on the New Testament, that is the Holy Mass, 1520', in *Works*, vol. XXXV, p. 100 (my emphasis in this and the following five quotations).
2 Calvin, commentary on Num. 19, *Commentaries on the Four Last Books of Moses*, translated by C. W. Bingham (Grand Rapids: Eerdmans, 1950), vol. II, p. 39.

3 Baxter, 'Poor Man's Family Book', in *Works*, vol. XIX, pp. 276–80, quoted by Mayor, *Lord's Supper*, p. 128.

4 *The Complete Works of Richard Sibbes*, edited by A. B. Grosart (Edinburgh: James Nichol, 1892), vol. I, p. 10.

5 HLS 118.

6 Ibid. 137.

7 See Dix's classic presentation of the issue, in *Shape of the Liturgy*, pp. 623–5.

8 K. Barth, *Church Dogmatics*, vol. IV. 1, p. 313.

9 Ibid., p. 315.

10 Ibid., p. 291.

11 See J. Moltmann, *The Theology of Hope* (London: SCM, 1967), pp. 197–208.

12 HLS 118.

13 Ibid. 140.

14 Ibid. 117.

15 Ibid. 39.

16 Torrance, 'Eschatology and the Eucharist', p. 326.

17 D. N. Power, *The Sacrifice We Offer* (Edinburgh: T. & T. Clark, 1987), p. 185.

18 *Baptism, Eucharist and Ministry*, Faith and Order Paper III (Geneva: WCC, 1982), statement on Eucharist, para. 9.

19 See G. W. Bromiley, *Thomas Cranmer* (London: Lutterworth, 1956), pp. 86–7; Stibbs, *Sacrament, Sacrifice and Eucharist*, pp. 21–4. For a discussion of Evangelical hesitation and a defence of the concept from the perspective of Reformed sources see B. D. Spinks, 'The ascension and the vicarious humanity of Christ', in *Time and Community*, edited by J. Neil Alexander (Washington, DC: Pastoral Press, 1990), pp. 185–201. For further discussion see J. M. Barkley, '"Pleading his eternal sacrifice" in Reformed Liturgy', in *The Sacrifice of Praise*, edited by Spinks, pp. 123–40.

20 On the related theme of Christ pleading his sacrifice see Stibbs, *Sacrament, Sacrifice and Eucharist*, pp. 29–31; Green (with Mascall), '"Eucharistic sacrifice": some interim agreement', in Buchanan *et al.*, *Growing into Union*, p. 188; Green, 'Christ's Sacrifice and ours', in *Guidelines*, edited by Packer, pp. 103–6; Saward's hymn, 'O Sacrifice of Calvary', *Youth Praise*, bk. 2, 214.

21 Knox, *Sacrament or Sacrifice?*, pp. 10–11.

22 For Calvin's views on Christ's mediatorial role in worship see *Institutes*, bk. IV, XVII, 17–18. For similar views in Luther see 'Treatise on the New Testament', in *Works*, vol. XXXV. For further development in modern Reformed theology see T. F. Torrance, 'The mind of Christ in worship: the problem of Apollinarianism in the liturgy', in his *Theology in Reconciliation*, pp. 139–214; J. B. Torrance, 'The vicarious humanity of Christ', in *The Incarnation*, edited by T. F. Torrance (Edinburgh: Handsel Press, 1981).

23 HLS 125.
24 K. W. Stevenson, *Eucharist and Offering* (New York: Pueblo, 1986), pp. 218–36 (p. 325).
25 Heron, *Table and Tradition*, p. 168.
26 Barth, *Church Dogmatics*, vol. IV. 1, p. 295.
27 Ibid.
28 Ibid., p. 351.
29 Ibid., p. 753.
30 Ibid., p. 320.
31 Ibid., p. 768.
32 See J. B. Torrance, 'Vicarious humanity of Christ', p. 145; T. F. Torrance, 'Paschal mystery', p. 118; Heron, *Table and Tradition*, pp. 167–70.
33 See ibid., pp. 174–5; Power, *Sacrifice We Offer*, pp. 173–5.
34 B. A. Gerrish, *The Old Protestantism and the New* (Edinburgh: T. & T. Clark, 1982), p. 96.
35 Cranmer, 'A defence of the true and catholic doctrine of the sacraments', in *Works*, vol. I, bk. V, XI.
36 See *Institutes*, bk. IV, XVIII. 17.
37 Ibid., bk. IV, III. 6.
38 Ibid., bk. IV, III. 1.
39 Ibid., bk. IV, III. 6.
40 Ibid.
41 Knox, *Sacrament or Sacrifice?*, p. 118.
42 For further discussion see C. J. Cocksworth, 'Eucharistic theology', in *The Identity of Anglican Worship*, edited by K. W. Stevenson and B. D. Spinks (London: Mowbray, 1991), pp. 49–68.
43 *PEER*, pp. 180–1.
44 Haweis, *Spiritual Companion*, p. 48.
45 Isaac Watts, 'When I survey the wondrous Cross', *Ancient and Modern Revised*, 108.

Bibliography

This is a select bibliography in which preference has been given to primary Evangelical sources. However, even here it does not seek to be exhaustive. For fuller bibliographical treatment see the writer's original thesis, 'Evangelical eucharistic thought in the Church of England, with special reference to the period *c*.1960–*c*.1980' (University of Manchester, 1989).

BOOKS, BOOKLETS AND ARTICLES

Adam, P., *Roots of Contemporary Evangelical Spirituality*, Grove Spirituality Series no. 24 (Bramcote: GB, 1988).

Andrewes, L., *Ninety-Six Sermons*, LACT (Oxford: John Henry Parker, 1841), vols. I, II, III.

Augustine, 'Homilies on the Gospel of John', Tract XXI, in *Nicene and Post-Nicene Fathers*, edited by P. Shaff, vol. VII (Grand Rapids: Eerdmans, 1956).

Aulén, G., *Eucharist and Sacrifice* (Edinburgh: Oliver & Boyd, 1956).

Avis, P. D. L., *The Church in the Theology of the Reformers* (London: Marshall, Morgan, Scott, 1981).

Baker, E. W., *A Herald of the Evangelical Revival* (London: Epworth, 1948).

Balleine, G. R., *A History of the Evangelical Party in the Church of England*, new edition with supplement by G. W. Bromiley (London: CBRP, 1951, first published 1908).

Barclay, A., *The Protestant Doctrine of the Lord's Supper* (Glasgow: Jackson, Wylic, 1927).

Barrett, C. K., *The Gospel according to St. John: An Introduction with Commentary and Notes on the Greek Text*, second edition (London: SPCK, 1978).

Barth, K., *Church Dogmatics*, edited by G. W. Bromiley and T. F. Torrance (Edinburgh: T. & T. Clark, 1956), vols. 1.2; IV.1.

Bateman, J., *The Life of the Right Rev. Daniel Wilson* (London: Murray, 1860), vol. I.

Bax, J., *The Good Wine: Spiritual Renewal in the Church of England* (London: Church House Publishing, 1986).

Bayly, L., *The Practice of Piety: or The Whole Duty of a Christian*, seventy-fourth edition (Exeter: J. Saunders, 1821), first published 1620.

✓ Bebbington, D. W., *Evangelicalism in Modern Britain: A History from the 1730s to the 1980s* (London: Unwin Hyman, 1989).

Beckwith, R. T., 'The Agreed Statement on eucharistic doctrine', *Churchman*, 87 (1973), 14–28.

'The approaching revision of Series Three', *Churchman*, 90 (1976), 289–93.

Christ's Presence and Sacrifice (London: CBRP, 1973).

'Do the alternative services legalize reservation?', *Churchman*, 85 (1971), 205–13.

'The ecumenical quest for agreement in faith', *Themelios*, 10 (1984), 28–30.

'An Evangelical looks at the Agreed Statement', *Faith and Unity*, 16 (1972), 49–52.

'Extended communion: one parish's experience: a response', *Churchman*, 100 (1986), 335–38.

'Lambeth 1958 and the "Liturgy for Africa" (I) and (II)', *Churchman*, 79 (1965), 248–54; 80 (1966), 33–40.

Priesthood and Sacraments: A Study of the Anglican–Methodist Report (Abingdon: MMP, 1964).

The Revised Series Three Communion: A Way Forward, LS 2 (Oxford: LH, 1979).

Rome, Canterbury and the Final ARCIC Report (Oxford: LH, 1982).

'A turning point in Prayer Book revision', *Churchman*, 89 (1975), 120–9.

Beckwith, R. T., ed., *Towards a Modern Prayer Book* (Abingdon: MMP, 1966).

Beckwith, R. T., and Buchanan, C. O., '"This Bread and This Cup": an Evangelical rejoinder', *Theology*, 70 (1967), 265–71.

Beckwith, R. T., Duffield, G. E., and Packer, J. I., *Across the Divide* (Basingstoke: Lyttelton Press, 1977).

Beckwith, R. T., Packer, J. I., and Buchanan, C. O., *Reservation and Communion of the Sick*, GMWS 4 (Bramcote: GB, 1972).

Beckwith, R. T., and Tiller, J. E., *The Service of Holy Communion and its Revision* (Abingdon: MMP, 1972).

Berger, P. L., and Luckman, T., *The Social Construction of Reality* (Harmondsworth: Penguin Books, 1971).

Bickersteth, E., *A Treatise on the Lord's Supper* (London: L. B. Seeley & Son, 1824).

Billings, D. D., *Alternative Eucharistic Prayers*, GMWS 16 (Bramcote: GB, 1973).

Services on Trial (London: CBRP, 1966).

Binns, L. E., *The Evangelical Movement in the English Church* (London: Methuen, 1928).

Botting, M., ed., *Pastoral and Liturgical Ministry to the Sick*, GMWS 59 (Bramcote: GB, 1978).

Bowmer, J. C., *The Sacrament of the Lord's Supper in Early Methodism* (London:
✓ Dacre Press, 1951).

Bowyer, L., *The Spirit and Forms of Protestantism* (London: Harrill, 1956).

Bray, G. L., *Sacraments and Ministry in Ecumenical Perspective*, LS 18 (Oxford: LH, 1984).

Brilioth, Y., *The Anglican Revival: Studies in the Oxford Movement* (London: Longmans, Green, 1925).

Eucharistic Faith and Practice: Evangelical and Catholic (London: SPCK, 1930).

Bromiley, G. W., 'Prayer Book development to 1662', *Churchman*, 76 (1962), 7–15.

Thomas Cranmer (London: Lutterworth, 1956).

Brooks, P., *Thomas Cranmer's Doctrine of the Eucharist* (London: Macmillan, 1965).

Brooks, T., *Heaven on Earth: A Treatise on Christian Assurance* (London: Banner of Truth, 1961), first published 1664.

Brown, C., 'The concept of Evangelical', *Churchman*, 95 (1981), 104–9.

Brown, L. W., *Relevant Liturgy* (London: SPCK, 1965).

Brown, R. E., *The Gospel According to John: I–XII*, second edition (New York: Doubleday, 1966).

Bruce, R., *The Mystery of the Lord's Supper: Sermons on the sacrament preached in the Kirk of Edinburgh by Robert Bruce in A.D. 1589*, translated and edited by T. F. Torrance (London: James Clarke, 1958).

Bucer, M., 'Confession of Faith concerning the Eucharist', in *Calvin's Theological Treatises*, edited by J. K. S. Reid, Library of Christian Classics vol. XXII (London: SCM, 1954).

Buchanan, C. O., 'Anglican Evangelicalism: the state of the "Party"', *Anvil*, 1 (1984), 7–18.

ARCIC and LIMA on Baptism and the Eucharist, GWS 86 (Bramcote: GB, 1983).

Encountering Charismatic Worship, GMWS 51 (Bramcote: GB, 1977).

The End of the Offertory, GLS 14 (Bramcote: GB, 1978).

Evangelical Anglicans and Liturgy, GWS 90 (Bramcote: GB, 1984).

A Guide to the New Communion Service (London: CBRP, 1966).

A Guide to Second Series Communion Service (London: CBRP, 1968).

Latest Liturgical Revision in the Church of England 1978–1984, GLS 39 (Bramcote: GB, 1984).

Liturgy for Communion: The Revised Series 3 Services, GMWS 68 (Bramcote: GB, 1979).

The New Communion Service: Reasons for Dissent (London: CBRP, 1966).

Patterns of Sunday Worship, GMWS 9 (Bramcote: GB, 1972).

Recent Liturgical Revision in the Church of England, GMWS 14 (Bramcote: GB, 1973); and supplements A, B, C (1974–8).

What did Cranmer Think He was Doing?, GLS 7, second edition (Bramcote: GB, 1982), first published 1976.

Buchanan, C. O., ed., *Essays on Eucharistic Sacrifice in the Early Church*, GLS 40 (Bramcote: GB, 1984).

Evangelical Essays on Church and Sacraments (London: SPCK, 1972).

The Development of the New Eucharistic Prayers of the Church of England, GLS 20 (Bramcote: GB, 1979).

Further Anglican Liturgies 1968–1975 (Bramcote: GB, 1975).

Latest Anglican Liturgies 1976–1984 (London: Alcuin/SPCK, 1985).

Modern Anglican Liturgies 1958–1968 (London: OUP, 1968).

Buchanan, C. O., Lloyd, B. T., and Miller, H., eds., *Anglican Worship Today* (London: Collins Liturgical Publications, 1980).

Buchanan, C. O., Mascall, E. L., Packer, J. I., and the Bishop of Willesden, ✓ *Growing into Union: Proposals for Forming a United Church in England* (London: SPCK, 1970).

Buchanan, C. O., and Pawson, D., *Infant Baptism under Cross-Examination*, GMWS 24 (Bramcote: GB, 1974).

Bultmann, R. K., *The Gospel of John: A Commentary* (Oxford: Blackwell, 1971).

Buxton, R. F., *Eucharist and Institution Narrative*, Alcuin Club Collections 58 (Great Wakering: Mayhew–McCrimmon, 1978).

Byworth, C. H. B., *Communion, Confirmation and Commitment*, GMWS 8, revised edition (Bramcote: GB, 1977).

Calvin, J., *Calvin: Commentaries*, edited by J. Haroutunian, Library of Christian Classics, vol. xxiii (London: SCM, 1958).

✓ *Calvin: Institutes of Christian Religion*, 2 vols., edited by J. T. McNeill, Library of Christian Classics, vols. xx–xxi (London: SCM, 1951).

Calvin: Theological Treatises, edited by J. K. S. Reid, Library of Christian Classics, vol. xxii (London: SCM, 1954).

Carey, G. L., *The Meeting of the Waters* (London: H & S, 1985).

Carey, G. L. and D. N. Samuel 'The ARCIC Agreed Statements...', *Churchman*, 102 (1988), 151–65.

Carus, W., ed., *Memoirs of the Life of the Rev. Charles Simeon, M.A.*, second edition (London: Hatchard, 1847).

Charley, J. W., *The Anglican Roman Catholic Agreement on the Eucharist with an Historical Introduction and Theological Commentary*, GMWS 1 (Bramcote: GB, 1971).

Rome, Canterbury, and the Future (Bramcote: GB, 1982).

. Clark, F., *Eucharistic Sacrifice and the Reformation*, second edition (Oxford: Blackwell, 1967).

Clements, R. E., ed., *Eucharistic Theology Then and Now* (London: SPCK, 1968).

Coates, R. J., 'The ministry of the sacraments and the occasional offices', *Churchman*, 74 (1960) 31–6.

Colquhoun, F., 'Charles Wesley's eucharistic hymns', *Churchman*, 63 (1949), 103–7.

'The Parish Communion', *Churchman*, 67 (1953), 19–23.

Cosin, J., *Works*, LACT (Oxford: John Henry Parker, 1851), vol. iv.

Couratin, A. H., *Lambeth and Liturgy* (London: Church Union, 1959).

'Thanksgiving and thankoffering', *Studia Liturgica*, 3 (summer 1964), 53–7.

'The tradition received', *Theology*, 69 (1966), 437–42.

Couratin, A. H., and Tripp, D. H., eds., *Liturgical Studies* (London: SPCK, 1976).

Cranmer, T., *Works*, edited by J. E. Cox, Parker Society Edition (Cambridge: CUP, 1844–6), vols. I, II.

Craston, C., ed., *Open to the Spirit: Anglicans and the Experience of Renewal* (London: Church House Publishing, 1987).

Cullmann, O., *Early Christian Worship*, Studies in Biblical Theology 10 (London: SCM, 1953).

Cuming, G. J., *A History of Anglican Liturgy*, second edition (London: Macmillan, 1982).

Cundy, I., *Obeying Christ in a Changing World* (London: Collins, 1977), vols. I, II, III.

Dale, P. E., *A Guide to Series 3*, GMWS 10 (Bramcote: GB, 1972).

Davies, C., 'Understanding the Real Presence', in *Word and History*, edited by T. P. Burke (London: Collins, 1968), pp. 154–78.

Davies, H., *Worship and Theology in England* (Princeton: Princeton University Press, 1961–5), vols. I–V.

The Worship of the English Puritans (London: Dacre, 1948).

Davies, J. G., and George, A. R., eds., *Essays on the Lord's Supper*, Ecumenical Studies in Worship 1 (London: Lutterworth Press, 1958).

Dayey, F. N., *The Fourth Gospel by the Late Edwyn Clement Hoskyns* (London: Faber & Faber, n.d.), vol. I.

Dillistone, F. W., *The Ministry of the Word and the Sacraments* (Toronto: University of Toronto Press, 1946).

Dimock, N., *The Doctrine of the Lord's Supper*, memorial edition (London: Longmans, Green, 1910).

The Doctrine of the Sacraments in relation to the Doctrines of Grace, new edition (London: Longmans, Green, 1908).

Papers on the Doctrine of the English Church concerning the Eucharistic Presence, memorial edition (London: Longmans, Green, 1911), vols. I, II.

The Sacerdotium of Christ, memorial edition (London: Longmans, Green, 1910).

Dix, G., *The Shape of the Liturgy* (London: A. & C. Black, 1945), first published 1943.

Dodd, C. H., *The Interpretation of the Fourth Gospel* (Cambridge: CUP, 1953).

Drury, T., *Elevation in the Eucharist* (Cambridge: CUP, 1907).

Two Studies in the Book of Common Prayer (London: Nisbet, 1901).

Duffield, G. E., *Admission to Holy Communion* (Abingdon: MMP, 1964).

Dugmore, C. W., *Eucharistic Doctrine in England from Hooker to Waterland* (London: SPCK, 1942).

Empie, P. C., and McCord, J. I., *Marburg Revisited* (Minneapolis: Augsburg Publishing House, 1966).

Ervine, W. J. C., 'Doctrine and diplomacy: some aspects of the life and thought of the Anglican Evangelical clergy 1797–1837' (Ph.D. thesis, University of Cambridge, 1979).

Fenwick, J. R. K., *Eucharistic Concelebration*, GWS 82 (Bramcote: GB, 1982).

Fenwick, J. R. K., ed., '*The Missing Oblation*', Alcuin/GROW 11 (Bramcote: GB, 1989).

Fitzmyer, J. A., *The Gospel according to Luke X–XXIV* (New York: Doubleday, 1985).

Frere, W. H., *Some Principles of Liturgical Reform* (London: John Murray, 1911).

Frere, W. H. and Douglas, C. E., *Puritan Manifestos* (London: SPCK, 1907).

Gayford, S. C., *Sacrifice and Priesthood: Jewish and Christian* (London: Methuen, 1924).

Geldenhuys, N., *The Commentary on the Gospel of Luke* (London: M. M. Scott, 1950).

Gerrish, B. A., *The Old Protestantism and the New* (Edinburgh: T. & T. Clark, 1982).

Goode, W., *The Nature of Christ's Presence in the Eucharist* (London: T. Hatchard, 1856), vols. I, II.

Gore, C., *The Body of Christ*, fourth edition (London: John Murray, 1907).

Gray, D., *Earth and Altar: The Evolution of the Parish Communion in the Church of England to 1945* (London: Alcuin Club, 1986).

Green, E. M. B., 'The doctrine of Holy Communion', *Churchman*, 76 (1962), 90–8.

✓ Green, J. B., *John Wesley and William Law* (London: Epworth, 1945).

Gregg, D., *Anamnesis in the Eucharist*, GLS 5 (Bramcote: GB, 1976).

⎪ Grisbrooke, W. J., *Anglican Liturgies of the Seventeenth and Eighteenth Centuries* (London: SPCK, 1958).

Hammond, T. C., 'The ministry and the sacraments', *Churchman*, 44 (1930), 209–16.

Hanson, R. P. C., *Eucharistic Offering in the Early Church* GLS 19 (Bramcote: GB, 1979).

Hardelin, A., *The Tractarian Understanding of the Eucharist* (Uppsala: Acta Universitatis Upsaliensis, 1965).

Hargrave, A., *But who will Preside?* GWS 113 (Bramcote: GB, 1990).

Harper, M., *Love Affair* (London: H & S, 1982).
This is the Day: A Fresh Look at Christian Unity (London: H & S, 1979).
Walk in the Spirit (London: H & S, 1968).

Harrison, D. E. W., *The Book of Common Prayer* (London: Canterbury Press, 1946).

Harrison, J., *An Answer to Dr Pusey's Challenge* (London: Longmans, Green, 1871), vols. I, II.

Haweis, T., *The Communicant's Spiritual Companion* (London: Samuel Swift, 1812).

✓ Hebert, A. G., *Liturgy and Society* (London: Faber & Faber, 1942).

✓ Hebert, A. G., ed., *The Parish Communion* (London: SPCK, 1937).

Heron, A. I. C. *Table and Tradition: Towards an Ecumenical Understanding of the Eucharist* (Edinburgh: Handel Press, 1983).

Hewitt, P. E., 'The place and purpose of the sacraments', *Churchman*, 73 (1959), 29–41, 76–86.

Hicks, F. C. N., *The Fullness of Sacrifice: An Essay in Reconciliation* (London: SPCK, 1946).

Hildebrandt, F., *From Luther to Wesley* (London: Lutterworth, 1951).

Hocken, P., *Streams of Renewal: The Origins of the Charismatic Movement in Great Britain* (Exeter: Paternoster Press, 1986).

Holeton, D., *Infant Communion: Then and Now*, GLS 27 (Bramcote: GB, 1981).

Hooker, R., *Laws of Ecclesiastical Polity*, Everyman's Edition (London: J. M. Dent, 1940), bk. v, vols. I, II.

Hopkinson, W. H., 'Changing emphases in self-identity amongst Evangelicals in the Church of England, 1960–1980 (M.Phil. thesis, University of Nottingham, 1983).

Houlden, J. L., 'Good liturgy or even good battlefield?', *Theology*, 69 (1966), 434–7.

Hughes, P. E., 'The place of symbolism in the word and sacraments today', *Churchman*, 72 (1957), 147–55.

Hylson-Smith, K., *Evangelicals in the Church of England 1734–1984* (Edinburgh: T. & T. Clark, 1989).

Jasper, R. C. D., *The Development of the Anglican Liturgy 1662–1980* (London: SPCK, 1989).

Jasper, R. C. D., ed., *The Eucharist Today: Studies on Series 3* (London: SPCK, 1974).

Jasper, R. C. D., and Cuming, G. J., eds., *Prayers of the Eucharist Early and Reformed*, second edition (New York: OUP, 1980).

Jeremias, J., *The Eucharistic Words of Jesus* (London: SCM, 1966).

Jewel, J., *Works*, Parker Society Edition (Cambridge: CUP, 1845), vol. I.

Johnson, J., 'The Unbloody Sacrifice and Altar', in *Theological Works*, LACT (Oxford: John Henry Parker, 1847), first published 1714, vol. I.

Joynson-Hicks, W., *The Prayer Book Crisis* (London: Putnam, 1928).

Kavanagh, A., *On Liturgical Theology* (New York: Pueblo Publishing Company, 1981).

Kibble, D. G., 'The Reformation and the Eucharist', *Churchman*, 94 (1980), 43–57.

King, J. C., ed., *Evangelicals Today* (Guildford and London: Lutterworth, 1973).

Knox, E. A., *Sacrament or Sacrifice?: Which is the Teaching of the Anglican Communion Office?* (London: Longmans, Green, 1911).

Lash, N., *His Presence in the World: A Study of Eucharistic Worship and Theology* (London: Sheed & Ward, 1968).

Laud, W., *Works*, LACT (Oxford: John Henry Parker, 1849), vols. II, IV.

Law, W., *A Serious Call to a Devout and Holy Life* (London: Dent, 1926), first published 1728.

Leaney, A. R. C., *A Commentary on the Gospel according to St. Luke* (London: A. & C. Black, 1958).

Leathem, W., 'Evangelical Catholicity', *Churchman*, 58 (1944), 165–72.

Leaver, R., 'A decade of hymns: reflections on the tenth anniversary of the "Anglican Hymn Book"', *Churchman*, 89 (1975), 108–19.

Lietzmann, H., *Mass and the Lord's Supper: A Study in the History of the Liturgy* (Leiden: E. J. Brill, 1979), first published 1926.

Lindars, B., *The Gospel of John* (London: Oliphant, 1972).

Lloyd, B. T., *Agapes and Informal Eucharists*, GMWS 19 (Bramcote: GB, 1973).

    Ceremonial in Worship, GMWS 75 (Bramcote: GB, 1981).

    Evangelicals, Obedience and Change, GMWS 50 (Bramcote: GB, 1977).

Lloyd, B. T., ed., *Lay Presidency at the Eucharist?*, GLS 9 (*Bramcote: GB*, 1977).

Luther, M., *Works*, vols. XXXV–XXXVII, *Word and Sacrament*, vol. I, edited by E. T. Bachmann and H. T. Lehmann; vol. II, edited by A. R. Wentz and H. T. Lehmann (Philadelphia: Fortress Press, 1960, 1959); vol. III, edited by R. H. Fischer and H. T. Lehmann (Philadelphia: Muhlenberg Press, 1961).

McAdoo, H. R., *Spirit of Anglicanism* (London: A. and C. Black, 1965).

Macdonald, A. J., *Berengar and the Reform of Sacramental Doctrine* (London: Longmans, Green, 1930).

    The Evangelical Doctrine of Holy Communion (London: SPCK, 1936), first published 1933.

McDonnell, K., ed., *Presence, Power, Praise: Documents on the Charismatic Renewal* (Collegeville, Minn.: Liturgical Press, 1980), vols. I, II, III.

McGrath, A., 'The Eucharist: reassessing Zwingli', *Theology*, 92 (1990), 13–19.

Mackean, W. H., *The Eucharistic Doctrine of the Oxford Movement* (London: Putnam, 1933).

Manwaring, R., *From Controversy to Co-existence: Evangelicals in the Church of England 1914–1980* (Cambridge: CUP, 1985).

Marshall, I. H., *The Gospel of Luke: A Commentary on the Greek Text* (Exeter: Paternoster, 1978).

    Last Supper and Lord's Supper (Exeter: Paternoster Press, 1980).

Martin, H., ed., *The Holy Communion* (London: SCM, 1947).

Mascall, E. L., *Christ, the Christian and the Church: A Study in the Incarnation and its Consequences* (London: Longmans, Green, 1946).

    Corpus Christi: Essays on the Church and Eucharist, first edition (London: Longmans, Green, 1953).

Maxwell, W. D., *The Liturgical Portions of the Genevan Service* (London: Faith Press, 1965).

Mayor, S., *The Lord's Supper in Early English Dissent* (London: Epworth, 1972).

Mitchell, A., *The Holy Communion* (London: CBRP, n.d.).

    'A liturgical essay', *Churchman*, 43 (1929), 51–62.

    This Service (London: CBRP, 1943).

More, P. E., and Cross, F. L., eds., *Anglicanism: The Thought and Practice of the Church of England* (London: SPCK, 1935).

More, R., *Freedom in a Framework: Some Possibilities with Series 3*, GMWS 40 (Bramcote: GB, 1975).

Morris, L., *Luke* (London: IVP, 1974).

Motyer, J. A., 'Principles of Prayer Book revision', *Churchman*, 76 (1962), 36–8.

✓ Moule, C. F. D., *The Sacrifice of Christ* (London: H & S, 1956).

Moule, H. C. G., *At the Holy Communion* (London: Seeley, 1914).

  Message from the Epistle to the Hebrews (London: Chas. J. Thynne & Jarvis, 1930).

Mowll, H. W. K., 'What is Anglican Evangelicalism?', *Churchman*, 64 (1950), 134–43.

Neill, S. C., 'The Anglican tradition in liturgy and devotion', *Churchman*, 59 (1945), 99–111.

⟨ New, J. F. H., *Anglican and Puritan: The Basis of their Opposition 1558–1640* (London: A. & C. Black, 1964).

Nockles, P. B., 'Continuity and change in Anglican High-Churchmanship in Britain, 1792–1850' (D.Phil. thesis, University of Oxford, 1982).

Nuttall, G. F., *The Holy Spirit in Puritan Faith and Experience* (Oxford:
✓   Blackwell, 1947).

Oulton, J. E. L., *Holy Communion and Holy Spirit* (London: SPCK, 1951).

Owen, J., *Works*, edited by W. H. Goold (Edinburgh: T. & T. Clark, 1862), vols. IX, XVI.

Packer, J. I., *The Evangelical Anglican Identity Problem*, LS 1 (Oxford: LH, 1978).

  Keep in Step with the Spirit (London: IVP, 1984).

  'Theological reflections on the Charismatic Movement', *Churchman*, 94 (1980), 7–25, 103–25.

Packer, J. I., ed., *All in Each Place: Towards Reunion in England* (Abingdon: MMP, 1965).

  The Church of England and the Methodist Church: A Consideration of the Report (Abingdon: MMP, 1963).

  Eucharistic Sacrifice (London: CBRP, 1962).

  Guidelines: Anglican Evangelicals Face the Future (London: CPAS/Falcon Books, 1967).

Parris, J. R., *John Wesley's Doctrine of the Sacraments* (London: Epworth,
✓   1963).

Parsons, M., *The Holy Communion: An Exposition of the Prayer Book Service* (London: H & S, 1961).

Peel, A., and Carlson, L. H., eds., *The Writings of Robert Harrison and Robert Browne* (London: George Allen & Unwin, 1953).

Potter, G. R., *Zwingli* (Cambridge: CUP, 1976).

Power, D. N., *The Sacrifice We Offer: The Tridentine Dogma and its Reinterpretation* (Edinburgh: T. & T. Clark, 1987).

Powers, J., *Eucharistic Theology* (London: Burns & Oats 1968).

Price, T., *Evangelical Anglicans and the Lima Text*, drafted by T. Price on behalf of the CEEC, GWS 92 (Bramcote: GB, 1985).

Rahner, K., *Foundations of Christian Faith: An Introduction to the Idea of Christianity* (London: DLT, 1978).

  Theological Investigations (London: DLT, 1966), vol. IV.

Ramsey, I. T., Lucas, J. R., and Peacocke, A. R., *Thinking about the Eucharist: Essays by Members of the Archbishops' Commission on Christian Doctrine* (London: SCM, 1972).

Ratcliff, E. C., 'The English use of eucharistic consecration, 1548–1662', I and II, *Theology*, 60 (1957), 229–36, 273–80.

Rattenbury, J. E., *The Eucharistic Hymns of John and Charles Wesley* (London: Epworth, 1948).

The Evangelical Doctrine of Charles Wesley's Hymns (London: Epworth, 1941).

Rodgers, J. H., 'Eucharistic sacrifice: blessing or blasphemy?', *Churchman*, 78 (1964), 248–54.

Rogers, E. J. G., 'The Evangelical Fathers and the Liturgy (with special reference to the Holy Communion)', *Churchman*, 60 (1946), 177–83.

'The Holy Communion in the Evangelical tradition', *Churchman*, 67 (1953), 11–18.

'Some liturgical considerations', *Churchman*, 60 (1946), 72–81.

Romaine, W., *The Scriptural Doctrine of the Sacrament of the Lord's Supper Briefly Stated* (London: J. Worrall, 1756).

Rowell, G., ed., *Tradition Renewed*, The Oxford Movement Conference Papers (London: DLT, 1986).

Russell, G. W. E., *A Short History of the Evangelical Movement* (London: Mowbray, 1915).

Russell Howden, J., ed., *Evangelicalism* (London: Chas. J. Thynne, 1925).

Ryle, J. C., *Expository Thoughts on the Gospels: St. John* (London: William Hunt, n.d.), vol. I.

Holiness: Its Nature, Hindrances, Difficulties, and Roots (London: James Clark, 1956).

Knots Untied, eleventh edition (London: William Hunt, 1886).

Principles for Churchmen, third edition (London: William Hunt, 1899).

'Where are we?', *Churchman*, I (1879), 30–8.

Sagovsky, N., *Modern Roman Catholic Worship: The Mass*, GMWS 34 (Bramcote: GB, 1975).

Samuel, D. N., *After the Fire: The Reconstruction of Evangelicalism* (Grimsby: Harrison Trust, 1980).

Agreeing to Differ (Grimsby: Harrison Trust, 1981).

Samuel, D. N., ed., *The Evangelical Succession in the Church of England* (Cambridge: James Clark, 1979).

Sasse, H., *This is my Body*, revised edition (Adelaide: Lutheran Publishing House, 1977).

Saward, M., *The Anglican Church Today: Evangelicals on the Move* (London: Mowbray, 1987).

Scales, D. A., *What Mean Ye by This Service?* (Cambridge: Truth and Faith Society, 1969).

Schillebeeckx, E., *Christ the Sacrament of our Encounter with God* (London: Sheed & Ward, 1963).

The Eucharist (London: Sheed & Ward, 1968).

Schmemann, A., *Introduction to Liturgical Theology*, Library of Orthodox Theology 4 (London: Faith Press, 1966).

Schnackenburg, R., *The Gospel according to St. John* (London: Burns & Oats, 1980), vol. II.

Schoonenberg, P., 'Transubstantiation: how far is the doctrine historically determined?', *Concilium*, 4/3 (April 1967), 41–7.

Schweizer, E., *The Good News according to Luke* (London: SPCK, 1984).

Scotland, N. A. D., *Eucharistic Consecration in the First Four Centuries*, LS 31 (Oxford: LH, 1989).

Searle, M., 'New tasks, new methods: the emergence of pastoral liturgical studies', *Worship*, 57 (1983), 291–308.

✓ Selwyn, E. G., ed., *Essays Catholic and Critical* (London: SPCK, 1926).

Shepherd, M. H., *Worship in Scripture and Tradition* (New York: OUP, 1963).

Sibbes, R., *The Complete Works of Richard Sibbes*, edited by A. B. Grosart (Edinburgh: James Nichol, 1892), vol. I.

Simeon, C., *Horae Homileticae*, seventh edition (London: Henry Bohn, 1846), vols. XI, xvi.

Simpson, J. A., 'The new alternative services', *Churchman*, 80 (1966), 26–33.

Smethurst, D., *Extended Communion: An Experiment in Cumbria*, GWS 96 (Bramcote: GB, 1986).

Smith, H., 'This is my body', *Churchman*, 46 (1932), 265–72.

Spinks, B. D., 'The ascension and the vicarious humanity of Christ: the Christology and soteriology behind the Church of Scotland's anamnesis and epiclesis', in *Time and Continuity*, edited by J. Neil Alexander (Washington, DC: Pastoral Press, 1990), pp. 185–201.

Freedom or Order?: The Eucharistic Liturgy in English Congregationalism 1645–1980 (Pittsburgh, Pa.: Pickwick Publications, 1984).

From the Lord and 'The Best Reformed Churches': A Study of the Eucharistic Liturgy of English Puritan and Separatist Traditions 1550–1663 (Rome: Centro Liturgico Vincenziano, 1984).

Spinks, B. D., ed., *The Sacrifice of Praise* (Rome: Centro Liturgico Vincenziano, 1981).

Stafford Wright, J., 'The place of the Lord's Supper in Evangelical worship', *Churchman*, 48 (1944), 68–75.

Stamps, R. J., '"The Sacrament of the Word made Flesh": the eucharistic theology of Thomas F. Torrance' (Ph.D. thesis, CNAA St John's College/University of Nottingham, 1986).

✓ Stephens, W. P., *The Theology of Huldrych Zwingli* (Oxford: Clarendon Press, 1986).

Stevenson, K. W., *Eucharist and Offering* (New York: Pueblo, 1986).

Gregory Dix – 25 Years on, GLS 10 (Bramcote: GB, 1977).

'LEX ORANDI AND LEX CREDENDI – Strange bed-fellows?', *SJT* 39 (1986), 225–41.

Stibbs, A. M., *Sacrament, Sacrifice and Eucharist* (London: Tyndale Press, 1961).

Stone, D., *A History of the Doctrine of the Holy Eucharist* (London: Longmans,
    Green, 1909), vol. II.
Storr, V. F., *Freedom and Tradition* (London: Nisbet, 1940).
    My Faith (London: SPCK, 1927).
Stott, J. R. W., *The Baptism and Fulness of the Holy Spirit* (London: IVF,
    1964).
    The Cross of Christ (Leicester: IVP, 1986).
  ✓ *I Believe in Preaching* (London: H & S, 1982).
    Evangelical Anglicans and the ARCIC Final Report: An Assessment and Critique,
    drafted by John Stott on behalf of the CEEC (Bramcote: GB, 1982).
    Your Confirmation (London: H & S, 1958).
Sydney Carter, C., 'The Reformers' doctrine of the Holy Communion',
    Churchman, 66 (1952), 92–6.
  ✓ Sykes, N., *Church and State in England in the XVIIIth Century* (Cambridge:
  ✓ CUP, 1934).
    Sheldon to Secker: Aspects of Church History 1660–1768 (Cambridge: CUP,
    1959).
Taylor, J., *Works*, revised by C. Page Eden (London: Longmans, 1850).
Taylor, J. R. S., 'Evangelicals and the Holy Communion', *Churchman*, 63
    (1949) 234–9.
    'The Holy Spirit and the ministry of word and sacraments', *Churchman*, 59
    (1945), 51–7.
    'The Reformation in worship: the ministry of the sacraments', *Churchman*,
    52 (1938), 100–5.
Thomas, W. H. G., *The Catholic Faith*, revised edition (London: CBRP,
    1952).
    The Principles of Theology (London: Longmans, Green, 1930).
    A Sacrament of our Redemption, second edition (London: Bemrose, [1905]).
Thornton, L. S., *Richard Hooker* (London: SPCK, 1924).
Tinker, M., *Restoring the Vision: Anglican Evangelicals Speak Out* (Eastbourne:
    MARC, 1990).
Tinsley, E. J., *The Gospel according to Luke* (Cambridge: CUP, 1969).
Toon, P., *The Anglican Way: Evangelical and Catholic* (Wilton, Conn.:
    Moorehouse–Barlow, 1983).
    Evangelical Theology 1833–1856: A Response to Tractarianism (London:
    Marshall, Morgan & Scott, 1979).
Torrance, T. F., 'Eschatology and the Eucharist', in *Intercommunion*, edited
    by D. Baillie and J. Marsh (London: SCM, 1952), pp. 303–50.
    'The Paschal mystery of Christ and the Eucharist: general thesis',
    Liturgical Review, 6 (1976), 6–12.
    *Theology in Reconciliation: Essays towards Evangelical and Catholic Unity in East
    and West* (London: Geoffrey Chapman, 1975).
Torrance, T. F., ed., *The Incarnation* (Edinburgh: Handsel Press, 1981).
Tripp, D. H., ed., *E. C. Ratcliff: Reflections on Liturgical Revision*, GLS 22
    (Bramcote: GB, 1980).
Venn, H., ed., *The Life and a Selection of the Letters of the Late Rev. Henry Venn*

M.A., edited by H. Venn, fifth edition (London: John Hatchard & Son, 1837).

Vogan, T., *The True Doctrine of The Eucharist* (London: Longmans, Green, 1871).

Wace, H., ed., *Church and Faith* (Edinburgh: Blackwood, 1899).

Wainwright, G., *Doxology: The Praise of God in Worship, Doctrine and Life* (London: Epworth, 1980).

Wakefield, G. S., *Puritan Devotion* (London: Epworth, 1957).

Warren, M. A. C., *Strange Victory: A Study of the Holy Communion Service* (London: Canterbury Press, 1946).

'Recent trends in Anglican Evangelical theology', *SJT* 3 (1950), 19–26.

Waterland, D., *A Review of the Doctrine of the Eucharist* (Oxford: Clarendon Press, 1880), first published 1736–40.

Watson, D. C. K., *I Believe in the Church* (London: H & S, 1978).

Discipleship (London: H & S, 1981).

Webber, R. E., ed., *Evangelicals on the Canterbury Trail* (Waco, Tex.: Word Books, 1985).

Welsby, P. A., *A History of the Church of England 1945–1980* (Oxford: OUP, 1984).

Wesley, J., *The Journal of the Rev. John Wesley, A.M.*, edited by N. Curnock, eight vols., second edition (London: Robert Culley, 1909–16).

The Works of John Wesley, 14 vols., (Grand Rapids: Zondervan [1958]).

Westerhoff III, J. H., *Will our Children have Faith?* (New York: Seabury Press, 1976).

Whateley, T. C., 'Eucharistic doctrine: the true road to harmony', *Churchman*, 45 (1931), 46–52.

White, J. F., *Protestant Worship: Traditions in Transition* (Kentucky: Westminster/John Knox, 1989).

Whitefield, G., *George Whitefield's Journal* (London: Banner of Truth, 1960).

Wilberforce, R. I., *The Doctrine of the Holy Eucharist* (London: Mozley, 1854).

Williams, R. D., *Eucharistic Sacrifice: The Roots of a Metaphor*, GLS 31 (Bramcote: GB, 1982).

Willis, E. D., *Calvin's Catholic Christology* (Leiden: E. J. Brill, 1966).

Wilson, D., *Sermons and Tracts*, seventh edition (London: George Wilson, 1825), vol. II.

Wilson, H. A. *et al.*, *Liberal Evangelicalism: An Interpretation* (London: H & S, 1923).

Wilson, T., *A Short and Plain Instruction for the Better Understanding of the Lord's Supper* (London: Rivington, 1822).

Wright, N. T., *Evangelical Anglican Identity: The Connection between Bible, Gospel and Church*, LS 8 (Oxford: LH, 1980).

Young, D., *Welcoming Children to Communion*, GWS 85 (Bramcote: GB, 1983).

Zwingli, U., 'On the Lord's Supper', in *Zwingli and Bullinger*, introduced by G. W. Bromiley (London: SCM, 1953), pp. 185–238.

REPORTS AND LETTERS

The Charismatic Movement in the Church of England (London: CIO, 1981).

Doctrine in the Church of England (London: SPCK, 1938).

Evangelicals Affirm in the Year of the Lambeth Conference (London: CBRP, 1948).

The Fullness of Christ: The Archbishop's Report (London: SPCK, 1950).

Keele '67: The National Evangelical Anglican Congress Statement, edited by P. Crowe (London: CPAS/Falcon Books, 1967).

The Lambeth Conference 1958 (London: SPCK, and Seabury Press, 1958).

The Liturgical Conference 1966: Report of Proceedings (Oxford: CIO, 1966).

The Nottingham Statement: Statement of the Second National Evangelical Anglican Congress 1977, issued by the Executive Committee of the Second National Evangelical Anglican Congress Statement (London: CPAS/Falcon Books, 1977).

'Oxford Conference of Evangelical Churchmen', *Churchman*, 52 (1938), 59–60.

'Oxford Conference of Evangelical Churchmen', *Churchman*, 72 (1958), 148.

The Oxford Conference 1975: Agreement in the Faith: Talks between Anglicans and Roman Catholics (London: CBRP, 1975).

Towards a Church of England Response to BEM and ARCIC, from the Faith and Order Advisory Group (London: CIO, 1985).

'An open letter concerning the Anglican–Methodist relations', February 1964, in *All in Each Place*, edited by J. I. Packer, pp. 15–16.

'An open letter concerning the eucharistic statement', *CEN* 18 Feb. 1972, p. 4.

'An open letter: on relations between the Anglican Churches and the Roman Catholic, Eastern Orthodox, Old Catholic and Ancient Oriental Churches, June 1977', in R. T. Beckwith, G. E. Duffield and J. I. Packer, *Across the Divide*, pp. 4–13.

'An open letter to the Anglican episcopate: ARCIC' (Bramcote: GB, 1988).

Private and unpublished correspondence of C. O. Buchanan at the time of and in regard to the Liturgical Commission's Second Series Communion Service (1964–7).

Index